D1134681

Cavan County Library
Withdrawn Stock

Integration in Ireland

Manchester University Press

New
Ethnographies

Series editor
Alexander Thomas T. Smith

Already published

The British in rural France:
Lifestyle migration and the ongoing quest for a better way of life
Michaela Benson

Chagos islanders in Mauritius and the UK:
Forced displacement and onward migration
Laura Jeffery

An ethnography of English football fans:
Cans, cops and carnivals
Geoff Pearson

Literature and agency in English fiction reading:
A study of the Henry Williamson Society...
Adam Reed

Devolution and the Scottish Conservatives:
Banal activism, electioneering and the politics of irrelevance
Alexander Thomas T. Smith

Integration in Ireland

The everyday lives of African migrants

Mark Maguire and Fiona Murphy

Manchester University Press
Manchester and New York

distributed in the United States exclusively
by Palgrave Macmillan

Copyright © Mark Maguire and Fiona Murphy 2012

The right of Mark Maguire and Fiona Murphy to be identified as the author of this work has been asserted by them in accordance with the Copyright, Designs and Patents Act 1988.

Published by Manchester University Press
Oxford Road, Manchester M13 9NR, UK
and Room 400, 175 Fifth Avenue, New York, NY 10010, USA
www.manchesteruniversitypress.co.uk

Distributed in the United States exclusively by
Palgrave Macmillan, 175 Fifth Avenue, New York,
NY 10010, USA

Distributed in Canada exclusively by
UBC Press, University of British Columbia, 2029 West Mall,
Vancouver, BC, Canada V6T 1Z2

British Library Cataloguing-in-Publication Data
A catalogue record for this book is available from the British Library

Library of Congress Cataloging-in-Publication Data applied for

ISBN   978 0 7190 8694 6 *hardback*

First published 2012

The publisher has no responsibility for the persistence or accuracy of URLs for any external or third-party internet websites referred to in this book, and does not guarantee that any content on such websites is, or will remain, accurate or appropriate.

CAVAN COUNTY LIBRARY

ACC No. C / 268965
CLASS NO. 325
INVOICE NO. 1483   /LS
PRICE £ 58·50

Typeset
by Action Publishing Technology Ltd, Gloucester
Printed in Great Britain
by CPI Antony Rowe Ltd, Chippenham, Wiltshire

Contents

List of figures

Acknowledgements

This book draws on a two-year research project, 'After Asylum,' funded by the Irish Research Council for the Humanities and Social Sciences (IRCHSS) Research Development Initiative Strand. We are grateful for the support of the IRCHSS and acknowledge the contribution of the Council to the development of innovative and exploratory research. We are deeply indebted to all of our research participants for the time they have given to us and their insights into the issues we raised. The process of writing an ethnographic book is always a difficult one: lives are rich and perspectives are meaningful; inevitably, therefore, much cannot be said.

In part, this manuscript was prepared while Mark Maguire was a Visiting Associate Professor in Stanford University's Department of Anthropology and he would like to thank Ellen and Tony Christensen for their friendship and hospitality and James Ferguson and Sylvia Yanagisako for providing such a stimulating environment in which to work. We would also like to thank Maura Parazzoli and Johanna Markkula for their helpful comments. Finally, we are indebted to the editorial staff at Manchester University Press and to the anonymous reviewers who helped us to shape the text.

Series editor's foreword

At its best, ethnography has provided a valuable tool for apprehending a world in flux. A couple of years after the Second World War, Max Gluckman founded the Department of Social Anthropology at the University of Manchester. In the years that followed, he and his colleagues built a programme of ethnographic research that drew eclectically on the work of leading anthropologists, economists and sociologists to explore issues of conflict, reconciliation and social justice 'at home' and abroad. Often placing emphasis on detailed analysis of case studies drawn from small-scale societies and organisations, the famous 'Manchester School' in social anthropology built an enviable reputation for methodological innovation in its attempts to explore the pressing political questions of the second half of the twentieth century. Looking back, that era is often thought to constitute a 'gold standard' for how ethnographers might grapple with new challenges and issues in the contemporary world.

The *New Ethnographies* series aims to build on that ethnographic legacy at Manchester. It will publish the best new ethnographic monographs that promote interdisciplinary debate and methodological innovation in the qualitative social sciences. This includes the growing number of books that seek to apprehend the 'new' ethnographic objects of a seemingly brave new world, some recent examples of which have included auditing, democracy and elections, documents, financial markets, human rights, assisted reproductive technologies and political activism. Analysing such objects has often demanded new skills and techniques from the ethnographer. As a result, this series will give voice to those using ethnographic methods across disciplines to innovate, such as through the application of multi-sited fieldwork and the extended comparative case study method. Such innovations have often challenged more traditional ethnographic approaches. *New Ethnographies* therefore seeks to provide a platform for emerging scholars and their more established counterparts engaging with ethnographic methods in new and imaginative ways.

Alexander Thomas T. Smith

Introduction

> My husband left – we didn't know where he went – and I was left with the children. Then men came into the houses and they were killing the different tribal groups. Then me, with my sister-in-law and the kids, we escaped it, we ran away […].
>
> It was not easy. You know Mosney feels like a prison. We knew we were there for refuge, but sometimes you would be there crying, just thinking the problems are too much for you. So, nothing for you to do. It was like that: I was just waiting for my papers, waiting for my papers, waiting for my papers. … So it's now six years, my status is still leave to remain after all of that. … The Church is my life now. If there is no Church, it is like you kill me. I don't have any other activities in my life now other than the Church. In spite of all that is happening to me here, I can say, 'This is home; this is the place that I can sleep peacefully.'
> (Former asylum seeker, interview, 2010)

As the Dublin–Belfast train passes between Balbriggan and Laytown some odd-looking buildings are visible beside the rail line. These buildings were once part of Butlins holiday village. First opened in 1948, Butlins offered a 'proletariat paradise' to young couples from Dublin and overseas Irish in the UK. Though Catholic periodicals initially castigated it as an alien intrusion, the camp quickly proved itself to be an immensely popular, cheap-and-cheerful tourist destination. At the height of its operation, it could cater for nearly 10,000 guests at any one time and had the capacity to accommodate several thousand of that number overnight in multi-coloured chalets. Many Irish people still remember visits to Butlins or receiving postcards from holidaymakers with colourful images of the swimming pool, the boating lake or the American Bar. In 1982, however, the Butlins camp was sold and became Mosney Holiday Centre. Eighteen years later the camp was bought by the state and turned into an accommodation centre for asylum seekers. The odd-looking buildings that are visible from the train are now the temporary homes of an astonishing variety of people who, in many ways, do not exist.

During the 1990s the numbers of people claiming asylum in Ireland grew at an astonishing rate: in 1992 there were thirty-nine applications for asylum; in 2001 there were just over 10,000 applications (see Mac Éinrí and White 2008:

153–154). Initially, neither the requisite legislation nor the resources were in place to 'manage' this form of migration, and asylum seekers were perceived to be too close to mainstream welfare and housing provision.[1] Moreover, the so-called Celtic Tiger economic boom put great pressure on housing capacity, and during the late 1990s serious consideration was even given to a scheme to house asylum seekers in floating hotels moored in Irish ports (Ruane 2000: 16). The so-called 'flotel' proposal was vigorously opposed, and in 2000 a system of direct provision was instead set in place. This system is characterised by an initial reception phase followed by dispersal to centres dotted around Ireland, a network of over fifty privatised and semi-privatised shadow villages.[2] Some are purpose-built centres; others are former hotels, guesthouses or hostels – there's even a trailer park. The largest of all the accommodation centres is the former Butlins holiday village.

Throughout Europe most asylum claims are refused in the first instance, prompting many commentators to argue that the primary function of asylum systems is to act as a deterrent against unregulated immigration (see, for example, FLAC 2003; Schuster 2005; Breen 2008).[3] In accommodation centres such as Mosney residents are provided with bed and board and, beyond this, they subsist on €19.10 per week per adult and €9.60 per child. They are not entitled to work or enter into third-level education.[4] As the former asylum seeker quoted in the above epigraph described it to us, life in Mosney is characterised by waiting – 'waiting for my papers, waiting for my papers, waiting for my papers'.

In 2008 Paul Rowley and Nicky Grogan produced the groundbreaking documentary *Seaview*. It explores the everyday lives of Mosney's new residents, lives lived in a space characterised by deadened time. Mosney is framed as an institutional landscape enclosed by fences and CCTVs, a place where the past ruptures the present in the form of mothballed tourist attractions and redundant toys. Time has a disturbed quality: people sometimes remain there for several years, yet at any moment their world might be shattered by an official letter announcing a future of integration in Ireland or deportation overseas. The film includes a young mother's reflections:

> A life of uncertainty, hopelessness, you don't know what will happen. It's no life to me, no life at all – you just live by the day. We are grateful for the accommodation, for the food, and most especially that our children are going to school, but that is not what life is all about. People are just wasting; governments are wasting in the name of the asylum process … And you can imagine if you have lived like that for five years, what kind of mother will you be when you eventually leave the asylum system? (Rowley and Gogan 2008)

Her question is an important one, because little is in fact known about what happens after asylum (see Phelan and Kuol 2005). Irish integration policies avoid references to asylum seekers or to the shadow villages in which they reside. Rather, integration is only for those with refugee status or leave to remain in the state. Metaphorically, the clocks in Mosney are frozen because deportation awaits the majority of its residents. During a newspaper interview one Irish government official cast the policy in simple terms: 'Integration can't happen without deportation!' (MacCormaic 2009: 9) Societal integration and state security are thus two sides of the same coin. But against the official logic of administrative order and control, many of Mosney's residents forge bonds that connect them to the world outside its fences. For example, a Pentecostal pastor based there described the role of his church to us thus:

> A lot of people here are from different backgrounds. A lot of people here are not really comfortable: a lot of stress, a lot of depression, a lot of troubles going through their minds. So, one of the things we do is to try to encourage them, try to let them see that there's a light at the end of the tunnel. There's no one here that really likes being here, and that's the truth. We reach out to the Irish community and have programmes with charity groups. [...] In any place that you find yourself you should be able to see home. [...] We are doing things to keep them busy, to make them feel they belong somewhere. (Interview, 2010)

While many of the pastor's congregation continue to be deported, others have gone on to lead new lives in nearby towns such as Dundalk and Drogheda. But little, as we have said, is known about what happens after asylum. This book represents an effort to examine experiences of integration, as former asylum seekers live their everyday lives alongside other migrants and 'locals' in fast-changing Irish towns. As Phenninx et al (2008: 7) note, across Europe research on integration has tended to be funded and policy driven rather than exploratory. Herein, we situate ourselves away from efforts to measure and compare integration and, instead, aim to offer insights into what integration means for the people concerned.

From 2009 to 2011 we gathered information on former asylum seekers in Drogheda, Dundalk and parts of Dublin. The project was situated in the towns and neighbourhoods near major asylum centres such as Mosney where refugees and those with leave to remain in the state have settled. Asylum centres are the temporary homes of astonishingly diverse populations, composed of individuals and families representing very different education levels, socioeconomic backgrounds and countries of origin. Many come from volatile and conflict-torn regions of Africa, especially Nigeria and the Democratic Republic of Congo. Our research was not, however, guided by an attempt to track the assimilation or 'acculturation' of particular populations in Ireland. Rather, this book is concerned with the everyday lives of former asylum seekers and other immigrants, their partners, families and children: the actually available sociality that shapes everyday life. Because many asylum seekers are from African countries of origin, the majority of our research participants identify themselves as Nigerian, Congolese or African-Irish.

The individuals we met suggested that we speak to their friends and relatives. In turn, those friends and relatives introduced us to others. We visited people's homes, participated in political campaigns, religious walks, church-based functions, activities in primary schools, and even beauty pageants. As frequently and as often as possible, we situated ourselves in the spaces and moments in which migrant subjectivities were engendered. We formally interviewed many dozens of people. Those narratives and interview extracts are available through-out this book. But, herein, we emphasise the observations and sensibilities that come from ethnographic research – the process of long-term study and immersion, and the reflexive engagement with the lives of research participants. Our work, however, is self-consciously partial: we do not attempt to speak for all the former asylum seekers in Ireland, for all African immigrants, or for all the towns and neighbourhoods in which they reside. We cannot tell the whole story. Former asylum seekers are, of course, often fearful of telling their stories. Even those individuals 'with status' remain worried about disclosing too much (Jackson 2002). Some do not wish to speak about the past because of the violence they suffered; others do not wish to speak about the past because of the ongoing structural violence they continue to suffer in their everyday lives.

There are many levels to ethnographic writing, and one important level is attention to the ways in which people craft their self-identities and represent what is important and meaningful to them. As the Anglo-Irish writer Elizabeth Bowen once put it, a concern for self-identity and appearances is symptomatic of an underlying fragility among those who are 'never certain that their passports are in order' (quoted in Kiberd 1996: 378). Herein we explore migrant subjectivities at intimate and affective levels, attending to the fragility of their lives and documenting the shifting political, economic and cultural terrain on which they stand. Our attention is to the context and meaning of their voices, and through-out this book the voices of former asylum seekers tend (almost without exception) to speak of a desire to succeed, to overcome barriers and become part of Irish society – in short, to integrate.

Breda Gray (2006) argues that integration is a deeply problematic concept because it necessarily raises a difficult question: what are migrants expected to integrate into? Gray's analysis of Irish integration politics and policies shows the ways in which refugees and other migrants are imagined as bearers of fixed and essentialised cultures and identities who must learn to be self-managing citizens capable of integrating into society. But Irish society is equally fixed and essen-tialised in policy. How, then, should we re-imagine this Venn-diagram-like model of integration to show the complexities of everyday life? How should we show the dynamic nature of migrants' everyday experiences while, at the same time, situating those lives amid the fast-changing towns and cities of contemporary Ireland? Our starting proposition is that if the fashionable and yet elusive term 'integration' is to mean anything – and that, of course, remains open to question – then it should be taken to denote policies and activities that transcend several different scales. Much has already been written about integration politics in Ireland (Gray 2006; Lentin and McVeigh 2006; Mac Éinrí 2007; Fanning 2009; Maguire and Titley 2010), but not enough has been written about integration experiences. If all politics is local, to borrow 'Tip' O'Neill's well-worn aphorism, then here we intend to emphasise the local experiences of integration politics. Of course, localities should not be ring-fenced and valorised as the sole and privi-leged site wherein the really real action takes place. Attention to the roles of government, policy making and the work of activists is doubtless also important.

That said; our central proposition is that government-level processes and lived experiences must be understood as imbricated, and locality is a central frame through which they come together in Ireland.

What specifically do we mean by locality? For the anthropologist Ulf Hannerz locality denotes the connections between friends and family, collegial and business relations, ethnic and other identities that produce and reproduce 'habitats of meaning' (Hannerz 1996: 22–25 passim). In this line of thinking, locality cannot be taken as a synonym for a neighbourhood or clearly bounded community: Hannerz does not consider localities as places where identities and histories are necessarily incarcerated in their own particularity. Rather, the notion of habitats of meaning encompasses the ways in which people make use of their cultural competencies, knowledge, cognitive and interpretative abilities in order to meaningfully interact with physical and behavioural environments. Thus, while some nostalgic commentators hold that the small, face-to-face communities of old are being broken apart and scattered abroad by the forces of globalisation, it is important to note that people live meaningfully and, therefore, in a sense, they live locally, no matter how mobile they might be.

We take Ulf Hannerz's comments on locality as a starting point from which to develop this work in two directions. The first direction aims to follow what Veena Das terms 'the descent into the ordinary'. In *Life and Words* (2007) Das argues that people learn about their worlds primarily through their experiences. Perspectives are, therefore, of crucial importance: people do not live in worlds that are available and structured as a coherent whole, but, rather, their perspectives are levelled upon available horizons (Das 2007: 4). In her ethnographic work on violence and memory in India, she attends to the voices that emerge from 'a frayed everyday life' (Das 2007: 9), experienced as limited, forever being remade. Drawing on the philosopher Ludwig Wittgenstein, Das takes 'voices' to denote more than mere utterances: her concern is with that which animates words and gives them life. Her ethnographic challenge, then, is to unpack the ways in which large-scale events and processes are folded into ongoing relationships and into people's experiences of the world. Occasionally, those voices may be heard on larger stages; more often than not we just hear words, disembodied and removed from their contexts – words without the shared experiences that would allow for meaningful conversations across cultural lines.

Throughout this book we aim to connect with and draw from the lived experiences of integration in Ireland. Following Veena Das, we wish to descend into the ordinary. But we also aim to follow a second direction. This book asks questions about how Irish localities are understood and lived in as diverse places, and about the ramifications of government policies. The everyday, for us, is the site in which we may perceive new ways of examining governmental and societal discourses on 'race', nationality or belonging, because in everyday life they acquire much of their sociocultural content.

The guiding principles that subsist behind government policies in Ireland genuflect to international neo-liberalism: a late capitalist discourse that pushes for government-at-a-distance and valorises the ostensibly value-free and efficient power of the market to order much of social life. But the powerful ancestors of contemporary neo-liberalism would hardly approve of their Irish offspring. Economic doctrines are rarely disseminated in a pure form, and governments around the world have localised the guiding principles of neo-liberal economic theory. And so too in Ireland, where the guiding principles of neo-liberalism have been blended into different and often competing sectors of society and compromised by powerful interests. In such a context there can be no 'value-free' economics, and arguably even it a pure form neo-liberalism is not value free and neutral. Indeed, herein we shall show that neo-liberal governing is cultural in its origins, cultural in its operations and cultural in its consequences. For example, we show the ways in which African drivers attempt to earn a living within a liberalised taxi industry, and we describe the ways in which multicultural schools interact with neo-liberal education policies – a troika composed of integration, inclusion and interculturalism – enacted in Irish ways and accented accordingly. Though it was not our original intention to study government policy, exercises of government power are important parts of everyday lifeworlds. Thus, in part, our work stands as a critique from the perspective of everyday life.

In towns and neighbourhoods around Ireland new identities are being fashioned within ordinary and everyday experiences, government policies are being folded into the moulds of local life, and the activities of former asylum seekers, new immigrants and long-term residents are shaping the future. All of this is adding even more texture to Ireland's already diverse localities.

Diversity and locality

After the train to Belfast passes by Mosney camp it continues to border towns such as Dundalk.[5] The partition of Ireland in 1921 resulted in the imposition of a border between the towns of Newry and Dundalk, and until 1947 all trains were stopped in order to facilitate immigration control and customs searches. During the late twentieth century the so-called Emerald Curtain was at one and the same time a fixed feature of living in Ireland and a deeply contested symbolic divide (Coakley and O'Dowd 2005: 4). This was illustrated vividly during the late 1960s and early 1970s when sectarian violence remade the ethnic geographies of Northern Ireland. Irish Government memoranda describe a sudden eruption of violence in 1969 and the consequent large-scale displacement of populations. During that year, over 700 'Northern Refugees,' as they were known, fled the violence in the North and were accommodated by the Irish Army. The following year, refugees again began to arrive over the border in 'ominous numbers', and, according to one official security report, the view at the time was that 'generally speaking dispossessed people create tremendous problems, social and economic, for host countries' (Garda Commissioner 1975: 9).[6]

The capacity of Army refugee centres was soon exceeded. Writing for the *New York Times* in 1971, Anthony Lewis described the scene in Gormanstown camp near Dundalk: '2,800 were jammed into the camp, many of them sleeping shoulder to shoulder on mattresses spread over the cement floor of an airplane hanger' (Lewis 1971: 4). Government security concerns structured the initial Irish responses to the Northern Refugee crisis, but by the early 1980s the crisis had abated and the refugees vanished from public consciousness. Towns close to the border, however, were left to deal with the integration of sizeable new communities.

The Good Friday Agreement in 1998 signalled the end of the Emerald Curtain, but the border quality and diversity of local life in Dundalk endured. In recent years – owing to currency fluctuations and its position on the line separating different jurisdictions – Dundalk has been slandered by the nickname 'El Paso'. Many asylum seekers entered Ireland by travelling first to the UK, whereupon taxis brought them from Northern Ireland to border towns such as Dundalk (see DeParle 2008: 1). Many other asylum seekers were dispersed to accommodation centres in the North East. Coterminous with the arrival of asylum seekers, from the 1990s onwards the demography of border towns such as Dundalk altered radically. The Celtic Tiger inflated an extraordinary property bubble in the Greater Dublin area, and Dundalk's location on the rail and road networks, together with its position as a 'hub' in the emergent Dublin–Belfast economic corridor, resulted in it becoming a dormitory commuter town for large numbers of new residents. The economic prosperity of the Celtic Tiger era also attracted a great variety of international migrants to Ireland, especially labour migrants from the former European accession states. Clearly, then, in the case of Dundalk, locality cannot be taken as a synonym for a clearly bounded community. Rather, Dundalk is composed of layers of diversity, and the perspectives of 'locals' often suggest a loss of familiarity with local life. The example of Dundalk is illustrative of the experiences felt in other towns where we carried out our research.

In Dundalk today the unlikely juxtaposition between different versions of Irishness inflects communication between political activists and community leaders. Former 'Northern Refugees' are often among the most vocal in demanding attention to the issues affecting 'new immigrant communities'. The following is an illustrative extract from an interview with a political activist and former displaced person:

I sit on a taskforce funded by European money … and I heard this mentioned around the table: 'the local Irish indigenous people'. 'Now that's a double-barrel insult', I said. 'Do you want to insult people any more?' […]

But it's not just about outsiders, because there's always an outsider. Someone comes in from the country and they're called a 'culchie'. But there's a political slant and bitterness as well. And we got that: 'Them Northerners took our jobs, took our houses, took this, took that.'

The Africans coming in and different foreign nationals coming in, they're getting what we got forty years ago: 'Sure, they won't work!' But they're not allowed work, and nobody knows that. 'They won't work; they're getting all our stuff.' Well, they're not: they're not allowed to cook their own food, and they're on seventeen quid a week, but people don't know that, so the ignorance that was there in '69, '70, '71 is still there with regard to foreign nationals.

You still have people saying to you that they were in a queue and they saw

Africans walking through and not paying. When I say, 'That's bullshit!' they suddenly say, 'Well, my sister seen it.' They don't get free cars; they don't get free anything. There's a whole myth ... and we need to break that down. (Interview, 2010)

'Local Irish indigenous people' is not a description that rolls easily off the tongue. It is symptomatic of both the absurdity of attempting to divide, categorise and name populations and the governmental pressure to do it anyway. Ironically, this activist, a Gaelic speaker and former political prisoner, versed in Irish literature and history, is the very kind of person most likely to refuse narrow-gauge categorisations. Moreover, to speak of 'local Irish indigenous people' is to use nation as the keyword, but a keyword that requires a semantic cloud of other words. 'Irish' is no longer good enough: one must also be indigenous – identity as a right of blood, identity as a people, population or 'race'. As E. Valentine Daniel once put it, 'In nationalist discourse, the question is not who is a Sri Lankan or who is an Englishman but who is a *true* Sri Lankan and who is a *true* Englishman' (1996: 364 [original emphasis]).

This book is a study of integration in Ireland and the processes and dynamics that obtain behind that term. It is also a study of how locality is imagined and how immigrants and others produce the local in ways that construct it (sometimes as *true* versions) and reveal it to be always-emergent and rarely as indigenous as it is assumed to be. This work aims to contribute to our understanding of these processes by examining work, civic and political activism; religious organisations and beliefs, education, and youth identity. The book is set out with chapters devoted to each of these themes. Each of the chapters pays careful attention to the everyday experiences of former asylum seekers and other immigrants, drawing out voices in the fullest ways possible. Threaded through the book are the stories and voices of individual protagonists (not all of whom are former asylum seekers), mostly from the Nigerian and Congolese communities. Political activists are also the mothers of school-going children; taxi drivers are also political activists; contestants in Nigerian and Congolese beauty pageants were raised in Pentecostal families. Their complex stories and experiences are just some of the threads that together compose the diverse tapestries of contemporary life in Ireland.

Voices and lives

Our work is an attempt to elicit the voices of former asylum seekers and other migrants as they live their everyday lives in Irish localities. We are interested in the individuals and families, co-workers, political activists, pastors and friends, all of whom live interconnected lives, share certain experiences and perspectives and, yet, present the world differently and often sceptically. In this section, we begin to tell some of their stories. All too often refugees, asylum seekers and other migrants have been presented in still images or as voiceless victims; too often their words have peppered journalism and official reports in disembodied and lifeless forms. Here, instead, we wish to elicit the voices within ordinary and everyday life. Our focus on the everyday is not driven by a romantic attachment to some local worlds that we imagine to alternately resist and accommodate forces originating elsewhere. Nor is the everyday a synonym for face-to-face communities that exist only as small parts of larger wholes. Rather, everyday life is composed of concrete relationships and abstract questions, perspectives and always-limited horizons, tacit knowledge, shared meanings, and the ever-present scepticism of the subject and the world.

'The suspicion of the ordinary', Veena Das argues, is 'rooted in the fact that relationships require a repeated attention to the most ordinary of objects and events, but our ... impulse is often to think of agency in terms of escaping the ordinary rather than as a descent into it' (Das 1997: 6–7). Following Das, we are also interested in attending to the concepts that arise from investigations of the everyday, 'pictures of what it is to make and remake a world' (Das 1997: 5), and the stories voiced by people themselves. The ethnographic challenge here is to show the complexities of the everyday, and our approach is influenced by the work of Ludwig Wittgenstein:

> 'The ground looked roughly like this.' Perhaps I even say 'it looked *exactly* like this.'– then were just *this* grass and *these* leaves there, arranged just like this? No, that is not what this means. And I should not accept any picture as exact in *this* sense.
>
> One might say that the concept 'game' is a concept with blurred edges.– 'But is a blurred concept a concept at all?'– Is an indistinct photograph a picture of a person at all? Is it always an advantage to replace an indistinct picture by a sharp one? Isn't the indistinct one often what we need? (Wittgenstein 1999: 172–173)

The challenge is to elicit voices in everyday life, voices within contexts that express different perspectives on the world. Those voices belong to people who have lost much in life and yet are attempting to make a new world in Ireland. No crystal-clear picture may be developed because they live interconnected lives in dense social bonds, families and networks. Their stories involve difficult journeys, practical actions, hope for the future and a variety of forms of 'self-styling' (Mbembé and Rendall 2002). But against the prevailing ways in which integration is framed in Ireland, their voices have the power to challenge the commonsense and taken-for-granted ways of the world.

Yinka, for example, frequently challenges the taken-for-granted ways of the world.[7] She describes coming to Ireland as a labour immigrant rather than an asylum seeker:

> I came in from Nigeria in 1999 when Ireland was still inviting people to come to work. I came in with my family. [...] I stayed here with my son; my husband has since gone back home. I came as his wife. It's difficult for someone who comes in as a spouse – in fact it's not difficult, it's impossible to work. If you come in as the spouse of a work permit holder you have to look to the work permit holder for every need that you have. And the relationship was strained from before. It was very highly abusive relationship. ... I have carried that stigma for so many years and I'm just now getting over it. So I looked to the Minister for Justice for the

opportunity to remain in the country with my child because we were both being abused. The Minister granted the permission to me for work. My husband was very upset: it was either that I was having an affair with the Minister for Justice, or somebody in the Justice Department was having it off with me . . . [*laughs*]

I lost my confidence. I lost my will to live. We were very poor and we had nobody to turn to. [*Later*] my sisters came from England and they wanted to set up a business. And I'm a trainer, that's what I do. All I wanted to do was to make some money to pay myself and then I could renew my papers and remain in the country. I look like I have a lot of confidence, but that's where I come from. I come from that point to the person I am now. (Interview, 2010 [our interpolation])

During 2009, Yinka campaigned as a Green Party candidate in the local and European elections. Throughout her campaign she made heroic efforts to reach voters and connect with a broad spectrum of local issues. Constantly busy, with a mind filled with new ideas, throughout the campaign Yinka was a whirlwind of activity.

Officially she was a 'new immigrant candidate,' a symbol of the changes occurring in the Irish political system. For many African immigrants in the North East, especially for asylum seekers and refugees, she represented their visions for change and offered societal hope during a period of deep economic recession and daily struggles. But Yinka's campaign was also a journey of self-discovery and empowerment, shown in her concern to offer herself as a role model for others. Throughout her campaign we witnessed her 'self-styling,' to borrow a venturesome concept from Achille Mbembé, her efforts to present herself to herself and to others in new and empowering ways. Yinka drew from her considerable personal and professional experiences and from her Pentecostal faith:

Shit happens, this is life. I find that with my knowledge of scripture, with the opportunity I have had, I am able to see how life can be. How by changing your thinking and your attitude – you won't necessarily have more in your pocket – but you may be happy' (Interview, 2010).

Yinka's desire to advance herself and provide an example to others drove her election campaign. She was also active in a great number of local affairs, especially so during 2009 when she mediated between African taxi drivers and 'local' drivers in a series of disputes in Drogheda. Disputes arising because of taxi deregulation and the entry of African drivers into the industry have erupted sporadically throughout the state during the past number of years. National industry policy, racialisation and societal discourses on belonging came together during these disputes, and as we show in the first chapter of this book Yinka's deep familiarity with the everyday lives of African drivers, together with her ability to appreciate public sentiments, informed the stances she adopted.

During the 2009 elections, Yinka was just one of several 'new immigrant candidates'. Nearby in Dundalk, Benedicta campaigned with a running mate on the Fine Gael ticket. Benedicta is also someone who frequently challenges the taken-for-granted ways of the world. She is a determined woman. This may be a rather plain characterisation, but it does describe her well. When one meets Benedicta for the first time the impression she elicits is of a busy woman with many things to do – important matters crowd her day. She is tall and striking looking. Even when she dresses informally she does so with care, as if she is always prepared to go to a meeting or stand up and talk in front of a room. She laughs easily and engages in conversation readily. It is hard to imagine that once she fled a conflict-torn region of Nigeria with little save the clothes on her back; it's harder still to imagine her sitting in an asylum centre and simply waiting for her papers for the better part of a year.

Benedicta has been in Ireland for over ten years. During that time she went from factory night-shifts to owning her own shop. But her *résumé* is not just marked by efforts to improve her own position. She has always been a charismatic individual, a seemingly natural leader. Indeed, it is possible to say that she has a migrant political career: early on, she took on the role of 'community leader,' representing Nigerian immigrants on local issues and acting as a voluntary mediator with a variety of institutions. Her language abilities, education background and self-confidence meant that she became an important 'go to' person. Later, she immersed herself in local politics and sat on a wide variety of committees. Later still, she twice stood as a candidate in the local and European elections.

> It took nine months, first of all, to have my application for asylum processed. I withdrew the claim and I put in the claim of a parent of an Irish-born child, but it still took nine months to get all that paperwork done. Once the paperwork was out of the way and my papers were due to arrive, I started looking for a job, but my degree wasn't recognised, so I ended up working in a factory. I was unhappy because I didn't go to university for six years to end up working in a factory. You know, I wanted, I mean, no disrespect to people who work in factories, but I just thought that I worked hard enough to do more. [...] Rather than work at that level, I wanted to work at a higher level – that is why I studied. So, for three months I worked there, and I was looking for an opportunity to get into Irish society, to really integrate, as that job wasn't really giving me that opportunity ... well because it was always the same answer: 'No jobs!' and things like that. I mean, I knew there were jobs, I just think it was because number one I was a Nigerian, and the attitudes to Nigerians and all that.
>
> I decided to set up a business of my own from the boot of my car, selling African food. ... I made some flyers and I distributed them to Africans I knew around the town and told them what I was doing. They were, like, you know, 'Oh very good, very good.' [...] I just told people give me a call whenever you want something delivered to your home, it was something as small as five pounds, you know. That continued like that, until eventually, I went to Dundalk ... and there was an African shop, the man was leaving town, so I took it over. (Interview, 2010)

From there, Benedicta became an evermore influential player on the local scene for African migrants, and in later years she ran as a candidate for local political office. Herein, we describe the local and European election campaigns of 2009 and follow the stories of Benedicta and her team of volunteers from the early days in the campaign to the final count. There is little doubt among those who know her that some day she will hold an important office. And, when Benedicta does gain such an office it will not just mark her successful integration or Ireland's successful integration of migrants, rather that Benedicta's upward mobility and leadership skills are a part of what integration actually means – she, among others, is giving social and cultural content to that word in Ireland.

Throughout the course of two years of sustained ethnographic research we constantly encountered the power of Pentecostalism in the lives of asylum seekers, refugees and other immigrants. And in their everyday lives, Pentecostalism offered useful tactics and powerful strategies (cf. De Certeau 2002; Lefebvre 1992). African taxi drivers reached to their beliefs in order to cope with their day-to-day experiences; political activists made use of religion to charge their campaigns; and, today, Pentecostalism offers alternative visions of education in Ireland. Reflecting on the extraordinary growth of Pentecostal Christianity in Africa, Achille Mbembé and Stephen Rendall were moved to trace the lineaments of *l'état de religion* – alternate structures of meaning that provide 'a means of psychic negotiation, self-styling, and engagement with the world at large' (Mbembé and Rendall 2002: 269–270). Our work suggests that Pentecostalism in Ireland does indeed offer alternate structures of meaning to African migrants, and the guiding principles and everyday practices of adherents establish a powerful critique of integration policies, especially those policies informed by neo-liberalism.

Pastor Femi was one of our key research participants, though to a somewhat lesser degree than the others. 'I gave my life to Jesus in the year 1986,' the pastor told us. And when he described his journey to Ireland he did so without any reference to governmental migration categories, processes or 'status'; rather, Pastor Femi related his experiences through *l'état de religion* – the invisible empire of global Pentecostalism and the route-ways thereof. 'That's one thing about knowing Jesus and Pentecostalism: anywhere you go you carry Jesus with you and you say, "Oh no I am not in Nigeria but I am in Ireland." So you go carry the Lord because there is a purpose for which God has brought you to that place' (Interview, 2010). According to the pastor, 'A lot of people especially in Ireland, they say, "Is that a strange religion?" and I try to tell as many people as I can that, "No, no, no – Jesus said he has not come to change the law but to fulfil the law".' The pastor is a missionary for his church and speaks optimistically about the many branches that have opened and are thriving. His church reaches out to people within the asylum system in centres such as Mosney:

> We let them realise that you are in a society that is not only there to be a taker but also a giver. We let them know that the society you are in now, you are to live as a good ambassador. 'You came into this society and they must see you as someone that is here to be helpful, not to be a burden to the government or the people, but your little contribution what you can do'. (Interview, 2010)

Throughout our interactions with him Pastor Femi spoke about Ireland in glowing terms. In some ways, the lacunae in integration policy and infrastructure presented him with opportunities: 'when I came to Ireland, I realised that, oh no, this is a society that you have to do these things yourself: DIY.' Now, he believes he has a role to deliver help, hope and the 'spiritual welfare' that is so needed during a severe economic recession. 'You know,' he told us, 'the average Irish person does not want to hear anything about church – that is the last place they want to go. Now that God has brought us here – even though you might say we came here as asylum seekers – we're here to work or for greener pastures, for any reason any one might want to aspire to it, but the bottom line is there is a purpose for God to allow that to happen' (Interview, 2010). We devote a chapter of this book to religion, the power of belief for African migrants and their efforts to re-enchant Ireland.

Bunmi is another of our key research participants whose story is woven into this text. Bunmi is a former asylum seeker who is raising her children in Ireland and working in a local primary school. She is a teacher, political activist, mother and writer. 'Initially,' she says, 'Dundalk was a very hostile … place. It's a border town, with Northern Ireland, and seeing a lot of black people was not something a lot of people were used to.' She singles out the negative influence of the media in particular:

> The media was very negative, coming up with crazy headlines, 'Asylum Seekers are Spongers.' And it was what people read, they were feeding them with misconceptions. So when I'm doing any project or talking anywhere I invite them to listen. And they carried the stories, and that started to get things going. And we had to deal with politicians – we wrote letters, made representations, and we were able to go through those stages. It was complaints, you know? Complaints that people were coming here to have babies. I had to say to them, if those people you are talking about are in their 40s or 50s well then maybe they are forcing themselves to have babies to get papers, but these are young women of childbearing age, and you can't stop them from having babies. There were myths that were being broadcast that the government was paying for our insurance – where do we get money for our shoes and our clothes? […] Well the majority of Africans don't drink, or smoke, or go to restaurants (that's a treat for us) – we cook, and we just don't go to Tesco. … With €200 a month I can buy food for the children and for myself. […] So that's how I buy myself clothing. That's what we love: we love to look radiant – and by nature we are flamboyant. (Interview, 2010)

In different ways from Yinka and Benedicta, Bunmi recognises the importance of self-styling, but she also devotes herself to presenting African culture and heritage to Irish schoolchildren:

> I started going into schools to tell them about cultural differences that have implications for education. You see the children were still coming home complaining, 'Oh, they call me a black monkey,' things like that. Well, we thought the best thing is to go into the schools, talk to the children and the staff. We introduced the international day to other schools: we'd cook some food, get dressed up and show them the vibrancy in our colours and all that. (Interview, 2010)

A chapter in this book is composed of an ethnographic account of everyday life in the multicultural primary school where Bunmi works. It was in this school that she began to work on a three-volume book, *Tales by Moonlight: African Stories for Children*. At the launch of that book she was praised by a government minister as a true example of integration. But, 'Integration to me is a two-way thing', she says, 'but the way the government have handled it ... is like assimilation, and they're two different things.' Against the taken-for-granted ways of the world, Bunmi aims to carve out a space for African stories and culture in the Irish education system and embody that very project, vibrantly, flamboyantly even. At her book launch, a teacher remarked that, 'There's a political dimension to storytelling', and Bunmi's storytelling conveys a personal political project that demands attention. Like Benedicta and Yinka, Bunmi is remaking her world in Ireland. Integration for her is a process driven in the everyday life she lives. 'None of my kids has ever opened their hands like this [*open-handed gesture*] to get welfare in this country. It's a pride to me.' This book includes a closing chapter on youth identity and suggests some of what the future holds for integration in Ireland. In a moment of deep economic recession, former asylum seekers and other immigrants are generating alternate structures of meaning in Irish localities, emergent forms of identity are being produced, and new sources of societal hope are available. This book represents an effort to tell the stories of these changes.

Notes

1 Most EU Member States now operate broadly similar asylum systems and a common European system is in the final stages of completion. However, important differences still exist between Member States, shaped by older international relationships and by domestic policies. Public responses to immigration levels in the 1990s together with acute housing shortages were formative influences in the growth of Ireland's asylum system. So also was the close relationship between UK and Irish immigration policies. Britain and Ireland have since 1922 shared a Common Travel Area and the immigration policies in both jurisdictions have consistently moved in lock-step. Thus, when direct provision was introduced in 2000 it was done so mindful of the possibility that Ireland might be seen to offer an attractive alternative to claiming asylum in the UK or in another Member State. In the words of then Minister for Justice John O'Donoghue, the aim was to minimise any 'pull factor for non-genuine asylum seekers' (Holland 2005: 4).

2 In 2010, in an effort to cut the costs associated with accommodating asylum seekers in Mosney, the Department of Justice, Equality and Law Reform's Reception and Integration Agency (which has responsibility for such centres) rolled out a plan to relocate 'single' asylum seekers to a Dublin centre. Throughout the summer and autumn of 2010 several protests drew attention to the very long periods of time that people spent in direct provision and the costs associated with simply waiting.

3 In 2008, over 70 per cent of asylum claims made in EU Member States were rejected at the first instance of the asylum procedure (Juchno 2009). Recent data from Eurostat indicate that over 98 per cent of applications in Ireland are rejected, the highest percentage in the European Union (Beesley 2011; Smyth 2011).

4 Many asylum seekers in Ireland remain in direct provision for very long periods of time. In 2008 an Amnesty International report found that as of the end of February 2007 1315 asylum seekers had resided in direct provision centres/sites for more than twenty-four months (Amnesty 2008; Breen 2008). During the same year, the European Commission published a Green Paper on the future Common European Asylum System. The Irish response included unequivocal statements, including, 'Ireland would **not** support any proposals at EU level dealing with access to the labour market for asylum seekers'; [*however*] Ireland would fully support [...] initiatives aimed at the development of integration initiatives for persons granted refugee protection or subsidiary protection status' (see Government of Ireland 2007: 4 [their emphasis; our interpolation]).

5 Chris Gilligan (2010) argues that Northern Ireland has been ignored in integration debates in the Republic and the UK. In each jurisdiction integration is imagined as something that begins and ends at the border.

6 The high water mark was reached on the night of 15–16 July 1972 when 5308 'Northern Refugees' were accommodated in the Republic.

7 Throughout this book the names of research participants used are pseudonyms, except in cases where people wished to be identified and gave their permission for their names to be used.

Taxis, deregulation and racism in Irish border towns

Some of them will look at you and open your door, but they don't intend to come into your taxi – they just want to leave a word or two with you, to annoy you, and then slam your door. 'Is it not enough for you to just pass me by and go and pick whoever you want to pick?' But they still want to leave words with you, saying 'f' words to your country, 'You are not welcome here!' It can be very painful, very frustrating, but the best we can do is to develop a strong mind: don't allow yourself to be pulled down; don't allow yourself to be discouraged. Telling yourself that you should expect this is not easy. Within ourselves we are trying to find an excuse for them, trying to justify their ill-treatment of us. These are the excuses: 'They never went out of this country, never met with this kind of intrusion of foreigners, so just give them some time and they will get used to it.' [...] It is not everyone that can take this, find the strength, or try to answer this, so many black taxi drivers come into the industry and then leave ... and go back on the dole. And these are the same people who accuse foreigners of coming here and grabbing the dole? They're talking about integration but never giving the room to integrate. [...] We have a saying in our language that means, 'Don't mind them. They think we're here to drive this for the rest of our lives.' So we try to use that as a consolation. Take it, take it for a while. So, we say to them – to ourselves, not directly to them – 'We met them here, and we'll leave them there.' (Taxi driver, interview, 2010)

When in Rome

On 21 September 2009, the County Louth-based radio station LMFM hosted a live debate on tensions in the taxi industry in Drogheda. Kevin Faulkner, representing the Drogheda Taxi Drivers' Association, alleged that his organisation was receiving complaints about foreign-born drivers who were not proficient in English and were unfamiliar with the geography of local neighbourhoods. Faulkner went on to say that those complaints could not be followed up because many such drivers claimed that their photographic identification had been lost or stolen, adding, 'They all look much the same to the general public' (McBride 2009: 25). His comments provoked a strong reaction, and the next day LMFM's

Michael Reade Show returned to the controversy. The following is an edited transcript of the exchange that took place between Kevin Faulkner, Michael Reade
and Fiona, a driver whose African husband also operates a taxi:

> KEVIN FAULKNER: People have the right to choose who they want to travel with
> ... There's no first-car system enforced by the taxi regulator on any taxi rank. ...
> Ninety-five per cent of people on that taxi rank are being compliant and that
> includes blacks and whites, or Africans and whites, whichever they like to be
> called. ... I have no problem with them, but when in Rome do as the Romans.¹
> [...] The public have a problem identifying the Africans in a taxi, because all
> they see is a head, and a shaved head at that, or a lady's head, so they cannot
> identify them. ... They are just going to have to grow up and face the situation
> that people have the right to chose. [...] There are a good number of cars out
> there that are not to a certain standard, and I don't want to go into it, because if
> I go into it I'll be called a racist. ... Let people judge for themselves what the cars
> look like, or what they're like when they get into them, or who's driving them.
> [...] The minute an enforcement officer appears in Drogheda all of the African
> drivers are gone off the rank, disappeared, gone! ...
>
> MICHAEL READE: Is it necessary when you're talking about the problems to
> mention what colour skin people have, Kevin?
>
> KEVIN FAULKNER: Yes, Michael.
>
> MICHAEL READE: Why is it necessary to say if they're black or not?
>
> KEVIN FAULKNER: Well, how do you want me to define the driver who has the
> problem?
>
> MICHAEL READE: But you've told us that it's not just the black drivers that have
> problems.
>
> KEVIN FAULKNER: Yeah, I said there are problems with Irish and Africans, with
> both.
>
> FIONA: So why are you picking on the Africans?
>
> KEVIN FAULKNER: Because the Africans are not complying – across the board
> they're not compliant. Most of my complaints are about Africans, I'm sorry to
> have to say.
>
> MICHAEL READE: So the majority of your complaints are about Africans?
>
> KEVIN FAULKNER: About the Africans, that's correct. Be they from the public or
> from another taxi man who is sitting behind an African taxi driver who hasn't
> his tamper proof stickers, or who hasn't got his photo ID up – he is not
> complying and he is taking money off that taxi rank that somebody else could be
> earning. ... I'm sorry Michael, but that's where the problem lies. It lies with the
> African drivers. As I said already, when in Rome do as the Romans do. ... People
> have the right to choose, and if they wish to assess the taxi before they get into it
> that's their right. And, until the taxi regulator changes that then it stays as is.
> (LMFM Podcast, 22 September 2009)

The flames fanned by this exchange spread in the form of a dramatic protest the following day. A large number of drivers assembled outside the LMFM station and a heated debate ensued, which was recorded live from the car park. One driver took the opportunity to challenge claims that African drivers were over-charging, pointing out that industry regulations demand that fare meters be used and, as a consequence, many people were interpreting being charged the exact fare as overcharging. In reply, Kevin Faulkner agreed that the meter should be used, but added that passengers frequently negotiated informal fares with 'local' drivers. He claimed that drivers were switching on the meters but still accepted a pre-negotiated price at the end of the journey. 'If the meter is on then the enforcement officer is happy,' he stated.

As the live debate continued, the LMFM roving microphone picked up a number of increasingly abrupt comments. Tensions rose when one African driver claimed that the focus on meter regulations and photo identification was a super-ficial attempt to avoid the underlying problem of racism. Those African drivers who commented turned to the ad hoc operation of taxi ranks, where no system of queuing obtained, even informally.[2] Other drivers pointed to their local connections with customers and supported their 'free choice.' Several drivers also claimed that they were abused and called 'white trash' by African taxi operators.

Yinka, the African-Irish activist whose campaign for local office as a Green Party candidate is discussed in a later chapter, joined the protest in the LMFM car park. She was careful to move away from issues of colour and went as far as to argue that racism has yet to become a societal problem in Ireland. Nigerians espe-cially, according to Yinka, operate an informal self-regulation system, and if anyone is known to be overcharging customers, 'We all pull that person out; we have ways of isolating the person.' The problem, she argued, is systemic and has been festering for many years. But, despite her intervention, the comments shouted at the microphone identified racism as the core issue. Kevin Faulkner attempted to bring together the main points in dispute and, agreeing with Yinka, drew attention to the broader structure of the taxi industry:

> KEVIN FAULKNER: The problem we have here – and Yinka said it right when she said it has been festering for a number of years – is there's the oversupply of taxis. People are finding it harder to make a living, be they black or white they're earning pittance. And the taxi regulator has caused this. And we're left to try and sort this problem here.

> [Following other comments] This is all about reduction in fares. When I get complaints about Africans overcharging they're really not overcharging. They hit customers for everything on the meter. [...] When they get to the destination and its ten euros, well if it's an Irish driver he'd say, 'Give me six.' (LMFM Podcast, 23 September 2009 [our interpolation])

But Faulkner's even-handed comments did little to conciliate the angry drivers in the car park. The last word went to a 'local' driver:

MICHAEL READE: Why should the queue system not change?

DRIVER: Why should it change? WHY SHOULD IT? There never was a first in the queue. The customer always had the option to go and get whoever they wanted, right? So it's only since these people here came on that they want to change what we've always had. If we went to Nigeria would they change the rules for us? No! So why should we do it for them? [*Loud applause*] (LMFM Podcast, 23 September 2009 [our interpolation])

The events surrounding the LMFM programmes were dramatic and captured local and national media attention. However, this was not the first time that issues of deregulation and racism came together in the Irish taxi industry. Six months earlier, taxi drivers engaged in a twenty-four hour strike over conditions within the industry and the refusal of the Commission for Taxi Regulation to place a limit on the number of licences. Drivers interviewed for TV3's evening news programme claimed that three of their number had committed suicide in Cork during 2009 because of work pressures. During an interview, Derry Coughlan, the chair of the Cork Taximen's Association, informed the news presenter that his association 'can only take in local Cork men' and their constitution did not allow 'non-nationals' to become members (English 2009). While he was careful in a subsequent newspaper interview to note that their constitution was open to change, Coughlan argued that most 'black' drivers were 'too new to our shores' and were untrained, adding, 'We are like a football club. You wouldn't take in a fella who can't play football' (English 2009). And to this day tensions continue to be recorded in many parts of Ireland (NCCRI 2007; Nee 2009; Gartland 2010; MRCI 2010).

During the weeks that followed the media frenzy over the LMFM radio programmes, An Garda Síochána (the police) attempted to crack down on unlicensed taxi drivers in County Louth. During this emotionally charged period, Fiona Murphy was invited to accompany Yinka to a meeting of African taxi drivers. The meeting was held in the downstairs room of an African food store. The room was clearly a domestic space, complete with a bed, kitchenette and a painting of a couple dancing next to the Eiffel Tower. The loud and angry voices of at least twenty African taxi drivers made the atmosphere in the make-shift bedsit claustrophobic and somewhat threatening. Yinka was warmly welcomed, and Fiona Murphy was introduced as a researcher who would be taking notes. Fear was the keyword. Drivers spoke of being worried about the possible consequences of telling their stories to the media and were fearful that bringing attention to their difficult circumstances would hamper citizenship claims. They feared for their children – would 'locals' seek revenge for perceived slights by attacking their children? There was also the more abstract fear of never being accepted, of always being an outsider.

'The problem on the taxi ranks is also the problem in the town at large,' said a driver at the back of the room to muttered words of agreement. The driver's statement was followed by a series of crestfallen comments about belonging and acceptance. 'Our children are Irish, mine are and yours are, and so we need to address the wider question of racism in the town,' a female taxi driver pointed out. Yinka called for positive actions to be taken: 'We can have a meeting with the Mayor, but I don't want to say there is racism in this town, because I am a community leader. Perhaps this would be better coming from you. You need to say what is in your heart,' she said. 'They say our cars are dirty, they say we rape, we kidnap,' said a driver angrily. His statement provoked irate comments, and fragments of experiences of racism, abuse and shame were recalled. 'Go home you filthy Nigger, I was told,' said one driver. 'I was attacked by a passenger and the Gardai didn't do anything,' alleged another man. Drivers recalled false accusations of overcharging in comments shouted from different parts of the room: 'This is not the price, I am not going to pay you, you black bastard,' and, 'You blacks rob and steal – go home!'

The drivers asked Yinka to attend the meeting in order to seek her advice, but she quickly took on the role of moderator, keeping the discussions on track and going as far as to ask Fiona Murphy to make a list of the key issues, which would then be brought before the Mayor. The list Fiona compiled included experiences of racism, perceptions of overcharging by African taxi drivers, queue jumping, accusations about the quality of the drivers' cars, and personation (the claim that all African taxi drivers look the same and can easily use one another's licenses). Once the list was completed, the room returned to its earlier, more unruly atmosphere, and the following rolling set of comments were made:

> DRIVER: This issue of using the meter is really affecting us. The Irish drivers are also claiming that we are ripping people off, but the meter is legal, local price is not.
>
> YINKA: I have already told the Mayor that black drivers are trying to be compliant with the law; there is no dignity left in this profession for Africans. We need to address all these lies. Irish people have had it too easy for too long, and this issue of queue jumping really needs to be sorted out.
>
> [ANOTHER DRIVER INTERJECTS]: The issue of the Gardai needs to be addressed, whenever you call them, they don't do their job effectively. But we can't prove this. They are constantly targeting us, asking us to move. We need to make them understand what we are going through. The Irish welcome people from the US and Europe, why are they like this to us?
>
> [ANOTHER DRIVER INTERJECTS]: People are constantly sticking their fingers up at me and calling me a black monkey.
> [Agitated murmurs spread across the room]
>
> YINKA: Name-calling does not mean anything: the real issue is the question of queue jumping.

The meeting proceeded with an attempt to identify and enumerate the African drivers operating in the region (thirty-seven names were mentioned[3]) with the aim of contacting them and encouraging them to act. The idea of forming an African taxi drivers' association was also mooted as was a suggestion to march through the town to raise awareness. One commentator agreed and hoped that a form of migrant consciousness might emerge among Irish people; after all, 'They themselves are plenty fighting for their papers in America and Australia.' This hope was dashed by another driver who painted a picture of the march that further sharpened the already racialised lines drawn through Drogheda. Yinka again made an effort to summarise and capture the sentiments: 'What we want is to live in this town peacefully, get them to stop calling us names, stop making it impossible for us to work,' she said.

Towards the end of the meeting those present revisited the incidents that sparked the radio show controversy and anchored the issues in the broader problem of the daily abuse visited on African taxi drivers. One driver demanded that the group carefully challenge all the allegations made against them and wondered whether there was any actual evidence of complaints. Another driver pointed out that many of his passengers had already asked him about the allegations made during the LMFM programmes, and the room boiled over with anger once more. It seemed that the discussion had gone full circle, and the meeting ended with promises of future action before everyone bowed their heads in prayer.

Here we take the dispute captured by the LMFM radio programmes as a starting point and aim to explore the taxi industry as a site of labour integration in Ireland. We wish to explore the ways in which former asylum seekers and other immigrants, especially from African countries, engage with this industry and in so doing negotiate in their everyday lives the tensions between economic and social mobility, racism and discrimination.[4] These drivers often make use of informal networks, struggle to make a living and face many of the same pressures as other, better established drivers. By attending to their working lives and experiences, we aim to draw attention to voices that are rarely heard and often only during moments of crisis such as the LMFM protest. Moreover, in order to attend to the voices of African drivers in towns such as Drogheda and Dundalk it is also important to understand the structure of the industry and the experiences of their fellow drivers. The comments shouted by 'local' drivers at the LMFM radio microphone sounded like an angry bubbling forth of hostility and prejudice, but their words also lack contexts and are separated from lived experiences. The majority of taxi drivers in Ireland must work increasingly long hours simply to maintain incomes that are below the average for industrial workers. Therefore, we should not just analyse statements: we must also examine the conditions that make statements possible.

Deregulation in the Irish taxi industry

Before 2000, the Irish taxi industry was tightly controlled, and only rarely or in the case of wheelchair accessible vehicles were new licences issued. Consequently, fewer than 3000 taxis operated in Dublin during the late 1990s, and the market value ascribed to a licence was over €100,000. Because demand greatly exceeded supply, many taxi licence holders were in a position to rent their vehicles to second drivers or 'cosies,' and a largely unregulated hackney sector expanded to meet the surplus demand. The industry also operated with fragmented administrative and fare structures, and rumours spread of undeclared incomes. At the same time, there were high levels of customer dissatisfaction over waiting times, together with concerns over safety and security: exactly who was your driver, and did the vehicle meet an appropriate standard?

In the late 1990s the Irish taxi industry presented a clear target for governmental intervention. The rationale behind this intervention was spelled out clearly in one of the key reviews of the Dublin taxi industry, which complained, 'The quality of taxi services (both driver and vehicle quality) are not directly observable' (Faber 1998: 5 and passim). This report called for gradual deregulation, quality-oriented policies and standardised practices, the display of fares and identification, and even the use of tachographs to record drivers' periods of duty and speeds. All of this was intended to lift the veil of obscurity and make visible that which was hitherto 'unseen.' Before deregulation, then, the taxi industry was unruly and occluded from the gaze of government, and recommendations to use regulatory instruments to make visible drivers' practices folded neatly into a broader campaign to transform the industry into one which would be governable, at a distance.

Here we are taking government (or 'governmentality') to denote the organised political mentalities, rationalities and interventions through which governable subjects and economic actors are produced (Rose 1999). This broad conception of government necessarily includes the powerful domain of economic theory. Neo-liberal economic theory underpins much of government policy in Ireland, and a competitive, open and liberalised market is understood to have effects at many different levels. On one level, the late 1990s was marked by the rapid expansion of the so-called Celtic Tiger, but public transport infrastructure lagged considerably behind economic growth. The deregulation of the taxi industry, viewed from the general position of national transport infrastructure, was perceived to be a means to lessen the burden on public transport by expanding the numbers of taxis, re-branded as 'public service' vehicles. On another level, neo-liberal theory works off the principle that free market competition has effects far beyond economic ones. Consequently, the deregulation of the Irish taxi industry was envisaged as a move that would increase supply to meet demand, but also increase quality, transparency and accountability. The situation was thus set to change.

In 1999, the government proposed to issue one additional licence to each existing licence holder and allocate 500 further licences for those wishing to enter the market for the first time. This proposal was challenged by hackney operators in a High Court review. In 2000, the High Court ruled that all citizens have the right to gain access to an industry for which they are qualified – and in one stroke the Small Public Service Vehicle (SPSV) industry, which includes taxis, limousines, hackneys and wheelchair accessible vehicles, was liberalised. Within a four-year period the number of taxis and hackneys increased by over 44 per cent nationally (Goodbody Economic Consultants 2009: 13).[5]

The *Taxi Regulation Act, 2003* provided for the establishment of the

Commission for Taxi Regulation, which became an independent body in 2004. Thereafter, the Commission (colloquially known as 'the Regulator') was responsible for instituting a system of governance whereby entry standards for the industry would be controlled and incumbent operators would be required to adapt and conform over time (Doyle 2010: 1–6). The new regulatory environment is one in which a national taxi meter is used, together with standardised fares. Furthermore, a national vehicle licensing system was introduced whereby one licence is now issued for one vehicle, and each vehicle is required to have a colour-coded, tamper-proof disc and standardised roof sign. Drivers are also required to issue receipts.

Historically, the national police force, An Garda Síochána, was the licensing authority responsible. This changed from 2005 onwards. Today, the Commission for Taxi Regulation jointly administers the system of licensing drivers and dispatch operators, and drivers must have secure identification cards. A customer's typical experience of this new 'regulatory framework' was explained to us by the Commissioner for Taxi Regulation, Kathleen Doyle:

> So if you get into a taxi now you will see on the dashboard a photo ID of the driver and the expiry date of their license and the details of their taxi number. And that means a passenger can get in with the comfort and knowledge that a driver actually is licensed: you can look at the picture and the driver. And, they also need to carry a smart card with them as well, which has the same information, and this is very, very handy. ... We have also enhanced this on the vehicles as well: there is a five number digit on the roof sign which is the license number, then there is a license disc, on the front and rear windows which is tamper proof and, again, that has the five-digit number. It has the expiry date of the license; it has how many passengers the vehicle is licensed to carry and the registration date of the vehicle. So that information is inside and outside, so when the passenger sits in, they can say, 'Oh yes, this vehicle is licensed,' and, 'Oh yes, that driver is licensed.' And, we also have information in the vehicle as well, which is the rights and responsibilities of the driver and of the customer as well. So, quite a bit of that enhanced information that we have put in place – just for general security. (Kathleen Doyle, interview, 2010)

Currently, there are over 26,000 small public service vehicles licensed in Ireland. At the time of writing, there were 754 SPSVs of which 509 were taxis in County Louth, including Drogheda and Dundalk, where much of this study was situated (Goodbody Economic Consultants 2009: 34). Entry into the taxi industry is open, and the costs associated with setting oneself up as an operator are not especially prohibitive, even for new immigrants. An individual must have the use of a suitable vehicle (which must be no more than nine years' old) and then apply for and purchase an SPSV licence at a cost of €6300. Applicants for SPSV licences are vetted by An Garda Síochána and must successfully pass a local area knowledge test. The costs of insurance, tax, taxi meter calibration and verification, the certification of roadworthiness and licensing must all be borne by the operator, and a recent report indicates that entry into the industry, if one already has a taxed and insured vehicle, requires an investment of around €7000.

Although barriers to entry into the taxi industry do not appear to be prohibitive, conditions within the industry are difficult. Survey data reporting on drivers' estimates of their incomes indicate that average gross earnings before tax are approximately €16,000 per annum after costs are deducted. Independent estimates, on the other hand, indicate that average gross earnings before tax are approximately €40,000 per annum after costs are deducted (Goodbody Economic Consultants 2009: 47). Those same estimates, however, show evidence of a decline in net earnings during the past number of years, especially in the Dublin region, concluding that this is 'a normal effect of competition' (Goodbody Economic Consultants 2009: 70, 73). While there is no reliable evidence of a collapse in drivers' incomes since deregulation, the typical taxi driver today earns significantly less than the average industrial income. In order to maintain their incomes drivers must work considerably more hours than their industrial-worker counterparts, and often they must do so in combinations of day and night shifts (Goodbody Economic Consultants 2005, 2009). Moreover, just under one third of taxi drivers operate their vehicles on a part-time basis or hold another occupation. The average driver works at least fifty two hours per week, and one in four drivers work over sixty hours per week (up from one in five in 2005). Also, the industry hits its weekly peak of activity on Fridays and Saturdays, especially during Friday and Saturday nights, and many of the fares in that period are carried by part-time drivers.

Today it is not difficult to get a taxi in Dublin or in border towns. For example, walking along one of the main taxi ranks in Drogheda one will see drivers sitting in their cars, sometimes for hours at a time. Some pass the time at the ranks by reading newspapers or books; others stand beside their cars chatting to one another. During weekend nights the number of cars at the ranks swells with part-time drivers, and the streets, especially outside popular bars and clubs, are often filled with lines of taxis cruising for fares. If one were to strike up a conversation with a driver there is every chance that he or she will say, 'There are more taxis in Dublin than in New York!'

Deregulation involved the dramatic transformation of an already atypical industry. As Elizabeth Hoffmann observes, driving a taxi in the United States is actually an unusual form of work: there's no designated office as such, incomes are uncertain and drivers are exposed to a great variety of people and risks. Also, personal characteristics such as likeability or humour play an important role in drivers' incomes in the form of tips (Hoffmann 2006). Aside from times spent at ranks or in contact with radio dispatch controllers, drivers' experiences are shaped by being at one and the same time 'on their own' and in brief but intense encounters with either regular customers or strangers. Hoffmann's research discusses 'street justice,' or the informal ways drivers have of unofficially supporting one another, assisting each other in risky situations, and thereby generating solidarity. Her work draws from data gathered in a Midwestern US college town and argues that despite the autonomous nature of the taxi industry there is a shared working 'culture' evident in street-level codes of justice.

If Irish taxi drivers were to identify with the notion of a work culture it would likely be with reference to the past, before deregulation. But neo-liberal economics and regulatory frameworks are also cultural forms. From their philosophical origins to the taken-for-granted language in which they are enunciated, economic theories and governmental rationalities are imbricated with social forms, societal institutions, and the dynamics of everyday life. The new 'regulatory framework' takes liberalisation to denote openness, transparency and accountability, but the taxi industry is alive with rumours, stories and street-level tensions. Much of this is connected to the pressures in the industry, which are keenly felt by established drivers, immigrants and other new entrants. And while these pressures are regarded by some as 'a normal effect of competition,' the human consequences are anything but normal. The French philosopher Michel Foucault once argued that neo-liberalism demands the perpetual trial of everything in the court of the economy. In a moment in which economic pressures are severe, there is good evidence to suggest that the struggle to make a liveable wage is condemning some taxi drivers to a terrible fate.

The vigil

On 13 July 2010, UNITY, a support group formed by taxi drivers, held a candle-light vigil in Dublin's Phoenix Park outside *Áras an Uachtaráin*, the residence of the President of Ireland. The vigil was held in memory of three drivers who committed suicide during the previous week. Their deaths brought to nine the number of drivers who took their own lives within a twelve-month period. More than 100 taxis were parked around the site of the vigil, and drivers, umbrellas up, stood with grave expressions on that unusually cold July evening. One of the drivers walked through the crowd handing out candles and pieces of paper to shield the flames from the breeze. A photographer circulated, trying to capture the scene from a good angle. In the centre of the group stretched a long row of crosses symbolising the numerous deaths and suicides within the industry. 'This is not a political rally,' said one of the organisers. 'It is purely an act of remembrance for our colleagues. We will stand in silence and finish with a prayer for them and their families.' For two hours, we stood in silence. As darkness began to fall, the scene became an even more poignant one, with the candles visibly flickering in the cold breeze. Several taxi drivers from outside of Dublin had made the journey to remember their colleagues. And at the same time as the Dublin vigil, Cork taxi drivers stood outside their cars for fifteen minutes to show solidarity with those in the Phoenix Park.

In an interview with the *Northside People* newspaper, John Ussher, president of the Irish Taxi Drivers' Federation, laid the blame for the deaths on financial conditions in the industry: 'Some taxi drivers are putting in seventy or eighty hours each week on the road and only coming out with the minimum wage,' he told a reporter, adding, 'Some taxi drivers can't make a living. They've had their cars repossessed, their houses repossessed, they've left the business and they've suffered strokes and heart attacks. Unfortunately, some people deal with it differently by taking their own lives' (*Northside People,* 22 July 2010). Ussher also apportioned moral blame to part-time drivers who were supplementing other incomes by operating taxis and, thereby, 'taking work from people who earn their bread and butter as a full-time taxi driver' (*Northside People*, 22 July 2010). The vigil was attended by approximately 100 people but attracted little media coverage. Although many taxi drivers are members of national unions, local associations, or national alliances such as John Ussher's Irish Taxi Drivers' Federation, there is no cohesive representative body. As a consequence, UNITY organised the vigil and notifications appeared on the website Irishtaxi.org. The notifications elicited a number of blog comments on working conditions and income levels. One driver asked:

> Why do 26,000 odd drivers quietly acquiesce to treatment which would cause an outcry if it was done to dogs? If you starve a dog, you are brought to court and charged with cruelty. Why is the present government allowed to get away with degrading and inhumane treatment of ordinary citizens who have been systematically deprived of their livelihood? (Irishtaxi.org, posted 14 July 2010)

For many such drivers, deregulation has come to mean more and more and yet lighter and lighter regulations, and the opening up of the market is understood to have swelled their numbers with new faces. Comments posted on sites such as the above are generally angry in tone and rail against liberalisation as a dehumanising process.

1 Taxi drivers' vigil, Phoenix Park, Dublin, 2010

During an interview with Fiona Murphy, Kevin Faulkner situated the tensions between African drivers and 'locals' in the shared context of severe working conditions:

> Now these Africans and the Irish people, they are struggling trying to get onto an overcrowded taxi rank. . . . So admittedly they don't work altogether, but as I said to you already, the Africans have to work nearly twenty hours a day to make ends meet. [. . .] God help the poor Africans, they are suffering more than we are because there is no first car system. People are passing them by, they see this, and this is where they are starting to become restless. And I just say, 'God help them!' (Kevin Faulkner, interview, 2010)

During the discussion, he spoke of the changes that had occurred in the taxi industry in Drogheda and narrated the story of those changes from the perspective of a 'local' driver. 'All of a sudden,' he said, 'we saw the Africans coming in . . . first of all there was one, two, three, and then they must have told their friends, "Come in, come in."' He went on to trace the connection between the African taxi drivers and the asylum system, as the following edited transcript shows:

> Mosney opened up around that time as well, and then when they were in Mosney for so long, they were told you have to go and seek accommodation in Drogheda. [. . .] They went for Irish citizenship. They could then do what they liked – they could drive a taxi or whatever. [. . .] There were all sorts of rumours going around, that they were getting subsidised, that they were getting €15,000 towards taxi licenses, which was untrue and unfair. . . . So these spurious claims were going around that the Africans were getting help from the Government. [. . .]
>
> So the problem that we had here then was that all these Africans were coming in. And the Droghedaians were then mixing with a different culture, a culture they never saw before. The only time they saw a black man was in the Lourdes Hospital – a doctor. . . . So they'd be coming to the taxi, and you'd see these black men, and at night-time, all you could see is these white eyes. And of course the ladies were really afraid and they wouldn't get in there, so they decided that they would take our own kind. Now that's how it started happening, and it's still happening. Every person that came along decided that they didn't want to sit in with an African, for whatever reason. They decided, 'Well, we will walk up through the rank until we get a white man.' (Kevin Faulkner, interview, 2010)

He went on to describe a series of meeting that were held to discuss the possibility of instituting a first-car agreement for the taxi ranks and described his close working relationship with an African driver who was acting as the local vice chairperson of the association, 'a sound man, very good, very good . . . well educated.' This first wave of African drivers were different, he argued, from the 'more aggressive' ones who subsequently began to operate taxis and frequently complained to passengers who walked past their cars in the rank. According to Kevin Faulkner, this more forceful attitude set light to rumours that spread 'around like wildfire.' And, rumours soon took on the form of complaints, which flooded into his association: 'This black fella said this, this black fella said that, this black fella charged me €10 and it should have been €5.'

KEVIN FAULKNER: So this went on Fiona, and the thing escalated with the issue of the Africans overcharging

FIONA MURPHY: Was it overcharging or was it because they didn't go along with the 'local price' and put the meter on instead?

KEVIN FAULKNER: [...] They find it very hard to get on in the business. They couldn't make ends meet. Because the more people that came on in Drogheda, the more people were struggling to survive. It's getting to the stage now where if you go down to that taxi rank without a radio link you are looking at less than two hundred euros a week for a forty-hour week.... Imagine if you get a fare ... and the fare comes to €6. Number one, the person will turn around to you and say, 'You're a fucking robber, you're a black fucking robber, I got it for €5 yesterday.' That's because they travelled with a white man – who are now under-cutting the blacks!

During the discussions, Kevin Faulkner pointed to the powerful role of rumours in the industry. He cited a variety of examples. The standoff in the LMFM car park arose following the spread of rumours about police spot-checks on licences and identification having led to African drivers 'disappearing.' Earlier, rumours alleged that government pressure resulted in higher than normal numbers of prospective African taxi drivers passing local-area geography tests. And, of course, rumours constantly circulate on the topic of identity and personation:

I have had a number of complaints with people confused with who was on that photo ID. [...] Because the rumours were going around that he had his cousin driving, his brother driving, and so on, and he had no license. These rumours were going around like wildfire around the town. So what happened was the public said, 'We cannot identify the blacks.'

At the taxi ranks identity is a theme with many memes: stories are told of crashes involving African taxi drivers who are subsequently 'switched' for the individual matching the taxi's licence; stories are even told of African drivers volunteering to take the blame for one another's fines.[6] Car crashes involving taxis do occur; and, as with most industries, there are some people operating taxis whose papers are not in order. But the widespread circulation of rumours about African drivers is deserving of attention beyond merely assessing the cred-ibility of any single rumour. As Jean-Noel Kapferer notes, 'The most important thing about rumours is not the question whether they are right or wrong, but that people deem them important enough to tell other people about them (quoted in Sökefeld 2002: 301). Simply put, a rumour is never just a rumour.

A variety of scholars have sought to unpick the ways in which rumours operate both as messages and as particular processes of dissemination (see, for example, Allport and Postman 1947; Rudé 1959; Shibutani 1966; Guha 1983; Sökefeld 2002; Bhabha 2004: 283–303). For example, Homi Bhabha attempts to isolate the enunciative aspects of rumours and their performative aspects, arguing that the enunciative aspects allow rumours to work like a social glue that binds people together, while the performative aspects result in a 'contagious spreading, an almost uncontrollable impulse to pass it on to another person'

(Bhabha 2004: 201). Certainly, one must avoid considering rumours to be half-truths representing hard-to-articulate feelings that spread virally among ordinary folk. Undoubtedly, there are times when rumours spread among well-educated elites. Moreover, in her ethnographic work on the violence that followed the assassination of Indira Gandhi in India in 1984, Veena Das borrows from Jacques Lacan to describe how, 'The peculiar nature of rumour – its lack of signature, the impossibility of its being tethered to an individual agent – gave it the stamp of an "endangered collectivity," … and led to the world being transformed into a "fantasmagoria of shadows, of fleeting, improvised men"' (Das 2007: 132). The crucial point that Das makes is that when everyday realities are shaken and altered rumours become a powerful social form. Their power and importance does not lie in their often-tenuous connections to some more actual events elsewhere, but, rather, in the lived experiences of their telling – rumours are events (Das 2007: 108, 119).

As taxis shuttle commuters, late-night revellers, business people and others around towns such as Dundalk and Drogheda, drivers and passengers share a mobile stage upon which to enunciate and perform rumours. Drivers spread rumours to passengers, and passengers spread rumours to drivers. The telling of rumours is a process that may involve improvising faceless and voiceless African drivers – archetypical figures fashioned in words to represent 'them Nigerians,' 'blacks' or 'non-nationals.' Taxi drivers have told us about occasions when passengers have spread rumours. On other occasions, we have been in taxis when rumours have been conveyed by drivers. There is an evident pre-scripted and performative quality to the way stories about African drivers are told or events involving them are described. After a time, most of them have been heard before. Events are frequently described as having been experienced by another person known to the teller. Moreover, the audience/participant is expected to respond in conventional ways. For example, one might express surprise, thus eliciting further information. It is our view that passengers are also likely to confirm the credibility of a rumour by sharing a rumour they have heard or describing a situation that they or someone known to them has experienced. It is also likely that the performance of a rumour will elicit knowing comments about practices considered to be typical of immigrants. However, if challenged on factual information or on their conclusions many drivers will instantly step away from the centre-stage and take care to avoid the perception that they might hold racist views. However, the performance of rumours also allows the ideological politics of immigration time on stage, depending on the audience reaction. And much is also dependent on the flow of communication, the always-emergent quality of performance. Yet, while it is important to analyse events and performances, it is also important to stand back and once again consider the conditions within the taxi industry that are opening a space for these rumours.[7]

We have discussed, above, many of the details of the process of deregulating the Irish taxi industry from 2000 onwards. Beyond those details, one of the most striking aspects of the process of deregulation was the scale of public discussions, media coverage and parliamentary debates. During the parliamentary debates over the *Taxi Regulation Act, 2003* the governmental rationalities and economic logic that undergird deregulation were on open display. In one especially illustrative set of exchanges in *Dáil Éireann*, Deputy Finian McGrath traced the history of deregulation back to 'Chicago school economists' and the transformation of the US airline industry in the 1970s, noting the 'ideological grounds' for the expectation that a 'competitor free market would always provide better and more efficient services' (*Dáil Éireann* 2003: 242). Later during the debate, Deputy John Curran spoke of his own academic lineage and what he learned from reading commerce in Dublin. The free market means a great deal, he argued, adding, 'I believe in it' (*Dáil Éireann* 2003: 246). And further, 'The market determines what is viable and what is not, it does not determine, and it is not easy to determine, the standard and quality of the service provided,' said Deputy Curran. This plain statement indicates a powerful discourse within which the market, governed from a distance, is understood as the site of verification and jurisdiction. Deregulation is understood as the use of regulatory instruments to standardise quality of service, responsibilise drivers as service providers, and govern the industry at a distance; the market is understood to determine which taxi operators would prove 'viable' and thus survive.

Deregulation and its economic and governmental rationalities have been judged to be successful by leading economists. For example, in a recent article Sean Barrett concludes that 'big-bang' deregulation 'remains a resounding economic success' and possibly even a model for emulation elsewhere (Barrett 2010: 65; see also Barrett 2003: 33–40). Barrett's analysis covers the possible objections to deregulation, including the question of whether it would lead to in-fighting among incumbent and new entrant drivers for fares that are becoming more and more scarce. On that point, drawing from the evidence of licence plates visible in a photograph taken at a drivers' protest against deregulation, he concluded that in-fighting had not occurred (Barrett 2010: 63). In contrast, we have found that the taxi industry is a deeply contested site, marked by divisions between established drivers, part-time drivers, new entrants and new immigrants. Evidence from other countries shows that the taxi industry is often identified by new immigrants as an accessible site of business opportunities and as a potential route to upwards social mobility (Das Gupta 2006; Mitra 2008). In Ireland, access to the taxi market is liberalised, but opportunities are increasingly scarce, and barriers to integration are not abstract notions but, rather, everyday, street-level and often brutal experiences. And, one may ask: is the taxi industry a potential route to upwards social mobility? From their ability to enter the market to the quality of their vehicles, the mobility of African drivers is closely shadowed by racism and rumours.

Bin Laden's taxi

African drivers operating in Dundalk and Drogheda have long been the subject of rumours and gossip. For example, as Kevin Faulkner observed in the previous section, rumours spread to the effect that African drivers entering the industry were somehow subsidised in order to gain employment after their asylum claims had been granted. Other rumours suggest that similar motives are behind African drivers passing industry entry examinations. However, the drivers' experiences of entering the taxi industry are clearly shaped by informal networks and the opportunities presented in their everyday lives. Tunde has been operating a taxi for over eight years, and he describes his entry into the industry thus:

> Here in Ireland, when I first got my government papers, I worked with [*a mobile phone company*]. That was until 2002. Then I was jobless for almost one year, so a taxi man I know, living in Drogheda here, he told me about the taxi industry and everything that I would need to know to go about it. I was jobless then, so I went to the Gardai for more information about it. They told me go to the taxi office to get more information about it. ... Which I did, I went back to them, and then they gave me the application form. I filled it, and they asked me to bring some references, which I did. Then they called me for interview – I passed it the second time. Now, then I had the certificate, and I was looking out where to go. Then I stopped a taxi to bring me home, and I started having a chat with him, telling him I wanted to do taxi driving and so on. (Interview, 2010 [our interpolation])

Tunde goes on to describe his subsequent interactions with the authorities and his efforts to develop a business plan in order to raise the money necessary to become a taxi operator:

> Then after that I ... went to the bank and spoke to the manager. They said to me, 'You are not working now. How are you going to pay back the loan?' 'I am not working now, but I want to set up my own business.' I said, 'If you want to offer me a job you can' – I cracked a joke you see. They said, 'OK,' so I applied for €7000, which they granted to me, so from there that's where I started. So I was able to pay for my insurance with the other €400, and then I used my car which is there. (Interview, 2010)

Tunde's first day at work as one of the original African drivers to operate in Drogheda is a day worth recording, because his experiences suggest how ignorance of the asylum system and migration processes opened a gap into which suspicion and rumour flooded:

> My first experience, when I started, here at the taxi rank in Drogheda? A man knocked, and I winded down my glass, and he showed me ID card and said he was a Garda. ... He went to the front of my car and checked it, all the details there, the road tax, NCT, insurance. He came back and asked about the insurance, and I said I don't have it yet, but I have the letters at home. He said, 'Its OK, you need to take them into the Gardai tomorrow,' and he gave my license back to me and left. So the next day, I went to the Garda station to show them the certificate. The Garda there was asking me, 'What offence did you do to be called in here?' I said, 'I didn't commit any offence.' ... But the man I was dealing with couldn't understand. ... I talked to another taxi driver, and he told me that because I was the first black man to start they were looking at me strangely. They thought I would not be able to afford the license and insurance. (Interview, 2010)

He is quick to refute any suggestion that African drivers do not comply with regulations, but also recognises the ways in which any incident involving an African driver can quickly draw in all drivers:

> So they should not generalise about the black taxi driver. We are all working to make a living, we are all paying tax. These issues we are talking about, well the meter should be the same. If you are not satisfied with my service, you have your right to demand my receipt and make your complaint. We are not coming here to mess up, we too we came here to integrate. [...]
>
> That is my fear now. I am afraid now. . . . When is it going to stop? Them now they are Irish, they are Irish, and I am Irish by citizenship. What about my children who were born here? What about them? So that is my fear: we don't know what will happen. We are trying to integrate into this society. We are doing our best, in spite of the mentality, 'Black people are no good, no good.' If I am no good, doesn't mean all black people are no good. I may offend you in one area, doesn't mean my wife is not good. They cannot say this, or generalise like that; they cannot say all are no good. (Interview, 2010)

Joseph, another African driver with several years of experience, takes up the issue of the taxi meter in the quotation below. He suggests that the semi-official narrative of African drivers using the meter in defiance of those who charge a 'local' price obscures a story of trial and error:

> [W]hen they come into the car and you go to put it on they say, 'No, no, no, don't put it on. Don't rob me, don't rob me.' And I say, 'How can I rob you, this is the meter, so you pay whatever the meter says?' And because of this they say, 'The Irish people don't use the meter.' And I say, 'Well they are the ones who are cheating you.' [...] So, OK, I will say that I did this twice or three times: I took people from the rank to their estate and I did not use the meter, so on getting there the guy said, 'How much is that?' and I said, '€6,' and he said, 'But you didn't put on the meter.' I said, 'People say, "Local run; local run is €6,"' now I am here saying, '€6 – I did not put on the meter'. He just opened the door saying this is a free ride. (Interview, 2010)

Joseph also speaks of the frustrations of working on the taxi ranks where no 'first car' system is in operation and his mounting anger as the months and years went by:

> On Saturday, I went to the rank. I was there for two hours. When I got to the rank there was only two cars, one in the front and me. So the one in the front took a run while I was there, and another car pulled behind me, which is a white guy. When the customer came he took the white one. That one went and come back again, and he took about four runs when I was in number one. So he made me mad, he made me feel bad as hell. I can't blame God for making me a black man, you know? It frustrates me, you feel bad, am I not a human being? (Interview, 2010)

Joseph's simmering anger spilled over one day, and while he asserted himself he also presented himself in striking ways:

> I was talking to a passenger in my car and they were complaining that we are here to take their jobs. OK, before that, this woman came to me at the rank,

'How much is to [*he says the name of the estate*]?' 'I said, 'It is €10.' She said, 'Rather than giving you my €10 I would rather give it to an Irish person.' She said that to me! So then to this lady I said, 'Would you prefer for us to be begging for money on the street? Because we are working; black people are working in this country and paying tax.' Then I said, 'What of the Romanians?' I am so sorry to say this, but I have never seen Romanians working. They are taking the social welfare and you see them on the street begging for money as well. So is that what they want from us to be doing? (Interview, 2010 [our interpolation])

We have proposed herein that rumours and incidents recalled are actually performative events. It is possible to extend this proposition by suggesting that when African drivers describe their experiences to one another or to 'outsiders' they too are selecting from experiences and memories. In this sense, recalling an experience is not simply an act by means of which facts are taken from the store-house of memory, but, rather, a cultural process which involves the presentation of self or 'self-styling' (Mbembé and Rendall 2002). Take the following account of an incident experienced by Victor, an African taxi driver:

I had a passenger sometime ago. This guy was actually going to the dole office, so he came to my taxi and he said he was going to the Social Welfare Office down there. From the moment that he came into the taxi he was blasting me, calling me all sorts of names – you know the f word and so on. Asking me, 'Oh Nigger, go back to your country.' 'Here I am doing my legitimate business, taking you to go and collect dole! The dole that I have contributed for you to take some, coz if we don't drive taxis you don't get the dole. And yet you have the guts, the effrontery to be calling me names?' So when I look at that I say to myself, what is going on here? Where are we? What sort of society is this? […] I don't know why or how they should look down on me because of my colour, so it's a terrible thing to live with and to cope with. (Interview, 2010)

These are the words of a driver wounded by racism, someone who is recognised and treated as different because of the colour of his skin. But his words also present himself as a person who is a cut above his tormentor, a person who is capable of social mobility – as the saying goes, 'We met them here and we'll leave them there.'

On a broader level, *Migration Nation*, the Government of Ireland's Ministerial Statement on integration identifies economic participation as a key indicator of integration. In this statement (and in similar policies internationally), integration is understood as a process that may be indexed and monitored by participation and upwards mobility. While racism is acknowledged to be a serious societal issue, processes of racialisation hover in the background of *Migration Nation*, while general social cohesion is given prominence as the core policy objective. Indeed, the statement aims to prevent 'the debate around integration becoming a "migrants only" discussion' (Office of the Minister for Integration 2008: 15). As we have shown in this chapter, this approach to integration is superficial at best – processes of labour integration and processes of racialisation are difficult to separate, especially in the taxi industry.

All of the African taxi drivers we interacted with in the course of our research experienced discrimination in one form or another. Some were hesitant to identify their experiences as racism; some drivers sought to brush off difficult experiences in favour of hoping for changes in the future. However, the over-whelming majority of African drivers recorded extremely difficult experiences and have no hesitation in labelling them clearly. Michael, a driver operating in Dublin, spoke to us about the rumours of overcharging by African drivers:

> The first thing I see, well it is not about the price – it's about the COLOUR of the driver. It is racism, FACT!! People can call it whatever they like, but it is pure racism when someone looks at you and say, 'Oh it is a black driver', and then goes behind you and finds a white driver. How is that nothing to do with racism? [...]
>
> To be very sincere, it is humiliating, degrading, and it makes you mental, it really does. Is it am I a subhuman being? But I refuse to accept this kind of theory that I am a subhuman being. No! But it affects you, because sometimes you are on the rank, and you see another guy taking about four or five fares before you – that makes you mad! ... I don't know where I sit with this. I always tell myself that God can give me the courage to accept the things I cannot change and the wisdom to change the things I can. I can't change this. (Interview, 2010)

Drivers such as Michael were always careful to partition their experiences of racism in the taxi industry from other interactions in society. They generally refused to generalise and often pointed to the great numbers of 'nice' Irish people (often denoting 'educated') with whom they have positive relationships. Thus, their saying, 'We met them here and we'll leave them there,' indexes a very partic-ular 'them,' improvised men and women who are archetypically drawing welfare benefits and are judged to be 'uneducated.' It is also noteworthy that many African drivers observed a lack of respect being accorded to all operators in the industry and witnessed abusive behaviour and even vandalism directed at 'local' drivers. Moreover, African drivers also recognised that economic hardships and the effects of deregulation were being felt by the majority of operators. As one Dublin-based driver put it:

> The taxi business or trade, its really tough, to say the least, there are so many things that you got to contend with [...]. There is no awareness from the govern-ment; ... the government has not helped the situation. So because over time, I have come to realise that there is a degree of racism here. We now know maybe it is ... because some ethnic minority are in the same trade competing with one another. So clearly, there is a case for racism out there. (Interview, 2010)

African drivers wished for the same solution, namely, that at the very least, ranks should operate a 'gentlemanly' system of queuing. The example of Dublin was frequently citied, where it was rumoured that all drivers encouraged passen-gers to take an African driver's car if it was the first in the queue. In formal and informal conversations with African drivers, we invariably noted the blending of seemingly contradictory sentiments: understanding and hope were usually mixed with anger and recollections of experiences of racism. However, any even-handed summary of those discussions would have to give prominence to the keenly felt pressures in the taxi industry and the experiences of naked racism. And, the words of African and other immigrant drivers often had a striking quality. The following are the words of Peter, who operates a taxi in Dublin:

> I have two kids. They are in school. I was married for some years and the marriage has come to an end now, I am just alone [...]. I work 'til five this morning had to wake up at seven this morning to take them to school, start work again after that – a lot of problems. I want to work and contribute to the country. I am here now, I don't want to take the dole, but we have cried out – nobody cares. [...] Maybe I can manage; I can work and earn €200 for the whole week, last week I made €230. You have to pay petrol, I have the kids, school time is nearly over now and I am just thinking about school books. [...]
>
> If you pass a newborn baby, a baby of six months old, who can talk a little, ask the baby how they feel about black taxi drivers and he will say, 'They are rip off.' Everyone, the whole of Ireland goes round, if you go around Ireland, and ask them, they will say they charge too much. [...] If Osama Bin Laden is a driver today, those people would prefer to get into Osama Bin Laden's car than into mine. They don't give a damn coz it is just this colour [*points to his arm*], I am telling you this from the bottom of my heart. (Interview, 2010 [our interpolation])

Liberalisation and racialisation

In a celebrated section of *Black Skin, White Masks* (1967), Franz Fanon recalls his encounter with the fact of his blackness. While walking down a street a child sees him and shouts, 'Mama, see the Negro! I'm frightened.' Fanon couldn't laugh or even offer a thin smile; nausea struck. He describes how a haemorrhage of black blood spattered his whole body with legends, stories, 'tom-toms, cannibalism, intellectual deficiency, fetishism, racial defects, slave ships, and above all else, above all: "Sho' good eatin"" (Fanon 1967: 112). While African taxi drivers operating in Dundalk, Drogheda, Dublin and elsewhere, focus on future upwards mobility and on their many positive relationships with Irish friends and neighbours, they could immediately identify with Franz Fanon's description of being enslaved by his own appearance. In their everyday lives, African drivers are called names, told to go home, accused of crimes, and are the subjects of rumours. The processes of racialisation in operation draw from history – 'they all look the same' was, after all, a problem of colonial rule – from popular culture and from specific societal fears.

The racialisation that we have documented thus far has no single locus or fixed point of origin. It is not possible to go behind the mask of political state-ments or government policies and reveal an ideological machinery of racism in operation. On the contrary, it is the very fluidity and multiform nature of racial-isation that makes it so powerful and insidious. Just as the state must be understood as the correlative of a particular way of governing and not a 'puppet show policeman' (Foucault 2008: 6), so too must we approach racialisation as an always emergent way of knowing populations linked to particular rationalities, mentalities and interventions (Gilroy 2000). These days so-called scientific racism has lost its claims to truth, but new forms of racism, especially forms articulated in the language of 'culture,' are ever present.

This chapter has shown some of the ways in which the liberalisation and deregulation of the Irish taxi industry opened specific sites of contestation between newer and incumbent drivers, often divided along racial lines. And we have noted a curious family resemblance between the neo-liberalism driving deregulation and the rather *laissez-faire* government policy on integration. Both policies are marked by an effort to govern at a distance; integration policy and liberalisation policies wilfully ignore processes such as racialisation. As the African taxi driver quoted in the epigraph to this chapter put it, 'They're talking about integration but never giving the room to integrate.' By this, he suggested that racism must be confronted, integration must mean more than a way of speaking about migrants, and real efforts must be made to understand the everyday experiences of the people who give content to the term integration. From racialisation to locality, and from integration to mobility, the following chapters further seek to unpick the everyday experiences of African immigrants in Ireland.

Notes

1 Interestingly, one African driver concluded, 'at the end of the day, there is a kind of adage in my language that says, "If you are a stranger, you have come to a new point in a land, you try to tread softly"' (Interview, 2010).

2 At some taxi ranks, especially in Dublin, informal systems of queuing operate and are often referred to as 'gentleman's agreements' because they have no legal standing and drivers using those ranks must agree upon the 'rules' and abide by them.

3 Currently, the Commission for Taxi Regulation does not keep data on the ethnicity of drivers. Thirty-seven names were recorded during this meeting, but the Drogheda Taxi Drivers' Association estimates that of 300 SPSV operators in the area at least 100 are African drivers.

4 A variety of scholars have documented the presence of racism in Ireland (Lentin and McVeigh 2006; NCCRI 2007). It is important to note that data on the level of racism in Ireland and, especially, data on racially motivated crimes and incidents are problematic. The National Consultative Committee on Racism and Interculturalism (NCCRI) was one of the bodies that used to keep data on reported incidents relating to racism, though that organisation has ceased to function due to funding constraints. NCCRI data tended to show fewer than expected incidents relating to racism. However, recent EU-MIDIS data show that Sub-Saharan Africans in Ireland are among the 'top ten' most discriminated against groups in Europe. Sub-Saharan Africans also recorded high levels of mistrust of the police and a general reluctance to report incidents (EU-MIDIS 2009: 9, 17).

5 It is, however, noteworthy, that data from the Commission for Taxi Regulation indicate a decline in the number of active SPSV drivers from 2008 onwards. Furthermore, the number of licences does not match the number of vehicles in operation, as many licences are not actually used (Doyle 2010: 14).

6 These rumours share a family resemblance with the rumours that asylum seekers receive preferential treatment vis-à-vis services such as healthcare or welfare benefits. The nature of the direct provisions system is not well understood by the general public, and into this knowledge gap rumours have flooded.

7 To this, one must also note the role of local media, from radio stations such as LMFM to local newspapers, which frequently pick up on matters associated with immigration and, indeed, tensions in the taxi industry.

2

Inside the politics machine

There is a zone of insecurity in human affairs in which all the dramatic interest lies; the rest belongs to the dead machinery of the stage. . . . The zone of the individual differences, and of the social 'twists' which by common confession they initiate, is the zone of formative processes, the dynamic belt of quivering uncertainty, the line where past and future meet. It is the theatre of all we do not take for granted, the stage of the living drama of life; and however narrow its scope, it is roomy enough to lodge the whole range of human passions. (William James)

The 2009 local and European elections took their toll on all of those who ran, especially 'new immigrant candidates.'[1] Brothers, sisters, friends, neighbours and sometimes even children answered phone calls, posted election materials and ran errands. Through thousands of these and other small acts they formed nascent political machines. During the 2004 elections, Benedicta campaigned in Dundalk as an independent candidate. She said that she found campaigning 'difficult financially,' and felt that she could not compete with the support levels enjoyed by other candidates. Despite all of this, voters responded well to her, but they didn't respond in sufficient numbers. During 2009, however, she was running on the Fine Gael ticket, and the support of a national political party, a campaign manager and an experienced running mate greatly increased her chances of success.

Each evening, regardless of the weather conditions, a small team of Benedicta's supporters gathered outside St Patrick's Cathedral in Dundalk at around 6.30pm. Fiona Murphy, in the role of researcher and circumstantial activist, attended regularly to help out and track the progress of the campaign. The volunteers were a diverse group who ranged in composition from long-time Fine Gael supporters to immigrants with little experience of Irish politics. There was always an air of enthusiasm as they gathered together and anticipated the work that lay ahead, and as the elections drew nearer the sense of camaraderie increased. Curiously, 6.30pm outside St Patrick's Cathedral was the favoured meeting time and place for the other candidates' campaign teams. The different volunteer groups betrayed their curiosity by eyeing one another warily, which had the effect of further enhancing each team's *esprit de corps*. Mary, Benedicta's campaign manager, organised the volunteers each evening, working off an election register to allocate streets and neighbourhoods to small groups. She grew up in a 'Fine Gael family' and was often described as a 'native of Dundalk.' She brought the confidence that comes from organisational experience and expertise to the campaign.

Benedicta's optimism and sense of hope was felt by everyone, and as the days and weeks rolled by awkwardness and hesitation dissolved into teamwork, routine and shared feelings of exhaustion. The constant door knocking, leaflet dropping and meetings soon took their toll: two weeks into the campaign Benedicta became ill. Fiona Murphy was one of the first people she contacted. It was nothing serious, she told Fiona, but it would be impossible for her to walk for miles through Dundalk's neighbourhoods. Instead, Mary, her campaign manager, would be helped by Christina, Benedicta's sister, and her brother in-law, Joseph.

That evening, Mary, Christina and Joseph marshalled the team at the usual meeting place and from there they began their slow progress through the town's neighbourhoods. Canvassing was difficult that evening: on several occasions doors were opened only to be shut again midway through the first, faltering remarks; on other occasions the lights were on but, apparently, nobody was at home. Rumour has it that during the late 1980s the former Taoiseach Charles J Haughey canvassed for a general election in Dublin accompanied by a man dressed as a gorilla. The actual experience of canvassing provides the only evidence to substantiate this rumour: the difficult first few moments in which one tries verbally to wedge the door open are moments during which Mr Haughey's gimmick would certainly prove its worth. Sometimes occupants from immigrant backgrounds, unused to the notion of canvassing or simply annoyed by the intrusion, slammed their doors with scarcely a word. However, there were also times during which Benedicta's volunteers wished that they could cut short the interactions. As supporters of a 'new immigrant candidate,' supporters who were in the main African-Irish, the volunteers were occasionally greeted with abuse.

That Monday evening Joseph stood alongside Fiona Murphy in the yellow half-light of a street lamp while Christina and a volunteer knocked on a front door. Fiona was lost in conversation with Joseph who was reminiscing about his migration from Africa to Poland almost twenty years previously, about his life with Christina running the African food-store they purchased from Benedicta and about their work for the Dundalk Polish Society.[2] They were interrupted by the piercing voice of an elderly woman. 'Africans are destroying Ireland,' she said, advancing out through the door towards Christina. 'They have no right to be here or run for elections!' The elderly woman then turned back into her house but stopped just short of slamming the door. She had evidently thought of something else and, at the same time, noticed that her audience was larger than she first realised. She turned and addressed the street: 'Africans have ruined America! Now they're here to do the same thing.' The statement was hard to fathom, and the volunteers stood for a while, stunned. 'Don't pay any attention: she is just an old racist,' said one of the younger team members. 'Jesus!' said another. And suddenly everyone began laughing. But the atmosphere was noticeably changed. The elderly woman's words signalled the presence of something which had hitherto been obscured by naïveté, or hope perhaps? Now the difficult realities of Irish politics and local sentiments seemed all too real and all too clear.

The team moved on, through an older red-brick neighbourhood known locally as 'little Belfast' and from there to a newer Celtic Tiger-era estate. At one house a young mother answered the door with her baby in her arms. She cried; her husband had recently lost his job, and she was worried that their house might soon be repossessed. Her story was by no means unique: nightly, the team encountered people wounded by the economic recession. 'I've lost my job and I'm falling behind on my mortgage payments,' one woman said. 'Go away! I'm not even going to vote in this election because politicians in this country have done nothing for us.' At one home the team waited for a few minutes before their knock on the door was answered. A tall man opened the door and fixed the team in his gaze. 'I'd leave as quickly as ye can,' he said quietly.

In yet another estate Benedicta's eldest daughter walked ahead of Joseph, Fiona and the other volunteers. This time, possibly in unconscious reaction to the earlier incident, the team remained close to one another. The door of a house opened and another elderly woman appeared. She was frail looking and leaned into a walking frame with something resembling a heavy shawl over her shoulders. 'Why did you come here?' she asked Benedicta's daughter. The woman may have appeared frail but she spoke in a clear, measured voice and maintained steady eye contact. 'What can you do for Irish politics that we can't do for ourselves?' The elderly woman did not give Benedicta's daughter the opportunity to respond: 'We don't need people from outside trying to tell us what to do,' she continued in an oddly reasonable tone. She then turned her attention to Fiona, 'And, where are you from?' Fiona simply replied that she had been assisting with Benedicta's campaign for Fine Gael during the past months as a way to research political participation. The elderly woman shook her head, 'You don't need to tell me about Fine Gael – I've voted for them my entire life; and newcomers cannot help!' She began slowly to close the door with, 'I don't want to insult you.' This woman could not be explained away as an old racist; nobody laughed. Her hostility was disturbing precisely because it was not composed of the blind hatred that one commonly associates with racism: she spoke as a person threatened by the newcomers she perceived moving insensitively through *her* world. This interaction spoke of frayed everyday worlds and wounded subjectivities. How could Benedicta and her volunteers ever hope to connect with this woman? Perhaps by gaining familiarity with the national politics that she evidently held dear, or through a process of becoming ever-more embedded within the locality? But her voice expressed a loss of familiarity with those very contexts. How, then, could they ever dream of representing her in local politics?

Benedicta certainly reflected on these questions. 'In 2004,' she recalled, 'a good number of people saw me as a Nigerian candidate,' but since then, 'I have worked to promote good relations in the town between immigrant and Irish people' (Interview, 2009). Benedicta saw the answer as lying in breaking the bonds of 'race' and difference and creating new bonds forged of local participation and familiarity. Her hopes resonated with the voices of other 'new immigrant candidates.' George, who ran for the Green Party in the North-East, had this to say:

> When they come to know you, they won't think you are black or immigrant, they will just say, 'He is a guy who will get the job done!, I was very careful not to set myself up as someone running just for immigrant issues, I tried very hard to show them this wasn't the case. [...] I saw the community as one. [...] I tried to deal with the issues, I tried to make myself relevant, and I didn't just do that for the purpose of the election, that's the way I am trying to live. (Interview, 2010)

Here, George and Benedicta show a similar concern to renegotiate the terms of their recognition in local politics. This is integration and political participation from the bottom up. But what they also reveal is how deeply their politics is embedded within their sense of themselves and their emotional investments, and together these form key parts of their lifeworlds.

The 'civic integration' of immigrants is framed as one of the most significant issues facing Europe.[3] In a moment in which texts such as Robert Putnam's *Bowling Alone* (2001) warn of declining voting levels, the hollowing out of societal institutions and the weakening of community ties, civic integration promises renewed social and democratic values – a machine for turning dangerous diversity into unity. The origins of contemporary civic integration, according to Christian Joppke (2007), are to be found in the Netherlands in the aftermath of the assassination of populist leader Pim Fortuyn in 2002. Thereafter, civic integration and companion ideas attained the status of a paradigm, facilitating an ever-greater cohering of European Union (EU) integration policy with migration management and border control (Maguire and Titley 2010). 'The logic of civic integration,' according to Joppke, 'is to treat migrants as individuals who are depicted as responsible for their own integration' (Joppke 2007: 247–248). Thus, within civic integration policies he detects the dead hand of austere neoliberalism. Research on civic integration is often characterised by efforts to define integration, generate typologies and indexes, measure social capital and even model the relationships between 'psychological predispositions' and civic and political 'opportunity structures' (Vogel and Triandafyllidou 2005: 14). Much of this work encodes a logo-centric belief that integration might be achieved if we could only clarify the definitions and typologies – as if the correct symbols and phrasing will illuminate and alter the world. Following Joppke, we argue that while civic integration is often delivered in a local accent it carries neo-liberalism within its grammar: immigrants are rendered as rational choice-makers with greater or lesser levels of social capital. This discourse prises political activism from its roots in the everyday; voices become disembodied words, and participation is rendered as lifeless signatures on policy.

In contrast to the approach which characterises civic integration research, in this chapter we follow the election campaigns of Benedicta and Yinka during the 2009 local and European elections. We describe their career histories as activists in Ireland and overseas and discuss the political system into which they sought entry. But, while we foreground two 'stories,' our work is also informed by numerous interviews with other candidates, attendance at rallies and a variety of meetings. The voices we attend to and the ethnographic moments we document offer a space in which it is possible to tease out the quotidian experiences of political activism and its interrelatedness with other aspects of life. From these perspectives we offer a sidelong glance at the Irish political system and civic integration. This chapter, thus, attends to the everyday in order to show the complexities and liveliness of immigrant political activism, an explicit challenge to the implicit neo-liberalism in a deadening civic integration discourse. Moreover, 'new immigrant candidates' described to us their suspicions that their activism was being used by political parties to gain access to new voters. They sometimes described themselves as pawns in other people's political games and worried that they would be forever trapped in the muted state of being a 'token.' Here we show the ways in which the lives of 'new immigrant candidates' are too complex and too alive to be simply assimilated into the existing political system.

Recently, an important body of social-scientific work emerged in Ireland on the topic of immigrant civic and political participation. For example, Fanning et al (2003, 2004) and Chadamoyo et al (2007) combine scholarship and activism to challenge political parties on their openness to diversity and call attention to institutional and technical barriers to participation. Related work such as that by Fanning, Howard and O'Boyle (2010) draws on qualitative data on candidates' motivations and experiences. Their interview data suggest that 'new immigrant candidates' were motivated by a desire to improve their localities and foster integration. They also explore the challenges of campaigning in localities where racism is present. Our work extends from these important efforts.

Our emphasis is less on the political system, as such, and more on political experiences. There is considerable precedent for this focus. Contemporary political science (and, indeed, economics) is marked by a move away from rational-choice theory and towards a greater appreciation of emotions and affect. Emotions, George E. Marcus (2002) tells us, have long been treated with suspicion in favour of a rational public sphere. Emotions give way to passions, and reason and justice must guard against ungoverned passions lest they result in violence.[4] Against the assumed rationality of politics, the affective turn in the social and natural sciences aims to show that political systems and voting behaviours are shaped by emotions and affect. Our emphasis on political experiences, then, is crucial to understanding civic and political participation in the fullest possible ways.

Rather than just recording the words of 'new immigrant candidates' in order to synthesise their experiences and challenge political structures – doubtless a worthy endeavour in itself – we also wish to explore a penumbral domain which is altogether more elusive. We have learned that political participation by 'new immigrant candidates' does not emerge against an always-already-present locality and objective political structures, but, rather, as a part of the production of locality and lifeworlds. At this scale, the local and the quotidian, political journeys are also emotional journeys of self-presentation and self-empowerment

– and this is often how they are understood and spoken about. Benedicta and Yinka struggled hard during their campaigns to raise money, organise supporters and materials, reach new immigrant voters and connect with their localities. Both candidates found themselves navigating a relatively unfamiliar world composed of such things as the formalised intricacies of campaign strategy and voting patterns. But Irish politics is also composed of the bonds of familial and political loyalty, and local and national sentiments. As such, Benedicta and Yinka's political engagements were emotional journeys through sentimental political landscapes.

Here is Benedicta's account of her longstanding engagement with politics and her motivations for running for local office in 2004:

> I have been very active in politics right from my student days in Nigeria. [*It's*] not new for me, just natural for me. When I heard in 2004 that non-Irish people could vote in the local elections and they could also run in the local elections, I just knew there was an opportunity there. But I knew very late, only about six months before, then three months before I decided to run, so it took three months to do all the work. It wasn't different this time around [*2009*]: I was fielded three months before the elections this time too. It is a very important part of integration – and you must give the Irish government that. I think it is one of the few countries in the world where non-Irish people can run for local elections. It is really wonderful that we can run, that people can vote and run in political campaigns when they are not even Irish citizens. Ireland must be commended for this; it is an important step to integrate people from non-Irish communities. Unfortunately, not all members of the migrant community have recognised that. (Interview, 2009 [our interpolations])

The quote above is the text of an interview carried out after the elections in 2009. Benedicta's words suggest a rational engagement with politics; her political self-presentation is of a long-time activist encountering a new and open political system with the skills and 'social capital' to participate. Her words convey the same optimism and present the same professional self as she did throughout the election campaigns. But, later in the same interview, her voice shifted when it came to describing what did and did not work:

> Support? Support all the way! My running mate was fantastic: he was one honest politician. [...] The way we advised some people to give my running mate number one and me number two ... that was where the plan fell. Some of the Fine Gael party members told me prior to the elections that they wouldn't be voting for me because I wasn't from here: that I was from the outside. They said, 'Why couldn't Fine Gael get a local woman and not someone from the outside?' Whatever outside meant to them, it has nothing to do with my life here in this town, no recognition of that, that I have my job, my family and everything here. The reminder is always there: people will always remind you, and ask: 'Are you going back home?' Home? Where is home? Home is not necessarily a geographical location. Home is where you have peace. I am raising my family here, I have my life here, and I have peace here.

Here, Benedicta connects political experiences with local prejudices, and she considers the meaning of home for someone who is frequently crossed off from the list of those who belong. Benedicta's response to thinly veiled racism is to reach for her own connections to locality and in so doing actively produce locality as webs of meaning and familiarity that do not have to be tethered geographically. The question of belonging elicits from Benedicta a desire to change what we mean when we say, 'local.' Her quasi-philosophical aphorism, 'Home is where you have peace,' seems inscrutable at first, or vague even. But this sentiment is deeply political. 'Peace' for Benedicta denotes a lifeworld in which one may live amid family, friends and neighbours, community and nation, in such a way as to make positive contributions to life rather than invalidating the lives of others. Here, politics is emotional politics.

A brief examination of the ways in which Yinka describes her personal and emotional investment in politics further illustrates the complex ways in which large-scale themes come to be braided together with personal histories and self-presentation. During a post-election interview she had this to say:

> You're disadvantaged because you're female and because you're black. Because of your name you're disadvantaged, and because they don't know you you're disadvantaged. And, you're disadvantaged because you don't have money. You are disadvantaged because, well just because. [...]

> I decided that people would try to pull me down, to injure me. I decided not to take their negatives into my heart. But even then I didn't have the confidence. I know I look like I do now, but I didn't start with the confidence to go into an estate and knock on the door and say, 'Hello, this is me. Here I am. Vote for me!' [...] Now I want to teach people, I want to hold their hands and say, 'You have a voice of your own.' [...]

> So how do we really become part of the Irish community? We have Irish passports, and that's not just a symbol: it is an indication that you will be welcomed into the community. Now people want to give back something to the community. (Interview, 2009)

Here, Yinka weaves together several of the challenges of navigating a dense and unfamiliar political landscape as a newcomer. Like Benedicta, she pushed herself to the limits of exhaustion to keep her campaign moving, often encountering hostility on the doorsteps and on the streets. But, surprisingly perhaps, she foregrounds her journey towards self-empowerment rather than describing political participation as an ideological commitment. But in so doing one can detect a political project: she sees herself as a potential model for emulation by others. She is also keen to portray a positive version of integration, one in which her journey illustrates the active contribution of immigrants to society, from the bottom up.

As we have described earlier in this book, Yinka speaks openly about her life-story. She came to Ireland from Nigeria in 1999 with her husband and teenage son and found herself trapped by the immigration status of being the spouse of a work-permit holder. Yinka describes years of domestic 'psychological abuse' suffered with little help from the Nigerian community or African churches. 'We were very poor and we had nobody to turn to,' she says. Her experiences in her

natal lifeworld were invalidated; her habitus was incomplete. Yinka felt stigma-
tised by her fellow African immigrants and sank into worries about her capacity
to raise her child and make a living. But she spoke to us about a critical moment
in her life during which she found the will to pick up the pieces and move on. A
friend based in London told her a story during a phone conversation late one
night. A Nigerian man, known to her friend, appeared before the courts because
of outstanding debts arising from his third failed business. The judge settled the
case quickly and then addressed the man, 'You are an inspiration to us all! Your
companies fail and yet you try again. Each time I see you, you seem so positive.
You're wearing a suit – you make me feel underdressed.' The details of the story
are sketchy and its veracity is unimportant. Yinka had an epiphany: you could be
drowning in debt and yet be positive in outlook; in the midst of failure you could
at the very least look good. What is at stake here is the power of appearances and
the emotional states they elicit. And even now, 'We live in this country poor – I
know I look OK! – but we live in this country poor.' A striking resonance may be
found in Elizabeth Bowen's masterpiece *Bowen's Court* in which she describes the
obsessive concern with appearances characteristic of the vanishing Anglo-Irish
ascendancy in Ireland, personalities who were 'never certain that their passports
were quite in order.' 'I think,' says Bowen, 'We are curiously self-made creatures,
carrying our personal worlds around us like snails their shells, and at the same
time adapting to wherever we are' (quoted in Glendining 1985: 139).

Yinka's journey into politics involved emotional self-discovery by way of a
recognition of the importance of appearances and the projection of confidence:
'Shit happens: this is life. But I find that with my knowledge of scripture, with the
opportunity I have had, I am able to see how life can be, how by changing your
thinking and your clothes and attitude – well, you won't necessarily have more in
your pocket – you may be happy.' She is now a well-regarded Pentecostal pastor –
perhaps 'a community activist more than a pastor' – and runs a business as a
professional trainer. 'I look like I have a lot of confidence,' she says, 'but that's
where I come from: I come from that point to the person I am now' (Interview,
2009). Yinka perceived campaigning for the policies she believed in as an opportunity to improve her self-worth. She hoped that others might one day follow her.
And even in the worst-case scenario she would try to look the part.

Yinka was well aware of what lay ahead: 'The first challenge is the challenge of
your name, the challenge of your colour. Not enough people know you or what
you stand for. Not enough people can trust you enough, which is understand-
able.' But by 2007,

> I had the Green Party in mind, their manifesto and what they stood for. I knew,
> 'I can buy that; I can sell their ideas.' It feels to me like they're talking about all
> the things that I feel also. I joined the party and decided I was going for the local
> elections. In 2008 I made my plan known to them. The Greens said, 'Yes.' By
> 2009, by March, I was ratified, I started ... campaigning. (Interview, 2009)

Awaiting Yinka was the complex and unfamiliar world of local Irish politics, with
its dense webs of clientelism, loyalty, emotions and sentiments. But she had a

purpose and was hopeful. She had, to borrow from Pierre Bourdieu, well-founded illusions.

A sentimental landscape

With characteristic gender bias, Sigmund Freud once proposed that all politics is an expression of the son's primal ambition to prove the father wrong. 'You will amount to nothing!' becomes the source of the son's ambitions to surpass the father figure and eventually reprimand him for his failings. Politics thus becomes revenge fantasies writ large. Although Freud, it is said, despaired that the Irish were impervious to psychoanalysis, he would have enjoyed the response a 1920s rebel politician gave to an English journalist. 'What are Sinn Féin's objectives on reaching power?' the journalist asked. Padraig (Paudie) O'Keefe replied, 'Vingince bejasus!'

The War of Independence ended with the Anglo-Irish Treaty of 1921, and the protracted and bloody civil war soon followed. But modern Irish political history shows curious forms of 'vingince'. While politics Irish style is certainly different to that of the British father figure it is more remarkable still for its extraordinary stability.[5] Four months after the civil war Ireland held its first free elections. *The Times* marvelled at the absence of bloodshed among, 'a people untrained, by the accidents of history, in self-government, and congenitally disposed towards political instability' (quoted in Lee 1989: 173). From that point onwards the core features of the political landscape took shape. Fianna Fáil and Cumann na nGaedheal (later Fine Gael) owe their origins to anti- and pro-Treaty factions respectively. Fianna Fáil emerged as much as a movement as a party, with a power base in western counties and especially among small farmers. Cumann na nGaedheal, most historians agree, appealed to the pragmatic interests of business leaders, the clergy and 'big' farmers (Moss 1933: 135). Tom Garvin thus observes,

> The emergence, for the first time in Irish history, of popular expression of two poles of Irish Catholic political culture: the vision of the Republic as a moral community, as a community of equals submerging individual identity and self interest for the common good on the one hand, and a non-magical, lawyers' pragmatic nationalism on the other, which saw Irish independence as a means to the construction of a commercialised, mechanical representative democracy. (Garvin 1991: 10)

Fianna Fáil entered parliament in opposition in 1927 and rapidly expanded thereafter. Their opponents went into decline. Following defeat in the 1932 general election, Cumann na nGaedheal merged with the small National Centre Party and the National Guard (the quasi-fascist so-called Blue Shirts) to form Fine Gael. Since 1933 the Irish political landscape has been dominated by these two parties. Little wonder, then, that many commentators still bemoan the absence of left–right politics in Ireland and the survival of 'civil war politics'.

Instead of the left–right distinctions regarded as the norm across Europe, socioeconomic stratifications have not dominated Irish politics. Rather, such differentiations have long been imbricated by history, ideology and a variety of local and societal sentiments and circumstances. This is illustrated by the history of Fianna Fáil, which governed Ireland continuously from the 1930s until the 1970s, sporadically during the 1980s, and as the majority coalition partner during the recent period of social partnership and the so-called Celtic Tiger. Fianna Fáil built a reputation as the masters of 'a machine-like style of politics centring around brokerage between citizen and bureaucracy and minor patronage' (Garvin 1974: 312; see also Komito 1985, 1989, 1992, 1993).[6] More recently, Fintan O'Toole discussed the relationships between nationalism and the localist style of Fianna Fáil:

> In its own ideology Fianna Fáil is the temporal wing of a spiritual entity. . . . Just as the catechism taught us that a sacrament is the outward sign of a state of grace, so Fianna Fáil as a party is the outward sign of an inner state of political grace. [. . .] By attaching yourself to a beautiful abstraction like the Nation, you can be on everybody's side, the rich and the poor, the farmer and the urban worker, and whatever you're having yourself. (O'Toole 1997: 101–102)

During the past two decades, political parties have remained dominant on the landscape. The two major parties, Fianna Fáil and Fine Gael, still retain the most powerful political machines. The Labour Party frequently threatens this dominance, while the Green Party and Progressive Democrats (now defunct) have largely held power and influence only through coalition with Fianna Fáil. There is a small socialist presence in the form of the Workers' Party and the Socialist Party. Sinn Féin, which is both nationalist and socialist in policy, has rarely threatened the position of the major parties. A variety of independent candidates also hold parliamentary seats, often on the basis of personal charisma with voters, and several have joined successive coalition governments. Currently, amid deep economic recession, the political landscape is on course for change. But, in the final analysis, Ireland has undoubtedly seen extraordinary stability since Independence.

Most major studies of Irish politics speak of a system characterised by a particular interface between the local and the national, composed of dynastic political families and personal charisma, brokerage and clientelism. And, running the length of the system is the powerful national influence of political parties with their appeal to versions of the Nation, that 'beautiful abstraction' which lends historical depth, coherence and legitimacy. This is a sketch, albeit a crude one, of the political landscape in which 'new immigrant candidates' must operate, complex webs of localism and nationalism, historical structures of feeling and day-to-day filaments of brokerage and clientelism. The complexities involved in navigating the Irish political system are illustrated by considering just two features: familial and clientelist politics.

A 2009 *Sunday Independent* study (McConnell 2009) showed that thirty-seven of the seventy-five Fianna Fáil members in parliament at that time have or have had at least one family member also serve as *Teachta Dála* (TD). A slightly more modest figure of sixteen members of Fine Gael showed similar ties and, as with

Fianna Fáil TDs, those links often extend back to the civil war. The numbers of dynastic families in other political parties, even adjusting for size, is much lower. While there is nothing especially unique about the presence of political dynasties – take the Bush or Kennedy families in the United States for example – the stability of the Irish political system does indicate that remarkable influence has been concentrated in the hands of small elites whose relatives are at a distinct advantage over new entrants into the system (O'Shea 2011). Moreover, several studies have pointed towards the important role of local institutions such as the Gaelic Athletic Association in fostering and facilitating political careers (see, for example, McMorrow 2010).[7]

In terms of the bonds forged by brokerage and clientelism new entrants are also at a disadvantage. During the 1960s political scientist Basil Chubb argued that clientelism involved the TD as 'the man in the know' 'going about persecuting civil servants' (1963: 272–286 passim). Two decades later, Lee Komito's exhaustive study of clientelism in Dublin concurred with Chubb, elaborating especially on the process of elections: 'The stereotype of Irish politics – the personal exchange between politician and voter in which the politician uses his influence to obtain state benefits for the constituent, and the constituent provides electoral support in return – is a justly deserved one. Politicians are thought to spend much of their time using their actual (or reputed) influence over the allocation of state benefits to build up personal followings' (Komito 1985: 6).

Brokerage and clientelism did not diminish with the economic boom of the 1990s – if anything those bonds were deepened and widened. Thus, it is these kinds of dense webs of relationships and significance that new entrants in to the political system must understand and therein tread, very carefully. Our ethnographic work is concerned with the national political system insofar as it concerns 'new immigrant candidates,' tracing their political careers and following their political campaigns. But our work focuses in detail on the 2009 local and European elections. Therefore, we must also briefly attend to the role of local government.

Dating back to the era of British rule, the system of local government in Ireland has undergone a great many changes during the past decades, such as, for example, constitutional recognition for local government in 1999, and, of course, the process of ever-deepening connections with the EU.[8] There are twenty-nine county councils in Ireland, five city councils and a large number of town councils. Local government is responsible for a great many services, from housing to water supply, and has limited powers within local economic and political geographies, from planning new developments to managing a variety of funds. Local government, then, plays a particular role in the county's political system. But before indicating the ways in which immigrant political and civic participation operate at that scale more details are required on the system and the style of 'localism' it engenders. Speaking of the relationships between national and local politics, JJ Lee reminds us,

> Firstly, the Irish [*national*] political system puts a premium on deputies of the
> same party competing within constituencies to persuade electors of the quality

of their service. Candidates in other electoral systems do not hesitate to remind electors of their concern for the constituency. But they do not normally have to descend into such vulgar levels of ingratiation as their Hibernian colleagues. Secondly, Ireland has almost no serious local self-government, in marked contrast to many western European countries. 'Local issues decided locally' are relatively rare in Ireland. Local issues are largely decided nationally, insofar as they are decided at all. (Lee 1989: 546 [our interpolation])[9]

Historians such as JJ Lee, together with a variety of other commentators, have long noted that the Irish political system could be described as having weaknesses at the scale of the nation-state and impoverished local self-government at the other end of the scale. Overwhelmingly, political scientists and historians agree that the system is characterised by activities in the middle: a curiously local form of national politics that is dominated by political parties and personified by local party representatives. However, importantly, unlike national elections, it is not necessary to be an Irish citizen to run for local government, nor does one have to be affiliated with a political party. The *Electoral Act, 1992* requires candidates to have had ordinary residence in the local electoral area for at least six months and they must be on the electoral register. Beyond that, all one needs is several hundred euros as a security deposit – and voters, of course. Elections involve a Single Transferable Vote (STV) system whereby voters may express however many preferences they wish within ballot limits and in rank order, sometimes cutting across party lines to support a candidate on the basis of individual characteristics.[10] During an election count, as we will describe below, the candidate with the highest number of votes is elected and their voters' preferences are then distributed among the other candidates.

But the story of immigrant political participation is not a straightforward narrative of increasing knowledge of the system leading to increasing participation. The Irish political system is difficult to crack for all new entrants, especially for those without party support, filial ties or 'streetwise' familiarity with the webs of brokerage and clientelism. During a post election interview, one 'new immigrant candidate' compared the 'blank sheet' with which she began her campaign to the know-how of those in major political parties: 'A wealth of ideas, a wealth of information, what to do, how to do it, which way to go – if you've never won, you don't know how to win.' This was commonsense, she argued, because, 'If I was contesting in Nigeria, if this was my local government in Nigeria and I decided that I wanted to contest the elections, I would have my family members surround me. I'd have my friends and the people I went to school with surround me – everybody from primary to secondary school to university. I would even have the people I met in my nursery out supporting me!' (Interview, 2009) These kinds of bonds of familiarity and this kind of wellspring of support was what the 'local' candidates enjoyed, she argued. She did not have those bonds. On the contrary, her experiences indicated a hostile public sphere shaped by many years of negative stereotypes and media coverage.

Even a cursory survey of the mainstream and tabloid media from the mid-1990s onwards reveals overt hostility directed especially towards asylum seekers:

'new racism' in the form of metaphors and mimetic forms that elicit intolerance, impossible-to-substantiate rumours, and oddly even-handed efforts to balance deracinated liberal multiculturalism against coverage of openly racist views (King 1999). Yet, even in this hostile context, immigrant identities were emerging in newly politicised forms. As we have attempted to show in this book, immigrants such as asylum seekers are themselves key agents for shaping integration. It is the efforts of immigrants on the ground to find work, raise their families and engage with their localities that give terms such as 'integration' social and cultural content.

Concomitant with the sharp increases in immigration to Ireland during the 1990s many non-governmental organisations (NGOs) challenged government policy and developed expertise in the area of migrants' rights, often employing immigrants or incorporating them as volunteers. At the same time a number of specific 'pro-migrant' NGOs (Statham and Gray 2005) developed out of religious charitable organisations with philanthropic assistance and now maintain a key role as interlocutors with government.[11] The recent work of Ronit Lentin and her colleagues in the Trinity Migration Initiative tracks the important role of migrant-led organisations and less formal migrant networks (Lentin, 2009; De Tona and Lentin, 2011). The development of these organisations and networks, operating at different scales and to diverse ends, indexes the growth of migrant political subjectivities.

A variety of studies point to the high levels of educational achievement and strong track records in professional organisational activities possessed by former asylum seekers and other immigrants before their arrival in Ireland (Chadamoyo et al 2007). Those individuals have brought their skills to bear on civic and political participation in Ireland. But research also shows that participants often have negative views of mainstream NGOs, which are understood to be competitors for scarce funding and sometimes exploitative of the skills and expertise of immigrants (Feldman et al 2005). Nonetheless, it is often the case that certain individuals from an immigrant background move seamlessly through the different levels of the third sector. Many of the 'new immigrant candidates' during the 2004 and 2009 local and European election cut their teeth in the world of migrant-led organisations and mainstream NGOs. During their migrant political careers, participation at that level was crucial to cracking the system.

It is also important to briefly attend to the display of politicised identities in a variety of other contexts and through different media. One may note, for example, the role of the multicultural weekly newspaper *Metro Éireann*, which was established by two Nigerian journalists, Chinedu Onyejelem and Abel Ugba in 2000. *Metro Éireann* continues to promote anti-racism commentary and call attention to migrants' rights.[12] Noting the important role of this newspaper as a contact point and source of knowledge and inspiration, one aspiring candidate recalled:

> I went into Dublin and spoke with someone in *Metro Éireann*. They explained to me: these are the political parties, and this is what to do – they explained all of it. And then he said, 'All of the political parties seem to have everyone they need

and not all of them are open to immigrants. The parties that are open to immigrants, well, most of them have their quotas filled. But if you are going to go into
politics and you want to have a good chance, then you want to have a look at the
parties and their objectives.' I went away with a party in mind, their manifesto
and what they stood for. I knew it feels to me like they're talking about all the
things that I also feel. (Interview, 2009)[13]

Media activities and migrant organisations and networks are more or less
significant features on the political landscape that immigrants encounter. But
even an extended discussion of these features fails to convince one that Ireland
has progressed from being a country experiencing dramatic, large-scale immigration for the first time in the 1990s to being a multicultural public space today.
Even after Ireland witnessed extraordinary levels of immigration from the former
EU accession states from 2000 onwards, migrants have been regularly conflated
with asylum seekers or simply perceived as temporary non-nationals, lacking in
authentic ties and legitimacy. In the run up to the 2002 general election all of the
major parties endorsed an Anti-Racism Protocol, vowing safeguards against
racism and xenophobia during elections. However, according to a report by
Fanning et al (2003), the political parties did little to encourage immigrants or
members of ethnic minorities to acquire membership. Indeed, at that stage the
Progressive Democrats Party debarred non-citizens of Ireland or the EU.
Moreover, in early 2004 controversy erupted when sixty asylum seekers residing
in Mosney requested Fianna Fáil to consider an application to establish a local
branch (*cumann*) within the asylum accommodation centre. Following a
protracted delay, they were informed that the request was to be refused on the
grounds that party rules prohibited the membership of those without residency
status (Collins and Williams, 2004; O'Connor, 2004). A follow-up report by the
same authors (2004; see also Chadamoyo et al, 2007) commended changes made
to the system of electoral regulations that allowed identification documents
commonly held by asylum seekers and former asylees to be used for voter identification, but there was little else to praise, except for relatively minor changes to
mission statements and publicity drives.[14]

During 2004 just six candidates from an immigrant background contested the
local and European elections, all of whom ran as independents. Two former
African asylum seekers were elected.[15] Although this may be regarded as a
generally positive outcome, one must bear in mind that those elections were held
coterminous with the 2004 citizenship referendum. The referendum sought a
constitutional amendment to remove the automatic right to citizenship by birth
in Ireland, *jus soli*, and thus the pursuant parental residence rights, in favour of
granting citizenship through a combination of blood and residence rights, *jus
sanguinis* and *jus domicile*. The amendment is widely understood to have been an
effort to restrict citizenship claims by asylum seekers with Irish-born children,
so-called IBCs. However, closer inspection reveals a broader governmental effort
to 'manage migration' in the light of evolving EU migration policy and in the
context of the British-Irish Common Travel Area, especially *vis-à-vis* non-
European Economic Area immigrant work permit holders (McDowell 2004: 16;

Mansergh 2004: 16; Lenihan 2004: 18; O'Halloran 2004: 6; see also Maguire and Cassidy 2009). The major political parties supported the constitutional amendment, but it is only by taking into account widespread anti-immigration sentiments that one may account for the astonishing 80 per cent of voters who also supported the amendment. The spectre of racism hovered throughout the 2009 elections.

Efforts, then, to narrate the increasing role of immigrants in mainstream Irish politics must not only describe the vagaries of the political system but also remain mindful of broader, societal sentiments towards immigrants. By way of just one example, Benedicta ran on the Fine Gael ticket during the 2009 elections, but this does not automatically lead to the conclusion that such parties are becoming more inclusive ideologically. Just two years previously, the Fine Gael leader (now Taoiseach), Enda Kenny, TD, addressed a meeting of his party and set out their migration strategy. He argued that Irish people could empathise with new immigrants because of their long history of emigration, but defined Irish people as, essentially, 'a Celtic and Christian people' (Finegael.ie, 2007).

Immigrants in the politics machine

Benedicta was not the only 'new immigrant candidate' standing for election in the North East during 2009. Yinka, who showed that she was a capable and energetic activist on the issue of taxi deregulation, also contested the elections in Drogheda as a Green Party candidate. Fiona Murphy followed Yinka's campaign and assisted her where possible. They first met in a town-centre McDonalds one Saturday morning, the day of a small Green Party rally. Yinka was two hours late for the informal interview but called and sent text messages at regular intervals. Upon arriving, Yinka bought a cup of tea and a doughnut, drew a quick breath and began to talk about the forthcoming elections. Yinka is a skilled communicator in front of an audience, but unlike Benedicta's consistently calm, measured style of speaking Yinka tended to speak quickly and change topic often during private conversations. That day, she was anxious about the forthcoming rally. As often happens during ethnographic research, Fiona abandoned the planned discussion and, instead, accompanied Yinka to the rally.

Yinka's car was packed with flyers and large campaign posters. Fiona managed to find room in the passenger seat among and on top of election materials. Yinka explained that vandalism was a major problem for her during the election campaign, so she kept a ready supply of replacement posters and flyers. Several times her posters had been pulled down, she said, and there were occasions during which she found them covered by racist graffiti or cartoon-like drawings. Nonetheless, she was in an optimistic mood that day. The rally was scheduled to take place near a town-centre hotel, and Yinka discussed her campaign during the drive, occasionally causing anxious moments on the road when recalling especially interesting gossip about opposition candidates. Together they unloaded some of the materials from the car outside the hotel. But it quickly became apparent that the rally had failed to draw significant numbers: a very small crowd waited in the hotel lobby. Not to be deterred, Yinka immediately suggested that those present should instead proceed up the town's main street and hand out flyers. By this stage, Yinka had spent several weeks struggling with inconsistent levels of participation from her supporters. Many of those who volunteered their time could only do so infrequently; others showed up once to an event or activity and vanished thereafter. The small scale and often ad hoc feel of Yinka's campaign served to compound the problem: new volunteers often stood back, cautiously examining activities before quietly slipping away at the first opportunity.

In all, only five people agreed to the new plan to spend the afternoon canvassing. Yinka and Fiona, together with a local Pentecostal pastor, his daughter and a quiet young man from Mauritius, divided up their roles. The Mauritian man volunteered to hold a large election poster, while Yinka and Fiona formed one canvassing team and the pastor and his daughter formed another. The main shopping street was busy despite the unusually cold weather that spring afternoon. Sometimes the passers-by grinned but shook their heads, but, more often than not, flyers were simply grabbed out of the volunteers' hands without comment. Yinka made heroic efforts to speak to people and never once seemed to lose enthusiasm. When she encountered people from an immigrant background she immediately asked if they were on the electoral register. If they said, 'Yes,' however, she immediately described her ambitions for local government with the air of someone confident that they had little alternative but to vote for her. Often, however, they expressed confusion about the elections and claimed that they had no idea that they were entitled to vote – this was the case for a great variety of persons from an immigrant background, from those still in the asylum system to those 'with status,' and from migrants from as far away as South America to those from the former EU accession states. Yinka quickly provided them with a photocopied page detailing the process of registering and talked them through the necessary steps.

Yinka also worked hard to connect with the general public as they passed her small canvassing team. While the 2004 local elections were overshadowed by the citizenship referendum, the 2009 elections seemed to take place in the midst of an economic and political storm. Noting the power of emotions and habits, Marcel Proust once remarked, '[A]n avalanche of misfortunes or illnesses occurring one after another without interruption in a family will not shake its faith in the goodness of its God or in the talent of its physician' (Proust 2004: 146). But deep anxieties have the capacity to shake even the strongest of faiths: potential voters were furious about the banking sector, collapsing property prices and swelling numbers of unemployed people. Immigration seemed to be yet another problem; integration was perceived as a luxury no longer affordable.

Many 'new immigrant candidates' discussed with us the ways in which their campaigns played out against the backdrop of an unprecedented economic crisis. In South Dublin a Green Party candidate's car was vandalised, an incident that was widely held to have been motivated by racism. But she believed that during crises people tend to look sideways or down for someone to blame, and she was determined that immigrants should not be victimised:

The actual canvassing? It depends on how you want to see it. I could choose to use this car issue and focus on it. I am not going to do that – that's not helpful. What I want to highlight is that people are not used to migrants and in an economic downturn you will find that people will blame people who are new that are not native ... and that puts you in a very vulnerable position, and there is nothing you can do about it. But also there are people who are very nice, warm, welcoming. (Interview, 2009)

Several commentators have noted that during 2009 the Fianna Fáil Party maintained a low profile in the local and European elections. As a Green Party candidate, Yinka was representing a coalition government party and consequently her position as a 'new immigrant candidate' was forgotten as potential voters lashed out against the government. She took much of this in her stride, and tried to steer interactions towards more favourable grounds. She spoke fluently about local matters, and took care to emphasise the need for environmental issues to remain high on the political agenda despite the economic downturn. The encounters were often bruising, and more than once Yinka confided to Fiona that despite her political beliefs her choice of party may not have been wise. Yinka, like Benedicta, harboured a sense that her party wished to appear diverse and aimed to attract immigrant voters, broad goals that her campaign would help achieve, whether successful or not. 'What have they to lose?' she asked. But for Yinka, several years of activism in the town and her growing profile at the interface between the locality and 'new communities' was at stake. The small group of volunteers shared the sense that while many flyers had been distributed few votes had been secured. Yinka, however, maintained her enthusiasm and was looking forward to the launch of a new Nigerian magazine in just a few days. She had been given the opportunity to address the launch and was anticipating a warm reception.

Several days later Yinka contacted Fiona and invited her to the launch of the Nigerian magazine. She planned to pick Fiona up at the train station and had set several hours aside before the launch for an interview. However, she phoned to apologise because she was running late and soon after phoned again to say that there was a change of plan. Instead, a friend of Yinka would collect Fiona and drive her to the launch where they could chat. Yinka's friend, it turned out, was, along with his wife, the co-creator of the magazine, a local Nigerian-born taxi driver who spent the journey alternating between discussing the increasing problems in the industry and chatting to his two children who sat patiently in the back seats. The deepening economic recession was resulting in ever-growing numbers of new part-time drivers, he said, and newcomers were taking what little business he had. He was volunteering to help Yinka because he perceived few other avenues through which to give voice to the problems experienced by African drivers. He was looking forward to Yinka's speech in a way that suggested a less-than-formal event was about to unfold.

The launch was scheduled to begin at 2pm, but at 3pm the taxi driver's two children were still busy connecting a large-screen TV and microphones to an amplification unit. Their father looked anxious and occasionally made suggestions, but it was clear that the two children were the technology experts. By 4pm the room was beginning to fill with well-dressed Nigerian men and women. Many of the women wore colourful traditional dresses, crowned with large head-pieces, and sometimes elaborate wigs. The event was characterised by a braiding together of political activism, the celebration of the cultural achievement that the magazine represented, and an overtone of religious solidarity. A great number of those present were Pentecostals, and one frequently heard praise to God for the successes of the day. One of the speakers invited to the launch was Yinka's friend Bunmi. Dressed in a traditional outfit, Bunmi took her place at a table positioned at the front of the room. After the creators of the magazine had spoken, she picked up a now-functioning microphone and began to speak in a slow, deliberate voice. 'Nigerian people, the people of the diaspora, need to work together,' she said before explaining: 'We need to face the way we are represented in Ireland. Too many negative images are circulating. The media is full of stories of people leaving Ireland because of the economy, but a lot of Africans are here to stay, particularly the children, and Irish people need to know that we are here to stay and do our part. We have to change these negative images and show them who we really are!' Bunmi then launched the magazine with words of hope and praise for those responsible. 'Praise God' and 'Praise Him' could be heard throughout the room. Some people bowed their heads; others clapped their hands quietly as they nodded in agreement. Tea and sandwiches were brought by teenagers, and the room soon filled with laughter, chat and even singing.

The time had come for Yinka to address the crowd about her political campaign. She called for attention but many of the men in the room were too engrossed in conversation to pay any attention. A pastor took up a microphone and demanded silence in no uncertain terms. Yinka then began to speak. She introduced herself in elaborate detail, but assured her audience with good humour that such an introduction was hardly necessary. She spoke about how Ireland gives migrants the opportunity to vote in local elections, and this was one of the few ways, she stressed, through which asylum seekers could have a voice in politics. Gesturing to her active role in local affairs during the past number of years, now, she said, was the time to bring more immigrant voices into Irish politics. She would represent their interests, she promised. As the applause began, Yinka shouted, 'Register now! And vote for me!' The pastor took the microphone once again and blessed her campaign. He touched her on the head as he prayed for her success. She kept her head bowed, and a small group of women standing to one side began to sing and sway gently.

Shortly after the launch ended Yinka was back canvassing on the streets with a few volunteers. She pressed flyers into the hands of passing townspeople and tried her best to bring environmental issues into the interactions as quickly as possible. A member of the catering staff from the Mosney asylum accommodation centre stopped for a while and spoke a few words in Yoruba to her. This buoyed her up, and despite the efforts of people to ignore her as they passed she continued to gently harass dozens of them with environmental slogans until it became too dark to continue.

The count

During the final days of the campaign Benedicta's team went into high gear. The volunteers had bonded as a group, and now the process of canvassing was a routine in which the component activities were completed quickly and without instruction. As a candidate for a major political party, Benedicta and her Fine Gael running mate could draw on the expertise and support of a semi-professional campaign manager. Benedicta was to concentrate on urban areas in Dundalk South and urge voters to give her running mate their second preference; her running mate, an experienced and incumbent local politician, would focus on rural areas. Political campaigns are about organisation, detail and presentation. Like the analogy the philosopher Wittgenstein once drew between learning a language and looking inside a locomotion cabin, to the debutant a political campaign is an unfamiliar world filled with hard-to-fathom activities and incomprehensible details. Knowing what to do and when to do it requires meaningful experience. Campaign management became more important as the day of the elections drew closer.

During the weeks leading up to voting day Benedicta's volunteers made hundreds of telephone calls, and countless letters and flyers were mailed to potential voters. Benedicta held several public meetings and rallies, all of which were well attended. She gave several radio interviews and participated in party press conferences. But the process of canvassing in Irish local politics is dominated by door-to-door canvassing, greeting the public on the street, and, in the popular imagination and folk-memory at least, by appearing anywhere people form in crowds. Memories of local and, indeed, national elections in Ireland have long conjured up an image of politicians addressing mass-goers outside church gates from aloft the boot of a car. Benedicta avoided standing on a car in favour of canvassing inside Pentecostal churches; she canvassed tirelessly on the streets and in the neighbourhoods and seemed to become ever-more busy the longer the campaign continued. She worked off the electoral register to target voters on the advice of the Fine Gael manager. She appeared to get on well with her running mate and seemed to be able to shift deftly from one local concern to another. Her ability to identify with people and present herself differently according to the audience grew as time went by. The volunteers witnessed Benedicta's political skills growing and they too became more confident in the campaign.

During the final days before votes were cast, Yinka's campaign began to falter. She was without the expertise of a professional campaign manager – her manager was a Nigerian taxi driver with little experience. Volunteer numbers began to drop off sharply. But she continued canvassing, often alone, until no more could be done. She became visibly tired, though her enthusiasm never diminished. When the voting day finally arrived, Yinka seemed almost lost for something to do. Now all she could do was await the results.

On Friday 5 June, Yinka, Benedicta and their volunteers spent the day reminding people of their promises to vote for them, while also ferrying people to the voting stations. The day was filled with gossip and lots of talk characterised by little expertise. Nothing would really be known until the election counts the following morning. The count in Drogheda was held in a large public building. Initially, people milled about, often cursing the poor weather and the possible effects this might have on voters. As time went by, however, the large hall became a quiet, sombre place. Candidates and their teams filled an anteroom where they watched the voting papers being tipped out of the boxes onto tables. Most of those present wore their party allegiance badges, and several people kept running tallies in notebooks. 'Wow, this is as backward as Nigeria!' said one of Yinka's volunteers. Several of the seasoned campaigners and managers grinned and then winced as if they had thought of a wonderful retort that could not be expressed because of the political implications. But, none of Yinka's supporters understood the process well, and a campaign manager from a major party, evidently confident of victory, took the time to explain the vote transfer process to them.

Yinka arrived. Her eyes were red from lack of sleep and the cumulative effects of weeks spent canvassing. 'I'm too tired for this!' she said after a while. 'I'm going back home.' Shortly thereafter one of her volunteers phoned her with an early tally. Soon word began to spread that Yinka had conceded.

In Dundalk a few members of Benedicta's team and her party campaign manager attended the count. She stopped by early in the day and seemed confident, but after a time she decided to return home and await phone and text updates. Benedicta's supporters were still hopeful as mid-afternoon arrived, though the count room was filled with discussions of an extraordinary performance by Sinn Féin. As a border town, Dundalk is an area with a long history of republican sympathies and a place where Sinn Féin have polled well, especially in the poorer neighbourhoods. But the extent of their success, even considering the political discontent fostered by the financial crisis, seemed to catch many experts off guard. In the absence of reasonable analysis rumours were beginning to fill the void: 'They've singled out Dundalk;' 'I've heard that there'll be a recount – something's wrong here!' As time went by it became clear that Benedicta's running mate would be re-elected. Benedicta's chances, on the other hand, were looking remote. She didn't get many second preferences, even from her running mate's voters – they expressed a preference for candidates from other parties rather than Benedicta. During the early afternoon she telephoned and thanked her team for their efforts but was sure, she said, that it was time to concede. Her final tally showed that she received roughly the same number of votes as she did in 2004.

Hope Alive

A number of weeks after the elections, Yinka planned a post-election meeting. She aimed to bring the African candidates together to discuss their experiences and the potential ways in which performances could be improved in the years to come. She decided to call the event 'Hope Alive.' Later, during an interview she described her motivations in the following terms:

During the elections I didn't experience too many negatives, but people were abused, people were attacked, cars were vandalised, people were spat on, people were called names, some people were told they were not welcome. They were not voted for. People were dejected, de-motivated, disappointed. 'We need to keep the hope in them alive,' I said. 'It's not just about politics – Hope Alive is about empowering them!' (Interview, 2009)

Most of the unsuccessful candidates who identified themselves as 'African' responded warmly to the idea and seemed especially welcoming of the opportunity to discuss the actual process of canvassing. She was explicit in her focus on African candidates, rather than opening the event to candidates from countries such as Poland – her concern was to unpick the particular challenges faced by 'visible' minorities. As the weeks passed, some of the initial enthusiasm began to fade as those who ran for election began to re-engage with their former work as local activists. And, many began to express the view that they would not campaign again. We listened to former candidates using terms like 'bruising' and 'wounding' to describe the process they had been through.

Yinka was insistent that the title of the proposed event, Hope Alive, conveyed her sense that none had actually failed, arguing that the profiles of individuals, communities and issues had been raised. In their ongoing work in neighbourhoods throughout Ireland, Yinka felt, African candidates needed to reflect on their experiences. Moreover, new candidates would emerge in the years to come, and the lessons learned in 2009 would be invaluable if they were somehow captured. She persevered. Posters and bookmarks were produced in the form of a collage made from candidates' election flyers. Invitations for an evening meeting were sent out, and speakers were chosen and contacted. The venue was a large hall in an industrial estate on the outskirts of Drogheda. As with the launch of the Nigerian magazine during the run up to the elections, the event mixed its stated objective with social celebration. Participants arrived gradually wearing either traditional outfits or their best church-going clothes – despite the fact that Yinka's invitations called for a 'light African' dress code. Perhaps they knew better, because a number of Embassy staff from various African countries arrived, as did a crew from Sky TV. Nineteen African candidates contested the elections, though not all attended the event. Each candidate was presented with a commemorative collage-poster and given time to reflect on their experiences.

In the main, the candidates who ran on political party tickets expressed some frustration with volunteer team numbers and the costs associated with their campaigns. Surprisingly, perhaps, many spent time reflecting on their lack of familiarity with their parties – they had taken care to verse themselves in policies and manifestos but found internal party politics difficult to understand and at times frustrating. Independent candidates, on the other hand, described the stresses of managing volunteers, the significant, 'wounding' financial costs and their constant struggles to get potential voters to register. All of the candidates spoke about the difficulties of door-to-door canvassing, from understanding and rearticulating neighbourhood-level concerns to their encounters with racism. Benedicta was also present at the event. When her turn came, she accepted the

2 Hope Alive, 2009

poster and addressed the audience in her customary measured and authoritative way. 'The numbers of candidates has increased since 2004,' she said, and 'It will double again the next time around!' The event was about hope, she argued, and there were plenty of reasons for hope. A small band began to play African music, food was available on tables, and the mood indeed became hopeful. Several people said, 'We need to meet again; we shouldn't leave it here.'

Following the Hope Alive event, the NGO Integrating Ireland held a meeting to capture the experiences of 'new immigrant candidates'. Mark Maguire and Fiona Murphy acted as rapporteurs for group discussions among the newly elected and unsuccessful candidates. All of those who ran considered themselves to have been unprepared for the complexities of the Irish political system. This, they felt, was compounded by the need also to educate immigrants about the system, registration and their voting rights. Many felt that the experience was positive in terms of what they achieved and positive in terms of their self-confidence and profile in local communities. But many also described the campaigns as 'wounding,' financially and personally. What if one stands back from the 2009 elections, then, and asks: to where from here? If the voting system can be explained better and voter registration is improved will more 'new immigrant candidates' be elected in the future? If we change the system and the symbols will the world follow accordingly? Perhaps, but reducing barriers to political partici-pation and producing policies that challenge racism is only a part of the story –

the rest of the story is composed of knowledge of those who ran. Against a neo-liberal solution for a complex problem, we must consider what may be learned by descending into the ordinary.

Myths and stories

The stories of Benedicta's and Yinka's campaigns and their emotional investments in Irish politics are not just illustrative case studies in political participation and civic integration. Stories, Michael Jackson (2002) reminds us, refuse the god's-eye view from above in favour of understandings and perspectives situated *within* the world. Rather than sifting through the cases of 'new immigrant candidates' in search of the commonalities that transcend each, we argue for attention to everyday and meaningful lifeworlds, 'For in telling stories we testify to the very diversity, ambiguity, and interconnectedness of experiences that abstract thought seeks to reduce, tease apart, regulate, and contain in the name of administrative order and control' (Jackson 2002: 253).

Across Europe, migration and integration policy are being 'up-loaded' to the competence of the EU. National differences and nation-state 'models' of integration are now folded into broader discussions about European civic integration. The EU's nonbinding 'common basic principles' for immigrant integration, for example, aim to create 'the opportunities for the immigrants' full economic, social, cultural, and political participation'. But integration into what, one might ask? For the EU Council the answer is clear: 'The principles of liberty, democracy, respect for human rights and fundamental freedoms, and the rule of law' (European Union 2006: 19). Discussions of common values have intensified in recent years. But these values are less than clear on closer inspection. When one thinks of the centuries of debates over precisely what constitutes liberty, or the crises in contemporary democratic participation, all that is solid melts into air. Moreover, this discourse serves not just to articulate Europe but also to construct it. Realist writers are illusionists, according to Guy de Maupassant, and perhaps, 'each of us simply makes an illusion of the world, a poetic, sentimental, joyous, melancholic, dirty, or lugubrious illusion according to our natures' (quoted in Bourdieu 1996: 331). EU integration policy and the current discourse on civic integration share a genre – the adherence to the game as a game to be taken seriously, and the *illusio* of the reality beyond, 'the world of common sense, the world of doxic experience of the common world procured by successful socialisation' (Bourdieu 1996: 227, 331 passim).

Christian Joppke (2006) argues that 'civic integration' marks an important policy moment in Europe in which the assimilative agency of the nation-state has been progressively written over. Today, cultural assimilation is spoken of in terms of integration into societal institutions, labour market access, language acquisition, adherence to the law, and political and civic participation. Whereas assimilation once meant, '*Je te fais disparaître*' ('I will make you disappear'), to borrow from Nicolas Sarkozy, now policy aims to produce self-sufficient, skilled and autonomous immigrants; now it is the state that should disappear. But this seemingly neutral and neo-liberal worldview is still haunted by a cultural spectre – commonsense values that are always elusive and cultural to the core. And whilst talk of national integration 'models' does little justice to the complexities of the current transformations at either end of the scale, it does remain important to attend to the specific ways in which integration is articulated and understood within Member States.

The well-known writer Roddy Doyle (2008: 100–130) captures something of the dynamic relationships between the logic of international migration management and the local and nationalistic worlds in which those efforts take shape. In the short story '57% Irish' Doyle's protagonist, Ray, is offered a position in the new ministry of arts and ethnicity. The job involves devising integration tests that will work to exclude immigrants. Ray develops a test based on affective responses to the song 'Danny Boy,' Riverdance and a goal scored by an Irish footballer during the 2002 World Cup. What Doyle captures in humour is the elusiveness inherent in conceptions of national integration. His essay also serves to remind one that even if integration is today spoken of in rational and neutral terms and studied quantitatively it remains a cultural concept used to frame cultural dynamics – an *illusio*.

Recent social-scientific research on immigrant civic and political participation in Ireland has challenged political parties and the political system to be more open to new immigrant participation (see, for example, Fanning et al 2010). Influenced by the current 'affective turn,' here we have extended this work away from political systems and towards political experiences. Our central premise is that much can be learned by attending to the everyday and to the interrelatedness of politics with other aspects of people's lifeworlds. Thus, the stories of Benedicta's and Yinka's campaigns and their emotional investments in Irish politics cannot be read as just illustrative case studies in political participation and civic integration, because the stories of people undermine the myths of states (Kapferer 1988; Jackson 2002: 28). A variety of studies of political integration in Ireland include the words of 'new immigrant candidates.' Their motivations for entering politics and their goals are ostensibly plain in their statements: to enhance integration, to contribute to local life, to challenge racism and discrimination. But mere words are not voices. For Veena Das voices denote not utterances but that which animates words and gives them life: the sociality of human bonds, the emotional and affective domains of frayed everyday lives (Das 2007 passim).

The stories of Benedicta's and Yinka's campaigns tell of two people who wished to enhance integration and contribute to local life, countering racism and discrimination by their actions and their very beings. But their stories also reveal the ways in which their political aspirations are embedded in their emotional lives, their senses of self and worth. When Benedicta spoke of 'home' as a place 'where you have peace,' she revealed that for her, political participation is about remaking the local such that it includes her life and her family. When Yinka knocked on doors and said, 'Hello, this is me. Here I am. Vote for me!' she argued that she was trying to reach out to others and say, 'You have a voice of your own.'

This sentimental politics closely tied to other aspects of their lives. Little can be understood about their campaigns without regard to the personal histories, or, for example, the important role of Pentecostal churches as spiritual forces and spaces of networks and bonds of familiarity. So much is overlooked if we do not attend to subjects and their worlds.

And the stories of Benedicta's and Yinka's campaigns cannot be judged to end without success, because such judgements can only be handed down from above. Benedicta and Yinka were born and raised in Nigeria and related many of their experiences to their formative years in that troubled country. When 'new immigrant candidates' tried to overcome the challenge of registering immigrant voters they did so mindful of the contrasting opportunities for electoral participation in Nigeria. As one Dublin-based candidate put it:

> Several of us encouraged people to vote. You see in Nigeria politics doesn't work, so why would people want to vote – because your vote doesn't count! [...] Politicians are seen as liars, cheats, devilish, no politician tells the truth – we need to change – you know? When I wanted to run, I got people to see what I intended; how far I had come, and [*that*] I allowed people to talk. (Interview, 2010 [our interpolation])

These political sentiments flow into transnational projects that stretch beyond the shores of Ireland. Personal histories and bonds cannot be stopped at the border by attempts to frame civic integration and participation in national politics. Investments in political and civic life in Ireland are credited towards investments in improving the political situation in Nigeria. Benedicta, Yinka and Bunmi have played an important role in setting up Action Congress in Ireland, an organisation that aims to encourage transnational Nigerians to set up local chapters. According to Benedicta:

> Action Congress is the only credible opposition party in Nigeria. Corruption is rife in Nigeria, so it is difficult. We decided to start it here so that whatever we learn from the Irish political system we can bring to Nigeria. I have learned here that politics can be clean. [...] We can marry the two: the Irish way of politicking and the Nigerian way, and bring our experience here to impact on Nigeria. It is a Herculean task, but it can be accomplished – we can teach Nigeria that politics can be done differently. (Interview, 2010)

Politics in Nigeria, Pentecostal churches, part-time campaign managers who are also part-time taxi drivers, from the ground up visions of integration, reimaginings of the local, self-presentation and appearances – these are all parts of the sentimental stories of 'new immigrant candidates,' stories that displace certainties and dissolve the myths of integration. Close examination of the Irish political system with a view to making it more accessible is a worthy endeavour, but we must also attend to the lifeworlds of those involved. Understanding the emotional and affective engagements of immigrant candidates may appear to be a sentimental approach but it is in fact crucial to any understanding of what is actually occurring on the ground. Attention to emotional politics, affect and sentiment may also speak to politics more broadly. During the course of our research we asked a senior political party figure to say when, exactly, she would be able to say that Ireland had achieved a good measure of political integration. This was her reply: 'When a black fella lifts the Sam Maguire Cup or wins a gold medal for Ireland, that's when they are going to be totally accepted in politics in this country.'

Notes

1 Using the label 'new immigrant candidate' or 'immigrant candidate' is problematic. Several research participants described themselves as immigrant candidates but occasionally resisted the label, arguing that they were first and foremost Irish candidates. Others described themselves as 'African candidates' to differentiate themselves from 'Polish candidates' who, arguably, experienced racialisation is different ways. Herein, and following Fanning et al (2010), we use the term 'new immigrant candidates' to denote those political participants who migrated to Ireland, often though not exclusively through the asylum system from the 1990s onwards, rather than returned Irish émigrés (one may add, of course, that Irish political history shows a variety of political figures from migrant backgrounds during the twentieth century). We keep 'new immigrant candidate' in quotation marks throughout to indicate the ambiguous and contestable nature of the label.

2 Throughout this book we are showing the interrelatedness of different domains in research participants' lives, from religion to education and labour to politics. The key sites in people's lives tend also towards the interrelated and poly-functional. Just as churches are sites of political participation so too are 'African' shops sites of sociality and activism (see Spiller 2001).

3 The EU *Handbook on Integration* (2009) narrows the concerns into the term 'civic citizenship.'

4 Little wonder then that *Punch*, the popular nineteenth-century magazine, once suggested that Irish passions resulted in tribunals composed of, 'accuser and accused – twelve paces apart to prevent accidents – a couple of judges and a surgeon' (*Punch* 1841: 153).

5 The lack of resemblance between Irish and British politics has been noted time and again by political scientists. Indeed, Kenneth Carty goes further in his preface to *Party and Parish Pump* (1983), noting that Irish politics has often been regarded as exceptional internationally. 'My attention was drawn to Ireland by footnotes,' he tells us, and, 'Over and over again the literature of comparative politics noted simply "except Ireland"' (Carty 1983: xiii).

6 Mart Bax's (1976) anthropological account of 'machine politics' explains how an effective politician was understood to 'have pull' within the world of official appointments, favours and interfaces with bureaucracy. Locals were not slow to ask the politicians to 'pull strings.' As one local jokingly put it, 'It's not for nothing that our national emblem is the harp!' (Bax 1976: 46)

7 Historically more than during the present day, one has to mention the role of the Catholic Church. Kenneth Carty in *Party and Parish Pump* (1983: 142), puts it succinctly, 'The Irish Church is an anti-intellectual, male-dominated, authoritarian, hierarchical organisation which rewards loyalty and faithful service. So are Irish political parties.'

8 Local government in Ireland emerged after Independence in a centralised form. A

Ministry of Local Government was established in 1922, appointments were made centrally, and the posts of County Managers were filled by civil servants, all to protect against, 'the evils of patronage, of family, local and political influences' (Kissane 2008: 23).

9 In concluding his classic work on Irish history, *Ireland: 1912–1985*, JJ Lee turns to the topic of party politics. 'Stability apart,' he tells us, 'The Irish have been nearly as sterile in government as they have been creative in politics. . . . The catch-all nature of the two main parties, now less ideologically distinguishable than in earlier decades, leaves both appealing to the total electorate, and therefore slow to take a stand against any pressure group. The party system has thus become inordinately exposed to extortionate demands' (Lee 1989: 454–546).

10 In Ireland 'proportional representation' is understood to automatically denote STV even though this is not axiomatic internationally (for full discussion see Gallagher 2008: 197–223).

11 Though, as Pauline Cullen (2009: 101–102) has noted, funding constraints and proximity to governing structures tends to compromise radicalism in such organisations.

12 Following the work of Chadamoyo et al (2007), Fianna Fáil launched a drive to recruit participation among immigrant groups.

13 Politicised immigrant identity formation is also available in a variety of literary works, that most sacred of 'truly Irish' endeavours (see, for example, Bourke and Faragó 2010). These voices disrupt the assumed homogeneity of the public sphere and often subvert the coherence of nationalist narratives: the stories of who we are. Such unruly politics has also been available in a variety of theatrical works, from Maeve Ingoldsby's *Mixing it on the Mountain,* a 2003 Calypso Theatre production in which Nigerian asylum seeker Solomon Ijigade played an African St Patrick, to Jimmy Murphy's *The Kings of the Kilburn High Road*, in which Irish emigrant labourers in London are played by a company of African actors. Arguably this small but significant genre reached an important moment with Roddy Doyle and Bisi Adigun's collaborative re-imagining of J.M. Synge's *Playboy of the Western World* in which the central protagonist, Christy Mahon, is rendered as an asylum seeker.

14 The ID cards issued by the Department of Justice, Equality and Law Reform to asylum seekers stated that these are not to be accepted for the purposes of legal identification. Thus immigrants legally entitled to vote were prevented from including their names on the register of electors. In 2004 the Electoral Regulations were amended to correct this situation.

15 Rotimi Adebari and Taiwo Matthews.

3

Enchanting Ireland

Our fields of experience have no more definite boundaries than have our fields of view. Both are fringed forever by a *more* that continuously develops, and that continuously supersedes them as life proceeds. (William James)

The Jesus Walk

It was still dark when Pastor Femi telephoned. Days earlier, the pastor invited us to accompany Pentecostal worshippers on a walk through the streets of Drogheda. He gave us precise directions to the church where we were expected to meet, 'a warehouse with a red door.' He told us that we should dress like the other participants in black and white clothing, and he teased us by suggesting that umbrellas would make wonderful accessories. By 6.50am on Saturday he was anxious to know if we were on our way. As it happened, we were driving through the right neighbourhood but on the wrong street. The pastor's phone call proved timely and he alternately ribbed us and provided directions until we found the church. Eventually, we parked our ancient Skoda outside the warehouse amid the congregation's well-maintained cars. A small number of black-and-white-clad worshippers huddled together under golfing umbrellas. It was cold, dark and raining heavily. Introductions were made with firm handshakes and broad smiles. 'We're mostly pastors from Drogheda and around,' said one man from under his umbrella, 'but there are many others coming.'

Shortly after 7am Pastor Femi arrived and opened the door to the warehouse. We were ushered into the church, which was basically a small anteroom filled with children's drawings and ringed by stacks of chairs. Immediately and without being prompted, some of the men began to set out the chairs. People soon filled the room to capacity, whereupon Pastor Femi asked that we each introduce ourselves. A variety of Pentecostal churches were represented among the congregation. He offered prayers for the day and outlined the intended route and sequence of events. At each special site, he said, a different pastor would lead the prayers. 'You should remain silent and respectful,' he said. We then filed out of the warehouse, through an industrial estate and towards the main roads. Because we had to wait on traffic before crossing roads, and because different people kept different paces, we ended up walking two-by-two along the footpaths with a variety of people. The experience of meeting so many new people in an industrial estate was all the more surreal because of Pastor Femi's injunction to remain silent. And it seemed that everyone had an uncontrollable urge to communicate, even if this meant confining ourselves to nods, eye contact and smiles – a silent *Esperanto*.

The first stop on the route was Drogheda's Anglo-Norman gates. The coeval fortifications of St Lawrence's Gate stood as a silent witness to much of Irish history, from Cromwellian massacres and the subsequent enslavement of Irish captives in Barbados to the eventual redundancy of town walls in the face of 'progress,' which for one nineteenth-century writer denoted, 'civilization and the mail-coaches' (D'Alton 1844: 85). As most of the town's inhabitants slept, a Pentecostal pastor placed a hand on the wet surface of St Lawrence's forbidding walls and intoned prayers for the people of Drogheda. He then turned towards the group and raised the pitch of his voice: 'People of Drogheda we pray for you. We pray that you will keep Jesus in your hearts.' Finally, he stepped back to the walls of St Lawrence's Gate, lowered his head and, touching the walls, announced: 'Now you will be known to us as the Gates of Heaven!' As if fused into one body, the congregation responded with nods and Amens.

The morning brightened and the rain eased a little as we walked silently away from St Lawrence's Gate towards the centre of the town. We paused, following Pastor Femi's lead, outside a branch of Allied Irish Bank. A mysterious sign hanging in a window next to the bank announced, 'WE HAVE BEEN SENT TO EXTERMINATE THIS RECESSION!' The authorless message was printed in black capital letters, except for the word 'EXTERMINATE,' which was printed in a bright red font. Members of the congregation smiled uneasily and gestured towards the ominous message: who placed it there, and what exactly did it mean? But the pastor leading the prayers outside the bank simply ignored the uncanny presence of the sign and proceeded to offer prayers. He prayed to Jesus and implored him to lift the country out of the recession. He prayed that we would all follow a better path in life and not place our trust in 'doomed economics.' And, as his prayers turned to the banking system his tone sharpened. Satan, he told us, had entered the Irish banks. The system must be cleansed: 'We will drive Satan out of the banking system!' Street cleaners passed by and eyed the group warily; the congregation chanted and swayed.

We proceeded, again silently, out across the river and then back to a bridge leading from north of the town. The morning traffic was beginning to build as yet another pastor led the prayers. He was more energetic than his predecessors, and the pitch of his voice rose and fell as he called upon Jesus to come into the lives of the congregation and into the lives of the people of Drogheda. Some people swayed, eyes closed; some clapped their hands slowly and gently while nodding in agreement; others raised a hand into the air when one of the pastor's prayers reached a high pitch. There was a feeling of energy, a tingling sense of collective effervescence. But occasionally one could catch a gaze as it wandered out to the passing cars to be met and returned in the bewildered looks of motorists.

Pastor Femi's injunction to remain silent was all but forgotten as the congregation spread out during the long walk to the next site. People introduced themselves, asked politely about one another or, more commonly, they simply moaned about the weather. We continued to walk uphill towards Millmount Fort, which surveys Drogheda from the top of a great mound that is rumoured to contain ancient passage graves. 'It's known locally as the cup 'n' saucer,' someone volunteered. We walked along the line of the fortifications and up to the Martello tower, journeying from the Norman-built defences to the summit where civil war shells once fell. This was Pastor Femi's chosen site. He recalled for us the history of the fort and those who at different times laid siege to it, from Oliver Cromwell's armies to the forces of the Irish Free State. 'This is a site of war,' he told us. 'It is a place where people made war in Drogheda.' 'But,' he said, 'it is also a place where people could be protected from war.' 'Let us all stand in front of this military site and pray for peace, and for peace for the churches, and for the people of Drogheda.' More prayers, chanting, swaying and silent clapping, but this time with music in the background: a song by Shakira could be heard through the door of a white Transit van in which two perplexed looking construction workers were eating breakfast.

We walked back down the hill to the 'peace bridge.' It was raining heavily now, and members of the congregation shared umbrellas. The roads were busy. We didn't stop long at the bridge – just a few short prayers. A few minutes later we arrived at the local Garda station, whereupon one of the pastors went inside to confirm with the police that we had permission to gather outside. This seemed to be excessive, but later that day Fiona learned that dissident Republicans were being detained in the station and a heightened security alert was in effect. In any case, the pastor re-emerged satisfied and proceeded to offer prayers outside the 'palace of justice.' 'We must look to these guardians of justice for protection. Our prayers should be sent to help them protect the town of Drogheda.' And from there we proceeded to a courthouse. 'This is a place where people suffer,' we were told. 'People here did wrong, but we should still pray for them – their lives will be better.'

It was now early afternoon, and as we made our way to the last site we passed through a Saturday market filled with stalls overflowing with flowers, knick-knacks and fruit 'n' veg. We walked in silence, but not because of Pastor Femi's injunction. The traders and customers stopped what they were doing to observe the long caravan of black-and-white-clad people. Without even a hint of irony, one grinning trader shouted, 'Yez should all be saying yer prayers!' A few jeered; there were some nudges and whispered comments; others looked on without reaction. We reached the final site, the regional hospital, tired and rain-soaked. This time the prayers were led by Pastor Nick from the Solid Rock Church. Originally from Belfast, Pastor Nick founded one of the first Pentecostal churches in the Republic (later, he spoke about the oddity of being a 'white' pastor with a largely African congregation). The pastor prayed for the doctors, nurses and the other staff in the hospital. But he went on to discuss several 'scandals' in the healthcare system, demanding better policy and better government, and praying for things to improve in the future.

3 Jesus Walk, Drogheda, 2009

We returned to the church via the industrial estate and made joking apologies for our old Skoda, which stood out among the expensive looking and well-kept cars. Now back to where we had started from we had time to reflect. Early that morning we departed from a church in an unobtrusive warehouse. Intoning prayers at important local sites, and walking silently from one location to another, the Pentecostal worshippers on the Jesus Walk tried, ever so discreetly, to enchant Ireland. We reflected on the power of the walk for those involved, their bodily praxis, affective and emotional engagements. And we wondered also about the ways in which locality was being remade during such events. In *Seven Winters* Elizabeth Bowen describes the 'minority world' of Irish Protestants by focusing on different appropriations of space, whereby Roman Catholics became, simply, '"the others," whose world lay alongside ours but never touched' (Bowen 1995: 508). Similarly, the silent movement of the Jesus Walk through deeply symbolic spaces and historical moments suggested to us the ways in which different value systems may share the same localities and yet be separated from one another by a gulf filled with different meanings, experiences, histories and practices – different ways of Being-in-the-world (Fischer 1999).

This chapter represents an effort to make sense of events such as this Jesus Walk and the everyday lives of the participants. We are concerned to show what is at stake for those involved. In obvious ways, our opening vignette describes Pentecostal worshippers engaging in a religious ritual. Much, therefore, must be said about Pentecostalism before appreciating its local articulations, from its central tenets and practices to its rapid rise and spread across the globe. However, this religious event cannot be bracketed off from other aspects of people's lives: such events and people's experiences of them are always embedded in lifeworlds.

For many, efforts to raise a family, make a home in the world or 'integrate' into society are made sensible through religious beliefs. At the same time, everyday life may provide the conditions for the possibility of their turn towards, away from or back to religion; and sometimes everyday life may challenge beliefs and either dissolve or reinforce them. At the risk, then, of turning experiences of the sacred into the profane, one may venture that culture exists both within and beyond religious experiences. Even if one holds that culture denotes 'traditions' and is an enemy to be faced as one journeys towards the sacred – as many Pentecostals do – culture tends to remain either as a dramatic foil on such a journey or as a limit on the horizon. But everyday life, too, is neither fully available nor comprehensible. As the famous pragmatic philosopher and father of American psychology, William James, once put it, 'Reality, life, experience, concreteness, immediacy, use what word you will, exceeds our logic, overflows and surrounds it' (quoted in Jackson 2009: 7).

Herein we show the important role that religious beliefs play in the lives of asylum seekers, former asylum seekers and other immigrants. We attend especially to the role of Pentecostal beliefs, embodiment and affective experiences, and to the spatial and temporal lineaments of people's everyday lifeworlds. We will show that religious beliefs play key roles in shaping integration, offering people a spiritual and worldly home away from home, while offering a measure of distance from mainstream society. But how do we begin this discussion? What language and conceptual frames should we use? After all, 'History, religion, spirituality, culture are shop-worn terms, devalued and dulled by the tasks we have assigned to them,' according to Michael Jackson (2009: 51). Jackson, like William James, argues that there is always a *more*: the penumbral wherein we experience ourselves and the world and the limits of both.[1]

As Jackson writes, 'What is at stake are those critical experiences, unfolding between what we take for granted and what we find we cannot control or comprehend.' What really matters, he argues, 'is not how we name them, but how we live through them' (Jackson 2009: 101). By describing the various Pentecostal churches and forms of worship, we explore the embeddedness of religious beliefs in the everyday, the force of the everyday in shaping religious beliefs, and the zone of indistinctness and indeterminacy that lies between and beyond what we call culture and religion.

It is illustrative to briefly return to the opening epigraph in this book, which is taken from an interview with a former Congolese asylum seeker:

> My husband left, we didn't know where he went when he left, and I was left with the children. Then men came into the houses and they were killing the different tribal groups. Then me, with my sister-in-law and the kids, we escaped it, we ran away. (Interview, 2010)

Like many asylum seekers who have experienced violence and trauma, she speaks of past events in a listless and disjointed way. Her story seems to lack verifiable facts, dates and recognisable persons, the very elements to which credibility is ascribed. This is not only because violence destroys language (Scarry 1985) but also because past events become estranged, taking on what Elizabeth Bowen once described as 'the trance-like quality of a spectacle' (Bowen 1975: 23; see also Taussig 1987: 132).

For this former asylum seeker, like so many others, the process of seeking asylum in Mosney involved feelings of imprisonment. 'Sometimes,' she told us, 'you would be there, just crying, just thinking the problems are too much for you.' But, 'The Church is my life now. ... If there is no Church, it is like you kill me. I don't have any other activities in my life now other than the Church. In spite of all that is happening to me here, I can say, 'This is home; this is the place that I can sleep peacefully' (Interview, 2010). When Mosney residents attempted to establish a Fianna Fáil *cumann* during 2004 it showed that political sensibilities cross the lines separating asylum seekers from those living after asylum in the world outside. Pentecostal churches also cross those lines and offer spiritual refuge, together with emergent and always-fragile forms of community. A Pentecostal pastor based in Mosney spoke to us about his efforts to help those condemned to simply waiting. He wished to show them the, 'light at the end of the tunnel.' 'In any place that you find yourself you should be able to see home,' he said (Interview, 2010). Especially for African asylum seekers, then, churches are present during their first experiences in Ireland and are midwives during the rare cases in which they are reborn with 'status.'

Thus far, we have shown the important presence of religion in the lives of our research participants. During the taxi disputes in County Louth, African drivers often ended their meetings with prayers and their efforts to define themselves against those opposing their inclusion were informed by religious sensibilities. With clean and relatively expensive cars they marked themselves off as different from 'local' drivers; with notions of proper behaviours they marked themselves off as different from those who were perceived to be racist and immobile. Even when confronting racism head-on, drivers' voices spoke from lifeworlds in which Being-in-the-world informs the conduct proper to human beings. Recall one driver's angry statement: 'I can't blame God for making me a black man, you know. It frustrates me, you feel bad – am I not a human being?'

One may also recall here our discussion of civic and political integration. We learned that being a Pentecostal pastor often required that one also fill the roles of community leader and activist, and being a leader or activist often requires a power-base within one of the African churches. When we began to write about these interchangeable roles we were tempted to think in terms of a form of pastoral power, which includes many roles, from activist to pastor and community leader, and blurs these roles one into another. To illustrate this, one might recall that Yinka's personal political project was almost impossible to understand without reference to religion; and, many moments within 'new immigrant' political campaigns were staged in churches, drawing from the support of congregations and appealing to them for votes. Religion, then, and Pentecostalism especially, requires attention in terms of its power and structure, nationally and internationally, its role in people's lifeworlds, and its role in enchanting Ireland.

The return of religions

According to many commentators, a famous *Los Angeles Times* report witnessed the birth of Pentecostalism in a shack on LA's Azusa Street in 1906. The report describes nights 'made hideous in the neighbourhood by the howlings of the worshippers who spend hours swaying forth and back in a nerve-racking attitude of prayer and supplication'. The journalist went on to describe how:

> An old coloured exhort, blind in one eye, is the major-domo of the company. With his stony optic fixed on some luckless unbeliever, the old man yells his defiance and challenges an answer. [...] Clasped in his big fist the coloured brother holds a miniature Bible from which he reads at intervals one or two words – never more. After an hour spent in exhortation the brethren present are invited to join in a 'meeting of prayer, song and testimony.' Then it is that pandemonium breaks loose, and the bounds of reason are passed by those who are 'filled with the spirit,' whatever that may be. 'You-oo-oo gou-loo-loo come under the bloo-oo-oo boo-loo;' shouts an old coloured 'mammy;' in a frenzy of religious zeal. Swinging her arms wildly about her, she continues with the strangest harangue ever uttered. Few of her words are intelligible, and for the most part her testimony contains the most outrageous jumble of syllables, which are listened to with awe by the company. (*Los Angeles Times* 1906: 1)

In fact, Pentecostal revival events had already taken place in the UK and in locations scattered across the United States.[2] Indeed, some commentators have argued that experiential practices are identifiable throughout the history of the Christian churches (Robateau 2001). Qualifications aside, the events witnessed by the reporter in 1906 were part of a fast-growing movement that today claims approximately 500 million adherents, mainly in the global south (*Economist* 2006: 48–50). These 500 million adherents represent very different beliefs and practices. Pentecostals may follow the Doctrine of the Trinity or be non-Trinitarian; there is no single, unifying Church; and, charismatic revival movements within mainline Christian churches are connected with the rise of Pentecostalism and are often enumerated as being composed of Pentecostals. What we are examining here are beliefs that are shared in part but simultaneously marked off as different from one another – they share a 'family resemblance' (see Anderson et al 2010: 15). The resemblances between the different members of the Pentecostal family are composed of varying interpretations of scripture and the rituals and practices that follow accordingly.

'Pentecost' is the fiftieth day after the second day of the Jewish Passover festival. It marks the descent of the Holy Spirit upon Christ's followers, which caused them to speak in tongues. It is ironic considering the tone of the 1906 *Los Angeles Times* report that the *King James Bible* records Peter assuring 'mocking' onlookers that the apostles were not drunk on 'new wine' (Carroll and Prickett 1998 (*Acts* 2): 13–14). For contemporary believers, Pentecost marks the descent of the Spirit, which ushered in an early-Church moment of prophesy and visions, spiritual gifts such as healing, repentance, baptism and glossolalia – speaking in tongues. In one sense, then, Pentecostals are understood to be conservative, reaching back in time for a more authentic Christianity but, in another sense, there is a liberal quality to their faith. When the reporter from the *Los Angeles Times* described the Azusa Street meeting he did so in the genre of the gentleman explorer, recording the irrational behaviours of the natives and the pandemonium of ungoverned passions. In describing affective and emotional engagements with faith as a 'frenzy of religious zeal' the reporter required the figuration of the savage together with its dramatic counterfoil – the rational Christian worshiper for whom emotional engagements and displays are excessive and perhaps even obscene. In contrast to this figure of the imagination, the worship practices of many Pentecostals are marked by liberal displays of enthusiasm and emotions.

In 1972 Walter Hollenweger produced a typology of Pentecostalism composed of (1) 'Classical Pentecostals,' who are independent of and opposed to the mainline churches; (2) 'Neo-Pentecostals' who remain within mainline churches and attempt to bring about spiritual renewal therein; and (3) 'Pentecostal-like, "non-white" indigenous churches,' such as those found in Africa and its diaspora and often referred to as 'white-garment' churches (Hollenweger 1972: 33–34). Various forms of Pentecostalism adapt to new cultural environments with ease, quickly becoming domesticated within local lifeworlds and changing accordingly. Flexibility and adaptability are also evident in organisational styles: some churches are simple backrooms with a single (often charismatic) pastor and tiny congregations, while others are 'mega churches' composed of millions of worshipers and run like corporations. Simultaneously loose yet coherent, adaptable and local and yet universalising and global, Pentecostalism presents a challenge to modern scholarship. In contrast to other work on this topic in Ireland, here we discuss 'classical' and so-called 'indigenous' churches to varying degrees even though there is some hostility between them (cf. Ugba 2009). We emphasise the global reach of 'classical' churches, suggesting the redundancy of category labels. And, in order to advance this discussion we must briefly explore the relevant scholarly literature.

Anthropologists have contributed towards understanding the spread of Pentecostalism and the lived experiences of worshipers. Joel Robbins (2004a, 2009, 2010b), for example, notes that despite the enormous numbers of local contexts into which it has folded itself the similarity between the processes of cultural change that it produces invites comparison. He describes these processes of cultural change in terms of their promotion of 'radical discontinuity with what has come before' (2010b: 159). Pentecostalism, he explains, tends to involve epiphanic and revelatory moments leading to conversion and the reformation of lives through radical ruptures (see also Meyer 1999). This presents interesting challenges to anthropology – a discipline synonymous with the study of human cultures – in that Pentecostal conversion often involves rejection of an objectified 'culture,' taken to denote stability, traditions, and sometimes even the demonic. Instead, according to Robbins, 'Pentecostals routinely enact the importance of rupture in ritual practices that aim to make disjuncture a constant theme in the practice of everyday life' (2010b: 161). However, one must remain mindful of the fact that the majority of Pentecostal adherents reside in the global south and there as elsewhere it often appeals to those whose everyday lives are already frayed and marked by ruptures, hence its popularity in those contexts. In looking at the case of Ireland one may easily call attention to the spread of Pentecostalism in Northern Ireland (Murphy 2002) and its appeal to a variety of 'new immigrant communities' throughout the island (Ugba 2009). But what else lies behind this? The Republic of Ireland has long been spoken of as a Catholic land, and the recent conflict in Northern Ireland has routinely been described as a 'tribal' and sectarian one. Yet, Ireland is also familiar with a narrative of change in which religion is cast as a figure from the past and in which the future is imagined in terms of modernisation and secularisation. We are drawn to Jacques Derrida and Gianni Vattimo's (1998: 6) important questions: 'Why is this phenomenon, so hastily called "the return of religions," so difficult to think? Why is it so surprising?' Here we are tempted to answer that there should be nothing surprising about the 'return of religions,' and attention to the everyday lives of worshippers, their rituals and lifeworlds, provides us with the intellectual tools to think about these phenomena.

In his recent book, *Shades of Belonging* (2009), Abel Ugba describes the lives of African Pentecostals in Ireland. He builds on earlier surveys (e.g. Ugba 2004) to paint a broad picture of new immigrants who identify themselves as African or 'black,' have migrated in order to seek political asylum, and who are mostly Christian and members of loose religious groups or churches.[3] Ugba's research is concerned with the broad category of African-led 'classical' Pentecostals who are independent of and opposed to the mainline churches. In keeping with an emergent line of scholarship, Ugba describes the growth of Pentecostalism in Africa, especially during the 1980s, against the backdrop of the disruptions to social and economic life pursuant to austere neo-liberal policies.[4] Pentecostalism, he argues, offered salvation from within the existing filaments of social relationships, and as people migrated so too did Pentecostalism.[5]

Importantly, Ugba calls attention to what might be learned from lived experiences. 'In the world of the Pentecostal,' he tells us, 'the natural interacts seamlessly with the supernatural and the lines that divide the transcendence from the ordinary and the sacred from the profane are sometimes blurred' (Ugba 2009: 85). His eloquent phrasing describes the emergence of newer 'prosperity' churches especially well. Since the 1960s new configurations of Pentecostalism have included Prosperity Gospel.[6] For these worshippers the accumulation of wealth, health, status and social capital are understood as matters of faith and in terms of faith. Ugba argues that Pentecostal groups formed by African immigrants in Europe tend to be 'either off-shoots or proponents of [*Prosperity*] Gospel in the African continent or have been influenced by them.' He goes on to describe prayers and songs in such churches in Ireland as being addressed not to an abstract afterlife but rather to various forms of integration in the here and now. 'Prayer requests and public worship sessions are dominated by issues connected with work and residence permit, visa and passport application, employment and financial worries,' he tells us (Ugba 2009: 97–98 [our interpolation]). Dress style, comportment and notions of self-improvement are the outward signs of complex belief practices. Here we add to Ugba's work, amplifying certain aspects that presented themselves most forcefully to us.

Routes and roots

> God commanded Moses that he should leave his town and go. And like Abraham he went to seek asylum – Abraham was the first asylum seeker! (Pentecostal pastor, interview, 2010)

From the late 1990s onwards African 'classical' Pentecostal churches spread throughout Ireland. Several of these churches, such as Christ Co-Workers in Mission and Gospel Faith Mission, were established by new immigrants in Ireland without financial support from overseas and with weak transnational links during their early years. Other churches, such as the Redeemed Christian Church of God and the Mountain of Fire and Miracles Ministry, were established deliberately as chapters of international church-movements. And, as one might expect, several churches may be characterised as splinters from existing ones (Ugba 2009: 105–109, passim). There is also a small presence of indigenous, 'white garment' churches, such as Cherubim and Seraphim and the Celestial Church of Christ. All of these churches owe their origins to faith movements in Africa and each creates and supports some form of a global ecumene for worshipers.[7] However, it is difficult to capture a still image of Pentecostalism in Ireland: this is a fast-changing landscape plagued by financial difficulties and competition, and a year can prove to be a very long time.

Some congregations meet in community centres, Gaelic Athletic Association clubs or schools; other congregations meet in local hotels or asylum accommodation centres. A significant number of churches are located in industrial warehouses. Inside these unobtrusive buildings one finds affective engagements of the body within worship, from gifts, healing and speaking in tongues to striking music, dance and material culture. All of these churches are evangelical to some degree, and the worshippers feel the force of religion in their daily lives and in their localities. Rather than attempting to place order upon this complex and ever-changing religious landscape, our work expresses the diversity while suggesting the depth of worshippers' experiences. Herein we discuss the origins of and everyday practices in Christ Co-Workers in Mission, we explain the ritual events in the Mountain of Fire and Miracles Ministry, and we describe prosperity preaching in churches such as the Redeemed Christian Church of God. We also describe Prosperity Gospel, ritual events and enchantments within Cherubim and Seraphim. The story begins in 1996 in Dublin's inner city.

Pastor Remba claims that he established the first African church in Ireland. In 1996 his Christ Co-Workers congregation of 'classic' Trinitarian Pentecostals gathered on St Augustine Street in Dublin.

> When I came here I felt a calling – something had to be done. It was very tough at the beginning: we had only forty five members. ... It was like a continuation of what we were doing back home [*in DR Congo*], but here we felt very strongly

that something had to be done. [...] Most of them, because they didn't have enough English, they were just at home. Most of them say to themselves, 'We are asylum seekers, we are refugees,' and they put a box around themselves. ... It was difficult at that time, but we asked ourselves: why do people just stay at home like that? Then we just started something and it grew and grew – just like that! (Interview, 2010 [our interpolation])

The Christ Co-Workers congregation was initially composed of Nigerian and Congolese 'real born again Christians,' together with a large number of persons who converted upon arrival in Ireland. Against the endless waiting of the asylum determinations' process, for many African migrants the Church offered hope and 'a link with home' (Interview, 2010). Within a few short months the congregation swelled and there was no longer enough space to accommodate them. Twice they were forced to move to keep pace with growth. Beliefs and a desire to seek out camaraderie certainly played a role in attracting new worshippers, according to Pastor Remba, but so too did the impact of the Church on the everyday lives of refugees and asylum seekers via its activism:

I remember that when we came we set up the African Refugee Network. The group is still there to advocate on behalf of refugees and asylum seekers, to refer people, or to help with the translation, or to bring someone to the doctor. [...] So in the Church we felt that the role of being a church is like an advocacy group [...]. With housing and with the doctors, we helped them register; with the Department of Justice, the Church was there. ... We did it, we even helped with free English classes, and we did it. (Interview, 2010)

There is little in these statements arguing for religion to be considered as a fragmented, sectional aspect of modern life (cf. Giddens 1991). On the contrary, during its early years Christ Co-Workers was available everywhere in people's everyday lives. During those early years, the Pastor recalls:

Once people got to know us and got to know our doctrine, they understood that we were not some kind of sect – just those kinds of religious groups who try to contradict what is already established. ... With the Irish community, it was like the fear of the unknown; it was a little bit difficult for some of them to approach us. Around 1999, we had a kind of mixed Church, celebrated some marriages, mixed marriages. (Interview, 2010)

During an interview, Pastor Remba described the challenges of integration in terms of his relationships with mainline churches. Although he worked towards ecumenism, he was also careful to point out the fundamentalist nature of Pentecostal theology and the evangelist mission:

We want to do our best to evangelise a lot of Irish people, and when they come to the Church they can have a place in our leadership team. [...] As a Church of the diaspora there are a lot of things we have to do to attract Irish people to our churches. Most of the time we look at it from only one side, but we have to approach them: they will not come if we do not go to them. Who are we, and what are we doing? We must try to invite them, and when they come we give them something to attract them. Not try to be less African but to try and change some things like for example the length of our service, you know? The punctuality in our services! We know you Irish people have a problem to be punctual but Africans can be worse than that. So an Irish person knows going to Mass that he will be there for forty five minutes something like that, but coming here, he can be here for two or three hours, something like that. We have a very good dynamic: . . . you cannot feel the two hours. (Interview, 2010)

Christ Co-Workers in Mission has travelled a long way since the late 1990s, from the early days during which forty plus worshippers gathered in a room in Dublin's St Augustine Street to today's evangelical spread through well-maintained websites, international networks and pastoral power: the charismatic individuals, music, dance and various affective experiences that make it feel alive and growing. But what exactly do these churches look like, where are they situated and what are the experiences available therein?

At first blush, the most striking aspects of the growth of African churches in Ireland are their locations and appearances. During the course of research for this book, more than once we found ourselves lost while searching for churches in large industrial estates. From Dublin to Dundalk, new housing and industrial estates mushroomed from the 1990s onwards, coterminous with the growth of the 'Celtic Tiger' economy. During this period, architects and planners often jokingly described Dublin as 'LA in the rain,' a label that serves as a fairly good description of car-dominated residential estates composed of relatively uniform detached and semi-detached houses. A similar pattern is evident in newer industrial areas: road-access by car dominates over other forms of transport; warehouses and businesses are often self-contained islands surrounded by car parks, and one never seems to find either a centre-point or a person familiar enough with the local geography to provide directions. These industrial estates are often the chosen locations for Pentecostal churches such as Christ Co-Workers in Mission.

DH Lawrence's *The Rainbow* opens with a description of farmers tilling the soil below a church on a hill. When any one of the farmers lifts their head from their work, their eyes immediately go to the church tower on the horizon and thus to 'something standing above him and beyond him in the distance' (Lawrence 2000: 3). What Lawrence captures in prose is the sheer presence of churches on European landscapes and in the spaces of everyday life – what Henri Lefebvre terms *l'espace vécu*. And, one may recall here the attention that Lefebvre gives to churches and religious spaces in *The Production of Space* (1991). Lefebvre goes as far as arguing that the theology and the institution of the Church rely on the concrete actuality of the churches (Lefebvre 1991: 43). It is interesting to think of these literary and philosophical discussions as one turns to African churches in Ireland. On weekdays, the African churches, situated in warehouses, community centres or above shops, draw little attention. But, on any given Sunday one might see cars full of well dressed African families arriving in an industrial estate; and one might hear the chatter of people and the strains of Gospel music. On Sundays, the unobtrusive churches are very much alive. They may not dominate the horizon and remind people of that which is above and beyond them, their architecture may not plunge one immediately into the worlds of sin and redemption, but they do represent 'actually lived and socially created spatiality, concrete and abstract at the same time, the habitus of social practices' (Lefebvre quoted in Soja 1999: 119). Henri Lefebvre's description of *l'espace vécu* resonates with the words of Pentecostal pastors as they explained their missions to us. Take for example the following extract from an interview transcript:

> If you read the Book of Revelation, the Bible talks about the dead church, the local church, and the living church. There are a lot of dead churches around. ...
> We aim to build up an aggressive Christian, and when we say aggressive Christian, you will notice these days that many young people don't go to church: the only time you will find young people in a church is during a burial or during weddings and all of those things. God is not happy about that! (Interview, 2010)

For this pastor the 'living churches' are composed of 'aggressive Christians,' and on Sundays one feels the force of their worship: 'good music, activity – it's *alive!*' (Interview, 2010 [original emphasis]) Moreover, unobtrusive African churches are very much alive in different ways throughout the working week. These poly-functional places are used for activities ranging from Bible classes to language classes, and from part-time crèches to media studios. Yet, the force of life in these spaces seems to be at odds with the locations which are chosen. What are the reasons that subsist behind the unobtrusiveness? One pastor provided a very straightforward answer to this question:

> We find that most of the places that are conducive for us are actually in the industrial estates. Because of, as you can see, the kind of structure we have here, and houses close by; because, firstly, we sing and we pray aloud, and because of the way the community is – we don't want to have a church there and houses there. [...] Using the industrial estate we found is the best option. ... All our churches are soundproofed, so we don't want to go against the law of the land. Like, the Catholics don't do like we do: they don't play music like we do. So that is why we use the industrial estate, though sometimes when we have a special programme we do mention it to the Gardai or something like that. Sometimes they do come around, not here but in some other places. But once they know it's a church then it's usually no problem. (Interview, 2010)

Many of the churches intend to operate unobtrusively on the landscape while reaching out from those sites through the lives and actions of worshippers. The churches also reach out across the globe through their connections with their international movements and associated networks, and in these ways religious and political situations in Lagos, Nigeria come to be seen as related to and coter-minous with life in Drogheda, Ireland. In everyday life a transnational ecumene is sustained, which may be fractured and incomplete but nonetheless real and meaningful. The churches often seek to complement their global ecumene with efforts to enchant their localities, such as the Jesus Walk we described at the beginning of this chapter, adding further layers of cultural meaning to the already dense layers of Irish spatial history. But what of the actual worship practices and rituals within the churches? We discuss a variety of events in Mountain of Fire and Miracles Ministry, and Christ Co-Workers in Mission illustrate some of the practices and rituals available.

Being in the Christian world

We walked from the train station in west Dublin to the industrial estate. One of the warehouses contained Mountain of Fire and Miracles Ministry, which was established in Ireland in 1998. It was early Sunday morning, and a service was about to begin. As we approached, a number of people were getting out of their cars. The men wore either expensive-looking contemporary clothing or 'traditional' West African suits; the women wore colourful dresses and sported Royal Ascot-style hats. A woman who was trying to strap a child into a stroller smiled at us and waved us towards the door. And each time the door opened loud Gospel music escaped. Inside, the church was essentially a large room, which had been converted to include a stage at the front and a mezzanine level at the rear. The background of the stage was composed of yellow cotton and an enormous projection screen. It had two levels and a side area for the band. There were several TV screens on the walls, together with Bible quotations and a large banner announcing, '2011: Year of Spiritual Investments.'

Immediately, we were struck by the music. A slender young woman wearing a long black cotton dress and headscarf was singing a Gospel Hymn. Her band had just reached a chorus as we entered, and she was singing with an arm held aloft. Her voice was extraordinary. She sang with enormous passion and the music seemed to go right into us. We were there to interview a senior pastor, so we waited at the rear of the room behind the TV cameras recording the service. Soon, however, a number of male pastors rushed about the room and asked everyone to move to the front and middle so we could experience everything. The congregation was made up of families and people on their own. The atmosphere was warm, and children strolled around near their parents, looking at one another quizzically and occasionally grinning up at adults. The music ended, and a pastor took the stage to outline the morning's events. 'We will study evangelism today,' he announced, listing the relevant chapters of the Bible. During the service, older children and teenagers were to go to the school at the back for Bible class, and parents should wait for them afterwards, he said. He began to sing, the band struck up again, and the church began to reverberate with music. As we looked about the room we saw people sway and dance a little, and several people, eyes closed, shook a loose fist in time with the music. The pastor stood at the podium on the lower level of the stage and began the day's readings. Two women wearing West African dresses smiled at us and passed us a copy of an annotated Bible. 'Mark 1:17,' he directed us, 'and I will make you fishers of men!' His passionate delivery was captured by the TV camera and projected onto the screen behind him and on those on the walls. Next we were guided to the Book of *Matthew*; then *Romans*. Members of the congregation followed his words with

Bibles open on their laps, and some wrote down his key lessons in notebooks. The readings blended into more Gospel music. Occasionally, the pastor read an important passage of scripture and we stood and recited the passage to our 'neighbours.' Unsurprisingly, the two women in front of us were more comfortable with the recitations. With broad smiles they introduced themselves, but then they closed their eyes and their countenances changed to serious ones. They recited the lesson from the Bible while wagging their fingers at us.

The first pastor ended his portion of the service with more music and proceeded to make a series of community announcements – a congregation member was expected to travel for several weeks and his house would be available; a concert was planned for the following Saturday night; and that Friday there would be a Jesus Walk through Glendalough. A second pastor took to the stage. He was thin, with an expressive face and a smooth voice. It was time for testimony. Five people clambered up on the stage. The first, a young woman, testified to an illness and the importance of Christ to her recovery. The second testimony was from a nervous looking young man. We wondered where we had seen him before. 'I drive a taxi in this good city of Dublin,' he said. 'Last night I drove a man to where he wanted to go, but when I got there another man put a gun to my head – the Lord saved me last night!' There were a few sharp intakes of breath among the congregation, and then several people clapped. Each person was allocated a few minutes for their testimony and a bell rang if they exceeded their time. The final testimony was delivered by a woman who was so filled with passion that she exceeded her time limit. The pastor had to gently wrest the microphone from her hand. He began to sing, and the band struck up again. The congregation swayed and clapped. He reached the chorus and raised his voice to a high pitch. The congregation, hands in the air, swayed as one. From time to time the TV camera fixed on us as we joined in.

Well over two hours after the service commenced, it was finally time for the senior pastor to deliver his sermon. Pastor Andrew took to the top stage and stood at the podium. He sang a Gospel Hymn, joined by the band. The topic of his sermon was evangelism, and he took inspiration from *Romans* – can you be more than a conqueror? He spoke eloquently, passionately and with great humour. He marked off Pentecostal worship from the empty gestures of other religions. He focused on self-empowerment in his congregation's everyday lives. 'You can't just go home after this and go back to your ways,' he said. 'If you are a true Christian, you must do more: you must have the faith, the confidence in your beliefs to evangelise others.' 'When I was studying philosophy in university,' he continued, 'we used to ask my professor, "Are you on the left or the right?"' He performed 'left' and 'right' with steps on the stage. 'She would never give us an answer – sometimes she was here, sometimes there.' 'Oh, Professor Awolowo, just answer the question!' Everyone laughed. 'You cannot be this way: you cannot advise others, teach or evangelise unless you have faith and practice that faith all of the time – the words you read, the music you sing, when you pray, it all has to be from your heart! And that is how you can be more than a conqueror.' An elderly woman in West African clothing sat to the side of the stage, nodding and gesturing throughout the service. And as Pastor Andrew reached his conclusion, she began to nod her head and sway in her chair in a trance-like state.

'We need new furniture,' Pastor Andrew said. 'It looks OK, but we can always make things better: just €90 will help.' 'This carpet he said,' looking down to the floor, 'and these cotton drapes, well you paid for them, and thank you.' The congregation clapped. 'I see the people who didn't give that much are only giving little claps,' he said with a grin. The congregation roared with laughter. Female congregation members walked about with velvet bags to collect tithes. 'Put your money in your hand and hold that hand to your heart,' said Pastor Andrew. 'They will only go to you if they see a hand on a heart.' New worshippers and guests such as ourselves were asked to follow an assistant to an upstairs room to leave our details. We were given a bag of church leaflets, notebooks, CDs and T-shirts. We explained the purpose of our visit, but a pastor still prayed for us to return. We rejoined the congregation amid more Gospel music, but the event was drawing to a close. We arrived at the church at 10am, and it was now approaching 2pm. We sought out the pastor who we had intended to interview, but he was providing advice to a long queue of people.

There are no typical African churches in Ireland; no description of an event will serve as a description of events in general; no world may be found in a grain of sand. Instead, depending on the location and the particular style of the pastors, one might either encounter an air of seriousness, a playful and energetic atmosphere or a mixture of both. Experiential religion seems to resist analyses and refuse categorisations. Nonetheless, Mountain of Fire provides an interesting example of the growth and power of African 'classic' Pentecostalism in Ireland. It maintains strong links with its parent-organisation in Nigeria and with other diaspora locations. Their attention to evangelism and the passion of their pastors has facilitated the growth of at least thirty-five active and self-financing congregations throughout the island of Ireland. Prayer, performance, embodiment and ideas fold into one another during rituals. Rituals and events are supported by websites and, as the example described above shows, are often televised live on open-access networks and recorded as CDs for worshippers. The websites are well maintained and provide a glimpse into their theology and practices. Mountain of Fire preaches the absolute truth of the Gospel, and often the objective of rituals is to drive demonic presences out of the body. By way of example, the Church's website includes an eight-step, do-it-yourself guide to the process of casting out a demonic spirit, which involves practised breathing, prayers recited loudly and from memory, and evoking the fire of the Holy Spirit and blood of Jesus by positioning one's hands on the organs of the body while naming them. Coughing, crying, yawning or sneezing are all taken as signs of the work of the Spirit. While these affective and emotional forms of worship are striking, it is also important to note that Mountain of Fire teachings seamlessly blend what might be assumed to be in the category of the sacred with the more 'ordinary' and everyday experiences of congregations. Pastors may instruct their congregations on the benefits (and dangers) of education, the benefits of a good marriage, the need for good communication at home or, for example, the dangers of evil in-laws. This blending of the sacred and the everyday is more obviously presented by the actual experiences of attending their events. The churches are financed by the congregations, they provide important social services; they are meeting places, schools, even venues for Gospel concerts.

Clearly, then, one must go beyond rituals, narrowly defined, and think about contexts and *events*, as such. The unobtrusive presence of many African churches bespeaks the hostile worlds in which worshippers perceive themselves – 'the way the community is,' as one pastor put it succinctly. In such local contexts, evangelism and enchantments emerge from intimate lived spaces embedded in transnational worlds. Visions of society and of integration, and practices that appear at the scale of the local but also flow out across a transnational world, must all be considered as conditions for the possibility of the particular worship practices and the church-events that we witnessed. But much may also be learned by close attention to events *as events*. Here, we draw loosely from the work of Veena Das (2007). Against approaches that imagine events as discrete, complete and available for textual analysis, Das looks to the ways in which the everyday provides the grounds on which events arise, while also looking to how events 'become located, embodied, or actualised' (Das 2007: 136; cf. Butler 1997). She quotes a meditation from Gilles Deleuze to the effect that, 'there are no private or collective events, no more than there are individuals and universals, particularities and generalities.' 'Which war,' he asks, 'is not a private affair?' (Deleuze 1990: 152) Deleuze challenges us to imagine worlds composed not of private individuals, singularities and their opposing categories but, rather, of interstitial and inter-subjective zones, often marked by indeterminacy. If we are to focus on church *events*, we must also look at the participants and their stories.

The following is an edited transcript of an interview with Pastor Femi. 'I gave my life to Jesus in the year 1986,' he told us.

> It was a wonderful day and a wonderful experience that I will never forget. I was born into an Anglican family, but there is a difference between religion and knowing Jesus Christ. You know a lot of people thought that just going to church will be enough, but there is more to it than that: it is about having a personal encounter and relationship with the All Mighty God – and that can only be achieved through knowing His son, Jesus Christ. So, I joined the Mountain of Fire back in Nigeria before I relocated to Ireland. [...] We have branches all over the world. (Interview, 2010)

The narrative here requires little interpretation. Before being born again, he recalls an upbringing in which religion was present but in a lifeless form. He was reborn into the liveliness of Pentecostalism, and he foregrounds the experiential even though his experiences are shared and embedded in a transnational ecumene. These same sensibilities were in the foreground for many of our research participants, some of whom struggled to phrase their experiences. For example, speaking of rebirth in the Redeemed Christian Church of God, one worshipper explained:

I left Mosney in 2003 and I decided, well, I love the Church because of the teachings. I don't know if you can understand what I am trying to say: like, if you grew up in a place that brought you so much fun and joy, and you enjoyed the presence of God there, I don't think you would like to move that far. That's what I have done. I like this place; I know what people here are going through, so I want to use my life as an example: 'Look if I can make it, you can make it!' (Interview, 2010)

For this man, having a place in the world includes both the Church and home. Yet, he found this difficult to articulate – he spoke of a sense of well being, something emotional and felt in and by the body, like a light shining upon one. His sense of the presence of God is real and yet elusive. The same sense of the penumbral was captured when our research participants spoke using common, shop-worn terms such as 'culture' and 'religion.' 'Where we come from we have culture, and now from that culture we have become Christians,' said one pastor.

And this society where we find ourselves the culture is totally different to ours: there are a lot of things that are strange to us, that we don't do, like drinking for instance, we don't really drink … because the Bible condemns that, you see, and we also encourage our children not to drink because it is against our faith. [...] We understand that these children are angels who behold the face of my Father, and that is *Matthew 18: 1–5*. We believe so much in children, whether we realise it or not someday we will come to depend on our children, they are a gift from God, your responsibility. But then there is death; and Heaven for some people, the Judgment Day, then He will say, 'Depart from me, you cursed, into the ever-lasting fire,' and that is *Mark*. However you spend your life you will give an account of it. Our faith is not our culture, or this culture here. I'm also a taxi driver here, and I see a lot of things on the streets, a lot of things every night, and I pray to God that our children will not take drugs and go this way. We have seen that God is real and Jesus Christ is alive. (Interview, 2010)

For this man, driving his taxi late at night and trying to raise his children as Christians, culture and religion are impoverished terms. Instead, he desires to capture *more*: a lifeworld in which beliefs and scripture are solid and yet always at the limit of that which is describable. He says, 'We still want the African ways of worship: they sing and dance – you can see the radiance … and the fire must be burning' (Interview, 2010).

During June 2010 we recorded several illustrative examples of Mountain of Fire congregation meetings, ranging from discussions with pastors to actual services, and noted a variety of practices, rituals and behaviours. For example, one morning Fiona met with Pastor Femi to carry out an interview and attend a lecture. She travelled to an industrial estate in Drogheda in which the Church was operating from an office building. Inside there was a large space for worship in a brightly coloured room and a crèche in an anteroom. Two middle-aged 'local' women sat chatting among several Nigerian-Irish worshippers and their children. Fiona was drawn immediately into conversation by a junior pastor, a short, thin and immaculately dressed man who held a gaudy tambourine. The pastor energetically moved the conversation from topic to topic until he noticed

Fiona's interest in studying the origins and spread of Pentecostalism. 'I'll explain the differences between religion and Pentecostalism,' he said. 'Irish people are not religious: they have no idea how to read the Bible for themselves – they need someone to interpret it for them!' he announced as if trying to provoke a reaction. Noticing that Fiona was unruffled by his sweeping statement and still interested in his ideas, he pushed even further. With a broad smile, he began to mimic a typical Catholic priest, blessing himself and reading from an imaginary Bible with great authority. His playful behaviour was certainly intended to provoke a reaction but behind that lay a serious effort to explain Pentecostalism. He argued that Mountain of Fire worshippers engage directly with the Bible and their beliefs. 'The way Irish people bless themselves on buses or trains, or as they pass graveyards, is only a small gesture and not enough to prove themselves good Christians,' he argued. Against hollowed-out traditions and empty gestures he situated the liveliness of Pentecostalism. We all have a choice to make, he said, 'You can choose to either live in the world or in the Christian world – and it's not possible to live in both.' He then went on to reflect on the economic recession: 'The recession is an act of God. If Irish people start to pray then things will get better. You see in Nigeria things like this don't happen because people pray, people pray and things always get better.' He spoke openly of his evangelical mission, and although mainstream society appeared potentially threatening to him it was, fundamentally, made up of people who should be saved.

The junior pastor's energetic discussion of Pentecostalism was cut short when Pastor Femi decided to begin his lecture. With great seriousness, he began to read passages from the Bible to the small group. He held the Bible in one hand and occasionally raised an instructive index finger to emphasise a point. The junior pastor swayed and raised a hand. But then, all of a sudden, he began to jump up and down and hop about shaking his tambourine. Pastor Femi was not in the least bit distracted by his colleague's movements and continued to read from the Bible. Even though Fiona knew that the junior pastor's movements were a display of this affective and emotional engagements with God, his incongruous and manic-looking performance suggested a comic effort to knock Pastor Femi off his stride. But Pastor Femi continued and turned his prayers towards Irish people and the Irish economy. The sacred faded into the profane until both became indistinct, and the ordinary and the everyday gave way to the eschatological. 'We need to pray to get out of this recession,' Pastor Femi told the congregation. 'It is only through prayer that Ireland will ever fully recover.'

While Pentecostalism has long been associated with individual transformation recent scholarship has also emphasised the imbrication of religious beliefs with work, politics and a variety of forms of activism. Moreover, as our research has already shown, Pentecostal beliefs in Ireland are active in enchanting local land-scapes, reconfiguring local populations as souls in need of saving, and understanding childhood and education as sites for religious instruction. The story, so often told, is that modern societies are on a pathway towards secularisa-tion, a future in which religion will play a sectional role, like a lifestyle choice, if indeed it plays any meaningful role at all. This story appears entirely foreign to the lives of most of our research participants. Indeed, the degree to which different Pentecostal beliefs and practices are capable of colonising more and more of everyday life is the real story. And this is illustrated vividly when we consider prosperity preaching.

Affecting integration

Anthropology has a long-standing though uneven record of studying embodiment: the ways in which people experience the world in and through their bodies (see, for early examples, Mauss 1935; Boas 1944; van Gennep 1960; Bateson 1975). By the 1990s, however, embodiment was positioned at the vanguard of disciplinary interests. In a seminal review written during that period, Margaret Lock recognised the growing interdisciplinary interest in embodiment and showed crude nature/culture divisions to be redundant: 'The body is no longer portrayed simply as a template for social organisation, nor as a biological "black box" cut off from the mind' (Lock 1993: 136).

Coterminous with these moves in Anthropology, the past two decades have also seen an explosion of work on affect theory, especially in neuroscience. For example, contemporary neuroscience studies the ways in which particular culture-bound sensory experiences, such as rituals, provide the conditions for mnemonic devices, or techniques that allow for extraordinarily rapid learning and remembering (Brown and Seligman 2009). At its simplest, affect denotes the evolved and embodied physiological and cognitive responses to the detection of significance (Neuman et al 2007: 9), but affect theory is informed by many different influences and positions. For some, affect is the driver of the body's innate responses to the world, while for other thinkers affect is the embeddedness of the body in an always-emergent world of humans and non-humans, complex sets of interlacements and assemblages (Gregg and Seigworth, 2010: 6–10). For us, the work of Michael Jackson (1988) has been especially influential. Jackson has long sought to show the ways in which creativity and freedom may be discerned in embodied experiences, conditioned and constrained by *habitus* and yet generative of new imaginings. With this perspective in mind, affect theory – especially as it illuminates ritual-like events – suggests to us ways of further exploring everyday life and the *more*, the penumbral of embodied experiences. When we consider Pentecostal churches that seek to bring the sacred and the everyday together we are met with that challenge of how to think about their events and practices. Here we are suggesting new ways of thinking and new conceptual frames. The need for new scholarly tools is highlighted when we turn to examine the growth of Prosperity Gospel.

During a Christ Co-Workers in Mission event we recorded the powerful affective and emotional engagement of worshippers within rituals in which the sacred and everyday were blurred and indistinct. The occasion was a Sunday service. After a short build-up, the pastor's citations from the Bible became ever-more urgent and almost angry in tone. His emotional charge seemed to touch the congregation and they began to sway with their hands held high. Soon the pastor was all but running up and down the low-lying stage shouting at the congregation through a microphone. Worshippers waved their hands in the air, some with their eyes closed. The people in the room seemed fused into one body. 'Beelzebub is everywhere,' the pastor roared. 'Shout it!' he demanded, and the room replied as one, 'Beelzebub is everywhere!' Some worshippers began to shake and screech; and the noise in the church became almost overwhelming. It was as if one's body couldn't fail but respond: there was a dangerous enemy, *it* had a name, and *we* could respond with prayer. We could feel people's energy as if it were within our own bodies. The pastor was sweating heavily, and he wiped his forehead with a white handkerchief. He lowered the pitch of his voice for a few moments, and the noise abated, leaving what felt like a strange pulse in the room. But soon he began again. 'Turn to the person beside you,' he commanded, and tell them, 'Beelzebub is everywhere!' The congregation responded without hesitation. 'Now tell them you will deny him, you will do everything in your power to deny him.' Again we turned to one another and followed his commands. And, again, there was no hesitation. The denials of Satan were issued fluently and angrily, mere words were transformed by emotionally charged voices. Then the pastor ran across the stage shouting, 'Success and prosperity will be yours if you can deny Beelzebub.' The congregation echoed with his words. 'Prosperity and success will be mine,' they said, and some began to fall back into their seats, exhausted. The worshippers at the Christ Co-Workers in Mission event were participants in a Prosperity Gospel ritual. The emotional and affective experiences they went through drove the message into their bodies. The pastor's words were felt; their responses came as powerful voices, shaped by one another in the moment of an event, deeply personal and yet inter-subjective.

Other 'classical' Pentecostal churches in Ireland include prosperity preaching in their events. According to one Redeemed Christian Church of God pastor:

> The RCCG is a full Gospel church. When I say full, I mean when you go through the Bible you see that the Bible talks about holiness, and the Bible also talks about people being rich. God is not glorified in churches being poor or people worshipping in a church being poor. So the Bible tells us that God is the owner of the whole earth. So, if he owns the whole earth then he is a very rich God – so there is no point preaching holiness and leaving prosperity behind! (Interview, 2010)

Pastor Femi also spoke with us about prosperity preaching in Mountain of Fire and was careful to point out that the goal was not simply to enrich worshippers but, rather, to see wealth as both something material, and thus important, and something available in multiple material and immaterial forms. 'If someone goes and steals he'll just get money,' Pastor Femi instructed us. 'This is prosperity, but in a negative way.' 'You see,' he said, 'God owns everything, and you don't have to jump the queue as long as you are with him!' And yet another pastor captured the basic philosophy thus:

> Success to me is not really about the amount of money that you have stocked up in your bank account. Success to me is when you are comfortably OK in every-

thing that you do. Success is when you are not going through any kind of pain – that is success. Other people think success is how much wealth you have acquired, but just try to be content and be satisfied with your present situation. (Interview, 2010)

Some of the churches we attended during the course of our research were registered companies; others were registered charities; but there was little correlation between the legal status of the organisation and the emphasis placed on prosperity and success therein. However, all of the churches collected tithes, and while the congregations tended to be composed of asylum seekers, refugees and new immigrants on low incomes, there was a commonly held expectation that one should make financial contributions to the running of the churches. In principle, one was expected to contribute 10 per cent of one's income in tithes, but in practice worshippers rarely reached that mark. Indeed, one of the churches we visited displayed on a television screen the weekly donations made by families. However, we found no evidence of churches preying upon congregations. Worshippers understood tithes in Biblical terms, as obligations and investments in futures in which godliness and material wealth were not separable from one another. As one worshipper explained:

> I donate what I can. The Church has envelopes and I put what I can into one each week. I don't feel the pressure to donate one tenth of my income, just what I can. I understand that the Church has employees, people who work here full time, and they need to be paid as well as the bills. I don't resent having to give this money: the Church wouldn't be kept alive if it wasn't for the generosity of its congregation. (Interview, 2010)

The idea that the churches might be homes to profit-making confidence tricksters would have struck our research participants as absurd. Some pastors spoke about the rigorous work involved in their financial control committees, while worshippers often noted the role of the churches in providing temporary assistance to congregation members in financial distress. What is at stake for pastors and worshippers alike is a shared and emergent disposition towards religion, culture and economy.

In an important recent essay, Jean and John Comaroff explore the connections between contemporary, 'millennial' capitalism and prosperity preaching. They draw on a scholarly tradition that stretches back to Karl Marx's identification of the intrinsic 'magic and necromancy' (Marx 2004: 29) in the transformation of the products of human labour into commodities to advance an argument about neo-liberalism. 'Neo-liberalism,' they argue, intensifies the 'abstractions inherent in capitalism itself: to separate labour power from its human context, to replace society with the market, to build a universe out of aggregated transactions' (Comaroff and Comaroff 2000: 305). In their view, neo-liberalism transforms cultures but is nonetheless a cultural mode of production and consumption. For many people throughout the world, formative experiences have been unsettled, and the once-intelligible workings of power and distributions of wealth are now hard-to-fathom, spectral and magical even. The Comaroffs argue that we are witnessing the rise of 'occult economies.' On one side, they argue that neo-liberalism strips bare cherished institutions, leaving the fingerprints of 'the market' in the place of certainty and intelligibility. This economic doctrine gained purchase during an era in which capital seems ever-more mysterious in its movements and free from the constraints of nation-states. Yet, on the other side, for all its assumed rationality, markets depend on socially produced abstractions such as 'confidence' and are troubled by rumour and gossip – one must never 'talk down' an economy. Comaroff and Comaroff wonder if any great gulf exists between the 'occult' mainline economies and new forms of Pentecostalism which promise seemingly alternate frames of interpretation: spiritual and financial returns on one's investments.[8]

In many ways, the Comaroffs' arguments are part of a broad effort to gauge the effects of cultural and economic transformations and dislocations via new forms of Pentecostalism. However, there is a great diversity in the available forms of prosperity preaching within global Pentecostalism, just as there is great unevenness in the global effects of cultural and economic transformations. In Ireland, one may note the conditions that give a local accent to Prosperity Gospel. One pastor spoke to us about this at length:

> Well when we first came, I mean Nigerians coming here from abroad, we are well educated. But when we got here initially, we found that before the integration most of them are put in maybe in hostels and they are given just €19 a week. We found that people laid back and enjoyed it; maybe they were just watching TV, wasting their life. So, we started preaching this from the altar, from the Church, 'You must do something to prove yourself in this society! Go to school, go to university, go learn, go and study, go and do some business.'
>
> My wife was a pastor in a church in Mosney, so ... we were teaching them how to go out and fend for themselves. Now ... from that particular place, Mosney, from that particular camp, you find people with their own businesses, they have their houses, some of them have gone to university; some have gone to do one trading or the other; you find people are settling down. But we have to find them, because people are wasting away their time. So when I first came here ... I started telling the other pastors, 'We have to stop this. We need to teach our people how to be integrated, how they can study, how they can work.' (Interview, 2010)

Many worshipers were quick to trace connections between the intimate emotional and affective domains of worship and their everyday lives. They also saw straightforward connections between Prosperity Gospel and their integration into society, with many seeing their own faith and associated decisions as models for emulation by others. Take for example the following extract from an interview transcript:

> I am here now, and I am working, and I know what it is like outside there. Getting your residence permit is one thing and getting a job is another – a paid job. [...] So that's what we are doing anyway, I mean it is not really easy anyway for a foreigner in a foreign land. ... From my own experience, because anything I do I try and bring in the kind of experience I had here to encourage people. ...

I thank the Lord most of them are trying their best, most of them are getting education you know, doing some extra lessons, some of the things I try to tell them to do at least to keep them busy, to make them feel that they truly belong somewhere. (Interview, 2010)

We concur with Jean and John Comaroff's assessment that new forms of Pentecostalism offer a way to gauge the effects of cultural and economic transformations and dislocations. Much more certainly needs to be said about 'occult economies' and what they in turn articulate about the magic that has always been inherent in capitalism. But like the Comaroffs, we eschew any suggestion of a perfect correlation between the rise of new forms of Pentecostalism and neoliberalism. Rather, we are describing an important set of correspondences that show people who are aware of the limits of 'culture,' 'the market,' and their opportunities for integration into society. Their engagements with Pentecostalism are the outcomes of their searching for *more*, journeys that have taken them into the domains of self-empowerment, emotion and affect and, at the same time, out into society to evangelise a world in need of saving and a landscape in need of enchantment. Seen in this light, Prosperity Gospel provides a sidelong glance at the notion of integration. Indeed, one may speak here of 'philosophies of integration,' to borrow from Adrian Favell (1998), through which people's lifeworlds are embedded in and inform their interactions with society. A person may be a former asylum seeker who regularly encounters obstacles to self-empowerment and wellbeing, but their journeys through life and landscapes may be spiritual and embodied as true and right. If the contemporary discourse on civic integration does not attend to these lives then it will remain, literally, lifeless. And it is with an analysis of the liveliness and enchantments of Cherubim and Seraphim, perhaps the most dramatic and different of the new Pentecostal churches in Ireland, that we conclude this discussion.

Enchantments

The Cherubim and Seraphim movement emerged in Nigeria. It is a Pentecostal church but of the variety referred to as 'non-white indigenous churches' or 'white-garment' churches (Hollenweger 1972: 33–34). Cherubim and Seraphim congregations in Ireland, as elsewhere, emphasise aspects of worship such as healing, song and dance, fasting, and the wearing of white garments. An outsider may well be struck by the unlikely juxtaposition presented by African worshippers wearing flowing white robes, fashioned to resemble angels, filing into an anonymous warehouse building. Indeed, the particular style of worship and material culture of Cherubim and Seraphim has attracted criticism from other Pentecostal churches in Ireland. Rumours continually spread about their activities. Indeed, on more than one occasion we were warned off Cherubim and Seraphim by research participants in other churches. One pastor openly described them as 'a cult' while another suggested that we should consider attending a 'reputable church' after Cherubim and Seraphim events in order to be 'spiritually cleansed.'

Cherubim and Seraphim are different from other Pentecostal churches in terms of hierarchy and rank. Grades such as prophet and prophetess are potentially available to all adherents. The Church has also undergone a good number of changes since its founding in Ireland. However, our objective here is not to follow the stories of change or individual biographies; rather, we were most struck by Cherubim and Seraphim's relationships to lived spaces and their aim to enchant the landscape.

Here in Ireland, members of the Church make frequent prayer-trips to certain mountains and beaches – they have a strong theological association with water. We attended several of their services, and one day arranged to interview the Prophetess of the Church. However, she telephoned to say that she would be late but suggested that we should ask to be admitted and await her there. Removing our shoes, we walked into the main church, which was a dark warehouse ringed with sacred pictures reminiscent of Catholic iconography and containing a small altar covered in flowers. We startled a middle-aged Nigerian woman. She was snoozing on a mattress in the corner of the church, wrapped in her white robes. We introduced ourselves and explained the purpose of our visit. 'I've seen you before, at the services,' she said. 'I've come to spend the day at the church to say special prayers.' She guided us around the church, and her words drifted out from there to different places in Ireland, special places with water. 'We don't go there to worship the sea,' she pointed out. 'No, we go there to worship in the same way that Jesus did.' Again, as she spoke she seemed to slip away from the here and now. This time she spoke of *Exodus* and described the departure of the Israelites from Egypt, the crossing of the Red Sea to the land of Canaan. 'We have a special relationship to beaches and mountains near the sea,' she said.

We continued to walk around the small church. The woman continued to speak of faraway places and distant times. She then turned to us and spoke of her own story. 'I am from Nigeria,' she said. 'In Nigeria we fast and we go to sacred sites, sometimes for days and days.' God, she said, played His role in her leaving Nigeria to come here, 'It was God's intention that I come to live and work in Europe.' She migrated to England first and could find neither work nor hope there. Soon she was fasting and praying for guidance. 'Jesus Christ appeared to me, coming out of the sea – He was wet – and I knew I should go to Ireland to find work there.' A few short days after arriving in Ireland she had a job and a place to live.

The Prophetess of the Church arrived. 'Yeah, we do have sacred places apart from the church,' she said during the interview.

> We do go to the beach and pray there like Jesus did. If you read the Bible, he always goes to the seaside, a lot. It's what you believe in. We go there as well for prayer. We go to a mountain as well. There is a mountain in Bray that we go to. So we do climb the mountain for special times. [...] We just pray, we pray for whatever, it doesn't matter if you don't have a special prayer, maybe you have a problem, you pray for it to be resolved. So maybe sometimes you have a special prayer, people have troubles, or they are depressed, or they need assistance to need pray. You can go with them and write their names and say, 'I am praying for this person.' God is forever there. (Interview, 2010)

We asked if the places are regarded as sacred, and she replied:

> I could call it sacred, anywhere you go to pray is sacred. It's not that we worship
> the sea, we go there to say a prayer you know. Wherever you are calling your
> God, at that point in time, that place is a sacred place for you. It is just like
> Moses, when God called to him and said off with your shoes because where you
> are is a Holy Land. So, wherever you go to pray at that very point in time it is a
> sacred place for you because it is where you are calling your God. (Interview,
> 2010)

There are many aspects of Cherubim and Seraphim rituals and practices that
demanded attention during our research, but none struck us more forcefully
than their relationships with space – their embodied enchantments of landscapes. In Paul Carter's magisterial study of spatial history, *The Road to Botany
Bay* (1987), he argues that space is not a stage on which actors perform from
scripts written by history. Rather, Carter imagines spatial history through lives
lived, never-ending journeys and unfinished maps – history as layers of possible
inscriptions. He gives an example of place-names to illustrate his point:

> Late in 1616, Dirk Hartog of Amsterdam and his ship, the *Eendracht* were blown
> on to the north-west coast of Australia. The skipper commemorated his invol-
> untary landing on a pewter plate, which he affixed to a post. The island where
> Hartog landed was named after him [...]. In 1697, another Dutchman,
> Valmingh, also blown off-course, found Hartog's memorial ... and appended a
> record of his own visit. In 1699, the English seaman, William Dampier, also
> visited this coast. He let the island retain its Dutch connection, but renamed the
> country to the east Shark Bay. In 1801, one Captain Emmanuel Hamelin discov-
> ered the pewter plate ... and named the place Cape Inscription. (Carter 1987:
> xxiv)

Irish landscapes have been continually named and renamed. Places and their
remembered histories have been written over time and again. Symbolic ancient
sites were re-inscribed by the Church, colonialism remade geographies, and later
still Anglicised signatures of colonial rule were given a lick of green paint (Kiberd
1996: 265). Today, new immigrants are living their lives, embarking on never-
ending journeys and adding new layers of spatial history. Cherubim and
Seraphim adherents sometimes go on pilgrimages to Israel but more often
remain in their new home and re-enchant their landscapes discreetly. Cherubim
and Seraphim worshippers have gone on pilgrimage in 'holy places' such as
Knock; Mountain of Fire worshippers have gone on pilgrimage in Glendalough;
and these and a variety of other churches have organised Jesus Walks through
Irish towns. These ritual movements through landscapes produce affective
responses from worshippers, wherein beliefs and senses of belonging are
embodied, sometimes politicised and often transformative (see also Eade and
Garbin 2007). 'In any place that you find yourself you should believe it is your
home,' one pastor told us. And during pilgrimages or Pentecostal walks through
Irish landscapes new homes are being made and enchanted. These walks include
people attempting to be successful, raise and educate their families and integrate

into society. The walks take place through hostile worlds guided by pastoral power. For those with faith, the walks embody an effort to remake the strange and hostile into potentially sacred places surrounded by souls in need of saving. But these embodied practices, rooted in everyday life, are always partial. Pastors encourage their congregations to strive for *more,* and religious beliefs are called upon to meet the challenges presented by everyday life.

Throughout the course of our research we attended numerous church events. Rarely did any of these events pass without pastors and the congregation offering prayers for Ireland. They offered prayers to halt the waning levels of Christianity or to lift the country out of the deep economic recession. 'We pray for Ireland every meeting; we pray for peace, because if there is no peace we can't enjoy our lives here,' one pastor explained. Time and again, pastors reminded their flocks that Pentecostalism offered them a religion that was alive and a connection to God that they could feel in their bodies. 'We don't *practise* religion, we do what the Word of God says,' one pastor told us. Against this, they situated the hollowed out traditions of mainline churches and the pointless worship of materiality for its own ends. Their mission was clear: to grow, prosper, reach out and save souls – an inversion of the missionary history of Ireland in which Africans figured as the souls in need of saving. Material wealth, health and wellbeing, success in education and proper behaviours could all be taken as signs of salvation. Understanding these ideas has important implications for understanding the role of the churches in integration.

As is well known, Walter Benjamin opens his thesis *On the Concept of History* with the story told by Edgar Allan Poe of a puppet-device that could play chess better than any challenger. In fact, the automaton was operated by 'a little hunchback' who guided the puppet's hand from within the device. For Benjamin the philosophical counterpart of the puppet was historical materialism, which had to enlist the help of a dwarf called theology that was 'wizened' and needed to be kept out of sight (Arendt 1973: 255). The image of the puppet and dwarf has been used by a variety of contemporary scholars to develop critiques of historical change, contemporary Christianity and capitalism (see, for example, Žižek 2003). If broadened beyond Benjamin's original intent, the image of the puppet and dwarf provides an interesting way of thinking about contemporary Pentecostalism (see also Robbins 2010a). Indeed, Benjamin's image of the automaton bears an uncanny resemblance to the descriptions Prosperity Gospel offers to explain the particular configuration of person, self and lifeworlds available in those churches: US preacher Charles Capps, for example, imagined the person as a central heating system through which personal power courses but who is controlled by a theological thermostat (Brandon 1987: 25; Coleman 2000: 28). Through Prosperity Gospel, then, one may configure health, wealth and societal integration as spheres of existence in which a spiritually empowered person may act. Theology here is neither wizened nor hidden, and attention to the everyday lives of African Pentecostals in Ireland may say much about the spirit in contemporary life.

Notes

1 Jackson uses the term penumbral (from the Latin *paene*, almost, and *umbra*, shadow) to denote areas outside of the settled self wherein one experiences limits. The penumbral is shadowed to a degree, uncertain, peripheral and yet a domain in which one may learn much about another.

2 There is a much older history of Pentecostalism in the UK dating back to the eighteenth century (Robinson 2005).

3 The 2006 census shows that more than 8000 people identified themselves as Pentecostal/Apostolic, while more than 5000 people identified themselves as Evangelicals and these data are likely to be underestimates. Ugba's (2004) survey was carried out from June to August 2002 and included a non-random sample of 182 respondents, fairly evenly split along gender lines. Over 60 per cent of respondents migrated to Ireland to seek asylum, while the remainder migrated either to work or study. Although eighteen nationalities were represented among participants, the overwhelming majority wished to be identified as African, with the remainder identifying themselves as 'black.' Over 71 per cent were unemployed outside of the home and yet just under half of all respondents indicated they had third-level qualifications. Importantly for our purposes, approximately 40 per cent stated that they were members of a religious group, while 20 per cent were members of ethnic/national associations. The general profile that emerges from Ugba's findings, especially with regard to religious affiliation is supported with the data arising from other studies. In 2003 the Irish Council of Churches estimated that 'Black Majority churches' included 10,000 African immigrants (ICC 2003), while the Presbyterian Church of Ireland estimated the number to be 30,000 by 2004 (McGarry 2004).

4 Naomi Haynes, for example, describes the 'villagization' of urban Africa, arguing that gift giving and mutual support have been reinvigorated in the face of globalization and austere neo-liberal policies (Bialecki et al 2008). Pentecostalism, she suggests, rests easily within everyday lives frayed by market and nation-state failures, lives in which societal hope seems to have all but evaporated. In these studies, Pentecostalism has been shown to travel 'along pre-existing daily social relationships ..., and shared migration, thus carrying its message like reliable and comforting luggage' (Poloma 2000: 3).

5 While he acknowledges the transnational dimensions, Ugba's research focuses specifically on Pentecostalism among immigrants to Ireland. Our work indicates that much more needs to be said about the transnational mobility of persons and beliefs – the shifting terrains of spirituality and sociality.

6 Also known as Health and Wealth, World Movement or Faith Gospel.

7 We use the word 'ecumene' derived from the Greek *oikoumenē*, which denotes the inhabited portion of the earth. Like Kopytoff (1987) and Comaroff and Comaroff (2000) we take it to denote an arena of constant cultural interaction and exchange.

8 Comaroff and Comaroff explain occult economies thus: 'As the connections between means and ends become more opaque, more distended, more mysterious, the occult becomes an ever more appropriate, semantically saturated metaphor for our times' (2000: 317–318).

4

Hallelujah Halloween

As the bees in swarming cling to one another in layers till the few are reached whose feet grapple the bough from which the swarm depends; so with the objects of our thinking, – they hang to each other by associated links, but the *original* source of interest in all of them is the native interest which the earliest one once possessed. (William James)

Telling stories

The foyer of the newly built hotel was busy. The occasion was the launch of Bunmi's *Tales by Moonlight: African Stories for Children.* The hotel was filled with invited guests from regional schools, together with the teachers, parents and children from St Joseph's, the primary school in Dundalk where Bunmi works. African women wearing colourful dresses and elaborate hats stood out among the crowd. Inside the main function room a group of schoolchildren rehearsed for a musical performance. Occasionally, a child broke rank and turned a cartwheel on the stage. Bunmi's daughters were full of nervous energy: they darted in and out of the function room to check the sound equipment, the arrangement of chairs and the lighting. A table at the side of the room held a supply of books, which had earlier been blessed by a Pentecostal pastor. The room quickly became crowded and noisy; the school children started to look jumpy.

Bunmi arrived wearing a bright purple West African dress and matching hat. Like a candidate for political office, she walked around the room, smiling, shaking hands and exchanging a few words with her guests. Teachers and principals from regional primary schools drifted into the function room and immediately clustered together to exchange gossip. Two principals stood next to the supply of books, audibly commenting on the usefulness of the 'resource' for multicultural schools. Bunmi progressed through the room, collected her special guests and mounted the stage. Immediately, spontaneous applause erupted from the crowd. The principal of St Joseph's Primary School called for attention. He spoke of the rapid transformations in Ireland, from its long history of emigration to the present situation wherein one in every ten persons is foreign born. This is a story of changes in schools, he said: 'Right now, 36 per cent of my pupils are migrant children – and that's three times the national average.' He went on to discuss the enormity of the recent changes in Dundalk, a border town where diversity has its own particular history. 'Bunmi,' he said, 'is someone deeply involved with the school – she has taken an active stance on multiculturalism.' 'Take international day,' he said, 'a great example of how we can celebrate our diversity and get children involved.' Then, in a solemn tone, he spoke of how Bunmi first came to Ireland as an asylum seeker and how she rebuilt her shattered world through determination and hard work. 'She is a great teacher, volunteer, mediator, and friend.' The crowd applauded loudly.

The principal introduced a government minister and 'native of Dundalk'. Beginning with a few suitable quotations from Irish literature, the minister spoke of the importance of books and the availability of different worlds in literature. 'Dundalk is a town that can now celebrate its African heritage and connections,' he said. 'It is fitting, now, that African stories should be told in our schools, places in which many of our traditional stories and literature have their roots.' He then repeated Bunmi's biographical details, suggesting that she stood as a 'true' example of what integration means. Loud applause followed. 'We can't afford to make the same mistakes as they made in the UK,' he continued. 'If we do not learn from history we will be doomed to repeat the same mistakes here.' 'You are a true African,' volunteered one of the invited guests on the stage. The room erupted in laughter and applause. Some people stood and clapped; others danced a little.

A teacher from the local primary school took centre stage and explained that she had coordinated literacy education in the school. She applauded Bunmi's role and recalled the African stories that she told to the children. 'I loved those stories,' the teacher said, 'and I knew we must find a publisher.' She recalled the moment during which she and Bunmi envisioned a book of African stories, complete with illustrations, to inspire all children with the power of storytelling. 'And there's a political dimension to storytelling too,' she said. 'Something very important can be done through stories.'

Finally, it was Bunmi's turn: she thanked everyone in turn and then began to speak about life in Africa, her decision to flee Nigeria and her subsequent journey to Ireland. She spoke of the difficult early years in the asylum system, first in Tralee and then in Dundalk. 'I always knew that I should volunteer,' she said. 'It is a way to get into the workplace, and now I have a new home.' 'At first, we were a small group of Africans here in Dundalk,' she recalled, and, 'we had to work hard to be accepted by the local community.' 'Look at Benedicta,' she said, commenting on the local and European elections. 'She's doing wonderful things. You should all look to her hard work – the personality opens the door but the character keeps it open!' There was more applause, laughter, chatting, spontaneous dancing, and a brief performance in song by the group of schoolchildren. Several people uttered a statement we heard often throughout our research: 'Every school needs a Bunmi!'

Within the education system, that powerful machine for generating societal inclusion, Bunmi's event sent out reassuring signals. This was integration expressed in a desirable form – an Irish version of integration, celebrated under the cultural star of literature and blessed by a government minister. But should this event be taken as a signal that all is well? The minister cautioned his audience that Ireland must avoid the mistakes made in the UK. His words echoed those of former Minister for Justice, Equality and Law Reform, Michael McDowell, TD, who argued that the absence of 'race'-based politics in Ireland was a positive sign. In contrast to other nation-states, 'we have handled it quite well,' he said (McDowell 2006: 59). The UK is thus configured as a failed experiment in multi-culturalism, which led to fragmentation rather than cohesion, parallel communities rather than fidelity to the nation and loyalty to the state. Therefore, when it comes to evaluating Ireland's approach to diversity in education we must ask: what makes Ireland's approach different, and how does this approach stack up against international examples? Moreover, to move beyond a superficial inter-pretation of Bunmi's launch we must attend to her personal story, the stories she wrote for children in Irish schools, and the stories of African-Irish parents and children as they engage with the education system in different and often surpris-ing ways. As the teacher in Dundalk noted, there is indeed a political dimension to stories. To borrow once again from Michael Jackson, stories have the power to disrupt the taken-for-granted knowledge of governing and order and, instead, show us the diversity, uncertainty and the imbricated nature of everyday experi-ences (Jackson 2002: 253).

Journeys and stories

'I arrived in Ireland in 1999 with my four girls,' Bunmi explained to us.

> We came because ... well, I won't go into details now. But, when we first came it was very, very difficult. It was so difficult to leave our country and come here, very, very stressful, and a highly emotional thing. It's different from, 'Oh, I'm going on holiday.' This is a situation where you are going somewhere that you've never been, somewhere that you don't have any family network and you don't know what you are going to face. [...] The cold was the first shock! [*Laughs*] I really pitied my children at the time though, because they were so small and we didn't have any winter clothes. They were going around with six layers at a time! (Interview, 2010 [our interpolation])

After the usual initial processing in Dublin, Bunmi and her family began their period in the asylum system in Tralee, County Kerry. 'We were afraid,' she recalls. 'We didn't know where they were taking us; we thought we were going into detention, and everybody was crying, the children were crying.' They arrived late at night in a house contracted by the Department of Justice, and the following day Bunmi and her family awoke to a new world. 'We had to go into town,' she remembered. She lowered her voice and continued, 'The reaction [*pause*], you know? People would shout, maybe they had never seen a black person before. ... They weren't always hostile, but they would stop us and it was too much (Interview, 2010 [our interpolation]).' Time passed and she grew more accustomed to 'Irish culture'. Indeed, Bunmi's story indicates that she was constantly one step ahead of official processes, and when it came to the education of her children she certainly stole a march:

> I came out of the house one day and heard the voices of children, so I traced their voices to a national school, went in and spoke to the principal. 'I'm looking for a school for my girls,' I said. He immediately admitted the two younger ones and recommended a school for the two older ones. But [*names her daughter*] found it very difficult to settle, because she is a very bubbly person. She wanted to make friends, you know, and expected that she would make friends easily. But it wasn't the case for her. Standing alone during breaks, sitting alone in class, nobody was talking to her, so she wasn't settled at all. And I thought, 'If she is not settled then others are suffering as well.' So it got to the point that when you wake them in the morning they are so reluctant, they don't want to go to school. I was concerned because they were children that were bright and loved school in Nigeria. So I had to come into school and spoke with the principal and sat down with the teacher to work it through. 'This is killing me,' you know? And we agreed that I would do a project on Nigeria and that way introduce [*names her daughter*] to her class. So I gave her clothes from Nigeria, and she presented the project, dressed in her Nigerian clothes; the teacher took pictures, and the whole class was very happy, and after that she made friends and became popular. So after that she joined the choir and the Gaelic [*games*], . . . and that really boosted her confidence, and since then she hasn't stopped. (Interview, 2010 [our interpolations])

Bunmi relocated to Dundalk during those early years. She made a point of visibly walking her children to school each day. She did her best to meet other parents and always invited them for coffee. She also began volunteering with a charitable organisation and with a refugee information service, quickly rising through the ranks to become a voluntary information officer. Within a few short years she had joined the cohort of semi-official trainers who crisscrossed Ireland providing workshops on multiculturalism and anti-racism training. A part of that work included visits to schools. 'You see,' she said:

> The children were still coming home complaining, 'Oh, they call me a black monkey,' things like that. Well, we thought the best thing is to go into the schools, talk to the children and the staff. We introduced the international day to other schools: we'd cook some food, get dressed up and go in, show them the vibrancy in our colours and all that. [. . .]
>   Initially I will say that my town was very hostile, a hostile place. It's a border town, with Northern Ireland, and seeing a lot of black people was not something people were used to. It was tough at the time: very racist incidents that we had to face, either physical or verbal. But when we started doing the school projects . . ., when children go home and tell their parents what happened, when they tell their parents' generation or their grannies' generation, 'There's black people coming into the schools to talk, and this is what they said . . .'. We told our stories to those children, we spoke our hearts out. So they knew we were talking from the heart, and it started getting better. (Interview, 2010)

Bumni began to volunteer in the literacy programme in her local primary school, St Joseph's, which was both a skills programme and a resource that aimed to promote reading in general – 'a book a week.' Bunmi browsed the collections of books in the resource room and noticed very few books about Africa. Those books about Africa in the resource collection were written by Europeans. She was not alone in noticing this. A teacher in her school noted the biases in texts throughout the education system: 'Different ethnic groups: that's one thing you don't see in the books. It's all white children in the books: ... all those stereotypical 2.4 children and what not' (Interview, 2010). But Bunmi decided to do something about the problem: 'I tried to write the stories I had heard as a child, trying to recall them.' 'I even called home,' she said, 'to speak with my father to remind me of some of the ones he told us when we were young.' The process was slow, but Bunmi noticed that after writing down several stories she was developing a thirst to write her own stories. With a small grant from the Office of the Minister for State for Integration, she published *Tales by Moonlight: African Stories for Children* in three volumes during 2008.[1]

Tales by Moonlight offers myths about the origins of things, such as why cats and rats do not get along. The narratives instruct children on important life lessons, such as why friendships are important, and why one should never trust a stranger. Bunmi intends the stories to speak to children from both Irish and African families. Thus, they are composed of African material but are shaped to elicit universal messages. Reading these stories allows one to gain insights into Bunmi's personal political project. She introduces volume two with the following statement: 'If we must talk of equality in education all children regardless of their cultural background must be fully integrated and included in our school systems. Apart from encouraging other children to learn about African cultures and tradition, this [*book*] will also help African children hold on to their cultural identity' (Salako 2008: ii [our interpolation]).

The stories resist categorisation as merely artefacts of diasporic consciousness. One may recall here W.E.B. Du Bois's 1903 treatise, *The Souls of Black Folk*, in which he wrote of the racial veil that covered the United States and provided the conditions for the possibility of segregated education. Famously, Du Bois describes the 'peculiar sensation' of being black, of 'measuring one's soul by the tape of a world that looks on in amused contempt and pity'. He describes this as double-consciousness: 'two souls, two thoughts, two un-reconciled strivings, two warring ideals in one dark body, whose dogged strength alone keeps it from being torn asunder' (Du Bois 1897: 5). But while many African-Irish people would recognise the peculiar affective sensations produced by racism and exclusion, the overwhelming impression one gets from Bunmi's project in *Tales by Moonlight* is of cultural self-confidence and empowerment. Several stories describe people and anthropomorphic creatures set in a land stalked by famine, yet the mythic quality of the stories lifts them out of their specific contexts. There is no sense of cultural impoverishment; rather, 'tradition' is the well-spring of empowerment. And empowerment, especially the empowerment of new immigrant parents, is crucial to the running of many schools in Ireland.

4 *Tales by Moonlight*

Ireland is in the middle of a momentous set of debates about the future of education. Questions are being asked about whether a largely denominational system is fit for the purpose of educating an increasingly secular and diverse society. The issues at stake are cast into stark relief when one considers the situation of schools in disadvantaged areas with high numbers of new immigrant pupils.[2] The substance of this chapter is an effort to explore everyday life in St Joseph's Primary School in Dundalk, a school which is attempting to meet the challenges posed by very diverse school-going populations in a locality marked by poverty. Herein, we attend to the voices of management staff, teachers and parents and to the roles of important figures such as Bunmi. Throughout this book we have signalled the importance of the everyday, and here we attend to integration at the chalk-face. But our ethnographic work here is not simply a study of curiosities in one particular school. Rather, St Joseph's is both diverse and disadvantaged and, thus, answers to the national profile of a school in which active and immediate issues are presented by pluralism. During every single school day, teachers, parents and children must work together to strike a balance between inclusiveness and effectiveness, empathy and discipline. The problems and prospects of this one primary school say much about integration and education nationally.

Learning to integrate

Currently, there are several types of primary education provision available to children in Ireland. First and foremost, there are national schools like St Joseph's, which are largely financed by the state and administered by (usually diocesan) patron bodies and local representatives. Secondly, there are non-profit multi-denominational schools such as those run by the Educate Together movement. Thirdly, there are *Gaelscoileanna*, which teach through the Irish language and tend to be run as voluntary organisations. Finally, there are a small number of private preparatory schools. A national primary school curriculum is taught in all schools, while the religious curriculum remains largely in the competence of churches. Today, the overwhelming majority of primary schools – around 90 per cent – are Roman Catholic.[3] The same pattern is evident to a different degree at post-primary or second level. The majority of secondary schools are state-funded to a high degree but are managed by religious or private organisations. The remainder are wholly state-funded community schools, or *Gaelcholáistes*.

The history of the Irish education system must be understood by attending to the powerful roles played by churches in the funding, management and day-to-day operations of schools. The 1937 Constitution of Ireland recognises the rights of parents and the roles of churches, especially the Roman Catholic Church, and limits the state to the job of 'guardian'. Indeed, one Minister for Education likened his role to that of a plumber who was called in 'only when something went wrong' (Browne 1998: 45; Kissane 2003).[4] The minister's seemingly graceless remark was, in fact, an expression of political nous. Post-Independence Ireland was configured as a Catholic country and a policy that aimed to render education unto the Church was deemed to be both pragmatic and appropriate. The majority could be catered for, minorities were in the minority, and diversity was largely ignored. Take for example the 1965 *Rules for National Schools,* which explicitly recognised the denominational nature of primary education (Williams 1999: 324). Therein, schools were required to identify periods of religious instruction to facilitate parents who wished their child to be excused from such instruction. However, the opt-out possibility masked a deep contradiction: religion was expected (and still is expected) to be integrated throughout the curriculum and evident in a denominational school's ethos.[5] This was an Irish solution to the problems of pluralism.

In one of his lesser-known short stories, 'A Minority,' Frank O'Connor explores 'race' and identity within Ireland's post-war denominational education system. In the story, Denis Halligan, a Protestant schoolchild, befriends Willy Stein, a war orphan, while opting out from Mass. Denis, fed-up with exclusion, decides to convert to Catholicism and hopes Willy might do so too:

> 'Ah, come on, Willy,' he said authoritatively, 'you don't want to be a blooming old Proddy.'
>
> 'I don't want to be a Cat either,' said Willy with a shrug.

'Don't you want to be like the other fellows in the school?'

'Why don't they want to be like me?' asked Stein.

'Because there's only two of us; and there's hundreds of them. And they're right.'

'And if there were hundreds of us and two of them, we'd be right, I suppose?' Stein said with a sneer. (O'Connor 1994: 187)

But Denis later discovers that Stein is not Protestant at all. To protect him from 'jeering,' the school and his adopted parents have lied. 'Stein is a Jew,' confides an older child. 'That's why his father and mother were killed.' Struggling with his identity and with the hollowness of his conversion, Denis lashes out:

He glanced round and saw Stein, thin, pale and furtive, slouching away from the chapel with his hand in his pocket clutching his slingshot. . . .

'Who's that?' asked Martha inquisitively.

'Oh, him!' Denis said contemptuously. 'That's only a dirty Jew-boy.' (O'Connor 1994: 189)

What O'Connor achieves is the creation of a cognitive map which guides readers from the large-scale and horrific histories of anti-Semitism and racism to the micro-scale of two young boys fashioning their identities and prejudices from imported material and that which is available on the ground. Identities are fashioned in everyday experiences, but those experiences are also imbricated by broader policies and systems. Frank O'Connor's writing captures the experiences of generations of opt-out children. His short story offers a prescient insight into the Irish education system, which from the 1990s onwards seemed out of step with an increasingly secular society and ever-more diverse student populations.

In 1992 and 1995 the government of Ireland issued key policy papers in which the roles of churches and religious instruction were diminished and the figure of the secular citizen seemed ever-more present, albeit hovering in the background (Government of Ireland 1992, 1995). These policies dovetailed with increasing demands for alternative forms of schooling, emanating especially from parents. Prior to 1998, the state funded only 15 per cent of the costs of establishing new schools. Generally, Catholic Church-owned land and resources filled the enormous gaps, and thus the system perpetuated itself in ways that presented inequitable choices to parents desiring non- or multi-denomination educations for their children. In 1999 the state agreed to fund the construction of all new schools, apparently sign-posting an era of state-funded secular education. Eight years later, however, data indicated that less than 2 per cent of primary schools were multi-denominational (see Mawhinney 2007: 394). Added to this, employment equality legislation enshrines the right of religious organisations such as schools to employ only those people who respect the ethos of the organisation. Moreover, schools are entitled to give preference in admissions on the basis of the faith of children where competition exists for school places and the need to maintain the ethos of the school can be demonstrated. In 2005 the United

Nations Committee on the Elimination of Racism and Discrimination recommended more non-denominational schools to protect against discrimination on racial grounds under the guise of protecting the religious ethos of schools (see Mawhinney 2007). During recent years, secularisation and new immigration have become imbricated, complex and often contradictory challenges to the traditional configuration of the education system.

In 2007 the *Irish Times* reported on the controversy surrounding emergency school provision in the Dublin region, suggesting that systemic issues were leading to the segregation of new immigrant children. Competition for school places was fierce at that stage, and immigrant parents were confronted with the challenge of securing admission for their children into schools that insisted upon prioritising Catholic children. The *Irish Times* reported that on 1 September 2007 some seventy new immigrant parents, described as 'mostly black,' attended a meeting with the Department of Education to resolve the issues. Later, the Minister for Education denied that there was any institutional racism at work. 'It might be a skin-colour issue, but it's not necessarily a race issue,' she said (Boland 2007: 1; see also Fanning 2009: 173). But the situation seemed clear to many commentators, Catholic schools were prioritising the enrolment of Catholic children, few non- or multi-denomination education options existed, and as a consequence new immigrant children were being excluded and forced to seek emergency school provision.[6] The end result was that when Scoil Choilm Emergency Primary School opened its door that same week in Dublin 15 the overwhelming majority of its pupils were from immigrant families – and, yet, the patron was the Catholic Archdiocese of Dublin.[7] Later that month, a multi-denominational Educate Together school opened in Balbriggan, County Dublin, a town near to Mosney asylum seeker accommodation centre, and admitted, according to the *Sunday Times*, '80 black children' (Sharrock 2007: no pagination). The headline of the news article read, 'Ireland opens its first all black school.' The same story was reported in other international newspapers. *The Guardian*, for example, recorded that one local politician likened the situation to a 'mini-Apartheid' (McDonald 2007: no pagination). Controversy and debate continues to this day, with the present Irish government negotiating changes to the levels of Catholic patronage of schools. A Forum on Patronage and Pluralism is expected to report to the government at the end of 2011. Clearly, however, immigration is one of the central issues which are challenging the Irish education model, and, whether wilfully or not, issues of 'race' are intersecting with matters of faith in Irish schools.

At the launch of Bunmi's *Tales by Moonlight* in Dundalk the minister who addressed the crowd lauded her as a true example of what integration means. 'We can't afford to make the same mistakes as they made in the UK,' he said. Ireland was thus imagined to be on a different path towards integration. And there is some justification for considering Ireland to be a distinctive case: the controversies over access to school places in an overwhelmingly denominational system are not available to the same degree in other European Member States. However, the minister's comments about the UK's 'mistakes' were delivered in a self-congratulatory tone for which there is little justification. Much may in fact be learned from international examples, and by attending to the experiences of integration in Irish schools we may begin to see the distinctive mistakes that Ireland is making. Our opening ethnographic vignette is also revealing in another sense. 'Every school need a Bumni,' people said. We heard this compliment many times throughout our research. But why does every school need a Bunmi?

Multiculturalism and its discontents

There are many approaches to diversity available in education systems around the world. In Ireland, comparison is often made with the UK and the United States. Multicultural policies in the UK are frequently described as failed experiments. Few, however, explore the motivations which subsisted behind those policies. For example, back in 1971 Father Bernard Coard's inflammatory pamphlet, *How the West Indian Child is made Educationally Subnormal in the British School System* documented failures to accommodate diversity and the resulting exclusion and underachievement experienced by immigrant children. To illustrate, one may recall Paul Willis's *Learning to Labour* (1977), which exposed the informal workings and social reproductions in a British school. Take for example the following extract in which a senior teacher describes the organised 'friendship groups' that were a part of the school's integration policy:

> We have got the ... European room, Bucknor, Grant, Samuels, Spence in the West Indian room and Singh, Rajit and co in the Asiatic room. So much for integration! There are three distinct rooms. You go into the white room and you will probably sit down and have a cup of tea made. You go into the Indian room and they are all playing cards and they are jabbering to each other, and then you go into the West Indian room and they are all dancing to records. In the West Indian room they are sort of stamping around, twisting. (Willis 1977: 47–48)

The teacher's frustrations fade into the racism he set out to challenge, as if there was something hidden but inescapable about the ways in which space, power and knowledge intersected. Paul Willis was among a new generation of scholars who focused on the 'hidden curriculum:' the ways in which curricula, structures and spaces encode norms, values and ideologies (see Lynch 1986).[8] According to scholars such as Willis, instead of generating societal inclusion, the machinery of education was reproducing social exclusion along the lines of classes and racialised divisions. And for immigrant children the experience of schooling was frequently harsh and exclusionary – they, to paraphrase W.E.B. Du Bois, were constantly forced to measure themselves by the tape of a world made in Britain. The work of activists such as Coard and a new generation of researchers led directly to the emergence of supplementary schools and several anti-racism and multicultural policy initiatives – imperfect policies, sometimes mistaken policies, but necessary interventions nonetheless.

The United States also has a long history of debates over the nature of multicultural education and equitable access to schooling. During the early 1970s, for example, US states such as Massachusetts attempted to reduce de facto segrega-tion in schools by transporting (or bussing, as it was known) mainly African-American children across district lines to schools catering to a majority of 'white' children. Irish-American neighbourhoods such as Roxbury in Boston exploded in violence, and for several years thereafter State Troopers were stationed at one high school. The bussing strategy was certainly a failed experi-ment, and there is good evidence to suggest that levels of segregation in US schools are higher now than they were during the late 1960s (Kozol 2005).[9] But access to schools was just one of a number of issues raised by diverse school populations. The 1970s also saw growing recognition of the cultural biases encoded in US school curricula and assessment systems (Labov 1972). But changes to the education system, especially curriculum changes, have proven to be controversial. Take for example Arthur M. Schlesinger's *The Disuniting of America* (1991), which argued that 'the cult of ethnicity' was undermining the foundations of the system. 'Our civilisation,' he argued, should not have 'guilt trips laid on it by champions of cultures based on despotism, superstition, tribalism, and fanaticism' (1991: 133–134). Ironically, Schlesinger's attack on multiculturalism reveals the hidden curriculum of the education system he set out to defend.

When the minister speaking at Bunmi's book launch alluded to 'the mistakes they made in the UK' he suggested to his audience that multiculturalism was a failed experiment. History may well judge multicultural education initiatives as failures but those experiments must be understood in their contexts and as responses to deeply encoded biases and institutional racism. Moreover, as we have already shown, Ireland's education system does not offer a *terra nullius*, untouched by issues of diversity and free from hidden curricula and forms of segregation. Rather, according to Lynch and Lodge, 'Irish schools have tradition-ally been characterised by homogeneity of student intake. There is a long tradition of segregation of students by belief, by different abilities, by racial affil-iation as well as by class and gender. Maintenance of separate educational (and subsequently social) worlds is an often unquestioned, institutionalised practice' (Lynch and Lodge 2002: 132).

From 2000 onwards the traditional approaches and institutionalised practices of the Irish education system were progressively reconfigured to cope with greater diversity.[10] 'Interculturalism' became the preferred rubric for discussing diversity in education. Interculturalism denotes activities to foster the inclusion of new immigrant populations, members of the Travelling Community, those with disabilities and those from disadvantaged backgrounds in the mainstream schooling systems.[11] Policy was informed by equality legislation, European Union (EU) directives, and international human rights law. And, if one fast-forwards to the recent *Intercultural Education Strategy, 2010–2015* the same discourse is evident. The education system is expected to play its role in societal integration by advancing the inclusion of diversity through interculturalism. The terms sound similar and the definitions provided are slippery. But intercultural education policy cannot be otherwise – because it masks deep contradictions.

Interculturalism is expected to inform practice throughout schools, but because of the denominational character of the actual system a religious ethos is also understood to be available throughout most schools. Integration, inclusion and interculturalism are the fashionable and elusive terms in which policy is expressed, but for many schools diversity is something which has to be managed in the everyday, and the deep contradictions between the rhetoric of policy and day-to-day experiences on the ground are readily apparent. Famously, one Minister for Education likened his role to that of a plumber who was called in only when something went wrong. Today's intercultural education policy today is also a hands-off one, characterised by government-at-a-distance. Integration is configured as something to be worked out, supported and repaired if necessary by those on the ground – principals, teachers, parents and children.[12] And that is why, 'Every school needs a Bunmi.'

What is the situation in schools with high numbers of new immigrant children? And how are principals, teachers, parents and children putting shape on integration on the ground? There are a number of key points to bear in mind when considering multicultural Irish schools. Firstly, figures compiled in 2009 indicated that almost 10 per cent of students in Irish primary schools were from 'an immigrant background.' Secondly, although data indicates that on average 'first-generation immigrant students' achieve education outcomes comparable to their Irish-born classmates, few reasonable conclusions may be reached by examining immigrant children in general (OECD 2009: 9, 13, 22). Thirdly, a recent report found that schools in urban areas and especially those with designated disadvantaged status had higher than average populations of pupils with an immigrant background (Smith et al 2009). Much may be learned, therefore, by considering the experiences of particular immigrant students in schools located in relatively poor or disadvantaged areas.

McGorman and Sugrue (2007) provide a detailed analysis of schools in Dublin 15, an area regarded as a 'unique case' because of its exploding school-age population. The picture they paint is of a fast-changing area, blighted by pockets of disadvantage and with a large and transitory immigrant population. Their work indicates a high level of student migration in and out of primary schools at different levels. 'Analysis of the ethnicity of those leaving and joining these class groups indicates a significant trend – that of Irish pupils leaving the schools and immigrant pupils joining [...]. The evidence suggests that these patterns, if not addressed, will result in ghettoisation and social segregation that is inimical to a rhetoric of inclusion' (McGorman and Sugrue 2007: 59–60 passim). The report records often heroic efforts by schools to cope with disadvantage and increasingly diverse populations. The voices of teachers show especial concern about the education attainment levels, discipline and general integration of 'African children' (2007: 67). African children reported significant problems but, McGorman and Sugrue conclude, 'Through their own agency, with adequate support, they are the prospect of a new tolerant and culturally diverse Ireland' (2007: 98). It is to the prospects for integration available in St Joseph's Primary School in Dundalk that we now turn.

Integration at the chalk-face

St Joseph's Primary School is located in Muirhevnamor, a large local authority housing development in south-east Dundalk and a designated area of disadvantage. Muirhevnamor is sometimes referred to as 'little Belfast' on account of the high number of so-called Northern Refugees who resettled there during the Troubles. Today, there is a high level of ethnic diversity among its 3000 residents. The landscape of Muirhevnamor is marked by poverty. The houses were built during the late 1970s in a series of cul de sacs composed of between fifteen and twenty dwellings. No matter what efforts residents make to maintain their properties, an air of neglect hangs about the estate. During the 1980s the Australian poet Vincent Buckley toured Ireland and was perplexed by the strange quality of housing developments that felt impoverished and yet materialistic and looked unfinished and yet used up (Buckley 1985). Muirhevnamor shares this strange quality, compounded by poor infrastructure planning. The estate is cut off rather than connected by major road arteries, and residents rely on the bus connections or local taxi companies to take them to the centre of Dundalk. During the mid-1990s Muirhevnamor's unemployment rate was estimated to be approximately 70 per cent. Many people found employment during the so-called Celtic Tiger boom but those gains have been lost in the decimation wrought by the recent recession. Reports on Muirhevnamor suggest that good relationships have been built up with local institutions and the police, but there remains a low intensity and everyday conflict with youths, 'boredom and drink' (Bowden and Higgins 2000: 69). The lone-parent families in the estate are sometimes targets of vandalism and abuse and so too are immigrant families. A republican activist in the area described to us in detail the 'off the radar' racism and abuse suffered by immigrant families who tend not to report incidents.

St Joseph's Primary School first opened its doors in 1979 and over the next three decades generations of diverse pupils were educated there, from the children of 'Northern Refugees' to Vietnamese refugees and from Traveller children to Romany migrants. During the late 1990s there was a significant increase in pupils from refugee and asylum seeking families, and all the while the school catered for impoverished 'local' residents. Today, the school resembles a large factory-campus and houses a community kindergarten in its grounds. Though St Joseph's has a sizeable playground, playtimes are staggered because the space is insufficient to cater for 500 pupils. Almost four out of every ten pupils is from a migrant background, and fourteen nationalities are represented in the diversity of accents that one can hear as children run about the schoolyard, playing football, hopscotch or singing and dancing in groups. According to the principal:

> Africans are the largest singular group. Initially, there was ... a belief among many of the Africans that they had to become more Irish than the Irish themselves. They thought that they should become Catholic, for example, or they thought that they should become enrolled in all the various ceremonies and everything. [...] We told people that it was their choice, that this is a Catholic

school with a Catholic ethos but part of that is that we are open to accepting different cultures, different religions – we have Muslim, Christian, non-Christian and they either opt in or out of our formal religious sessions. But we are not proselytising: we are not trying to make good little Catholics out of everybody. We want to provide the best possible service for everyone, and to give them the freedom to do their own thing. (Interview, 2010)

In this denominational school in a disadvantaged area with a high immigrant population, integration is being worked out at the chalk-face.

Over the course of several months during 2010, we spoke informally with teachers and interviewed several of them; we ran focus groups, observed classes and generally hung around. It did not take long to form an impression of a school facing enormous challenges. In the relaxed setting of their staffroom, teachers spoke of the poverty and drug abuse in the surrounding neighbourhoods, but there was little despondency. Rather, the school functioned in a highly organised manner. Each morning the staff gathered together for a brief meeting, a white-board was filled with planned activities and notes, and teachers began their classes buoyed up by the *esprit de corps*. St Joseph's is also an outward looking school. Staff could often be overheard discussing continued professional development activities or 'Incredible Years' training.

The principal and vice-principal managed the school's affairs efficiently and with a surprisingly light touch. They often dropped into the staffroom to chat with teachers and check on the progress of a student or on the general performance of a class. The informal style was possible because of the underlying level of organisation. The light touch of the senior staff was also evident in their dealings with students. During the course of our research the principal and vice-principal handled a variety of extremely sensitive situations with little fuss. Moreover, many of the teachers were well known to parents in the surrounding neighbourhoods and did their utmost to include parents in school life.

For almost a full school year, Fiona Murphy attended a 'senior infants' class composed of fifteen pupils. Some of the children were immigrants from Africa, the Middle East or the former European accession states, while others were born in Ireland of either Irish or immigrant parents. However, identity categorisations based on migration studies were of little use in framing quotidian classroom experiences. Ethnic differences, it seemed, appeared in complex ways. Some teachers recorded their efforts to stamp out racism immediately upon encountering it, often by calling upon parents to help deal with situations. One teacher explained:

The most time, you would see it in a child that comes from a background that might be a little less well off. ... What I mean by that is people in less fortunate situations – financially or socially. When there is an element of frustration at home and maybe there is unemployment at home, and in Irish society now there is a lot of blame put on immigration for unemployment, and there may be references made at home and comments made at home which the kids are then repeating in the yard. Well, I have rarely seen racism in the kids who are more settled or their home environment is more relaxed, you would rarely hear a comment from those kids. (Focus-group interview, 2010)[13]

Other teachers noticed the nuanced ways in which ethnicity and 'race' mani-
fested themselves to pupils and responded in measured ways. During a
focus-group interview one teacher recalled, 'I was out in the yard today and one
white kid came over and said, "Teacher, teacher that chocolate-brown boy over
there fell over."' The staff at the focus-group interview laughed at the story and
recalled similar moments during which the seriousness of events had to be
weighed and responses measured to fit the situations. In general, openness and a
willingness to explore issues with students characterised the teachers' responses
to racism. One teacher even described the school as a site with a layered history
of ethnic interactions and suggested that this was the lens through which they
viewed diversity:

> The children of the families who came down here during the Troubles played
> together in the yard like the African children play together today. Everybody I
> suppose, but children really seek an identity – two things they want: identity and
> belonging – and that's what they really seek more than anything else in the
> school setting. So the [*Northern children's*] identity was quite hidden, because it
> wasn't open or safe for them, but that gradually came, just settled in, belonging,
> and becoming part of the school, similarly with the African community.
> (Interview, 2010 [our interpolation])

For a number of months, Fiona acted as a circumstantial teaching assistant,
helping out with the lessons and different exercises, reading stories and from time
to time assisting the children in the acquisition of English language skills.
Religious instruction was available but in a form that engaged the body more
than the theological soul: sometimes religious-themed songs were played and the
children danced to the beat rather than to the message. Irish language classes
occurred each day, wherein some of the children struggled, with those who
migrated to Ireland most recently finding the instruction most challenging. The
classes were not without their problems, and throughout the school significant
difficulties were described by teachers. Some, for example, described 'bright
classes' in which they had to struggle to maintain standards while simplifying the
style of communication for new immigrant students, especially those for whom
English was not their first language. Others dismissed those claims and suggested
that language levels were an issue throughout the entire education system. In that
vein, one teacher remarked, 'I must say my African children, their language is no
problem, their English is no problem, and they are bright as well! They give the
class a bit of spark!' (Focus-group interview, 2010)

One of the most important 'intercultural' issues that teachers and parents
faced together was discipline. When African children first began to be admitted
to the school in large numbers, teachers found it difficult to appreciate cultural
mores regarding eye contact. African children tended to avoid looking at teachers
directly, especially in situations in which they were being disciplined. Teachers
took this as a sign of disrespect, but the pupils understood eye contact with an
adult as a disrespectful gesture. During an interview, the principal of St Joseph's
described the important role that Bunmi played within the school as a mediator

for these and other issues of cultural awareness and translation. But there were also problems around corporal punishment. According to the principal:

> African parents would have come and said, 'Well, we expect you when our children are misbehaving that you beat them.' We explained that we could not do that. And again, I remember the old days: when I began teaching we did beat children. I am not saying it was right, it was just the culture at that time, and we know in retrospect that it was very wrong. But at the time we didn't know it was wrong because we had been brought up in a culture where if someone misbehaved, they were spanked. If you go back to Victorian times, I believe, teachers used to bring children out first thing in the morning and they used to administer corporal punishment in preparation for anything that would accrue thereafter. So, you know, whether it is progress or change – you can call it what you will – and I would like to think that it is progressive change [...]. But we are all biased by virtue of the fact that we all grew up in a mono culture for a long, long time in a mono religious culture as well, means we are blindfolded for want of a better term, the only way that can be improved or widened is by exposure. (Interview, 2010)

The principal's open-mindedness translated into an informal policy of dialogue with parents – and again Bunmi played a key role. And the principal's way of framing the issues as cultural ones were echoed by many parents, as the following extracts from a focus-group session show:

> I realise that the fundamental style, the original style of Africans towards discipline is the one the Irish have got in the past ..., but eventually they dropped that and they come to the European laws of what should be done [...]. At the same time, there is still a conflict in that area, I realise, but at the end of the day the authorities put too many rules on the part of the child, but when the child becomes bad they put it back to the parents. ... I am not saying corporal punishment ... but some common-sense discipline must be applied to make them get on line and do the things that should be done. That is one major problem of the Africans in the system. That is what I realise. (Focus-group interview, 2010)

Several parents also noted (as did teachers) issues of discipline that were crosscut with gender. Male schoolchildren, for example, were understood to adjust poorly to female authority figures. However, the broad issue of the disciplining of male and female children dominated discussions. A parent had this to say:

> I remember [*in Uganda*], they used to beat me all the time. If my mama was still alive now she would still beat me – there is no age limit to stop beating. Beating is a good thing, a good discipline [*she demonstrates a slap on the wrist*]. [...] You are afraid that they will go to the teacher and say, 'Oh, my mama beat me,' and the police will come and take the child from you. So I don't want to beat the child because the child will tell and they will report me. That makes us feel uncomfortable, but in African life, we beat children, we beat them. (Focus-group interview, 2010 [our interpolation])

During a discussion with parents, Bunmi elaborated on the key issues, speaking from the heart as both a parent and teacher:

> We have to work twice as hard as Irish parents in bringing up our kids because of the cultural issues here: it is so permissive to so many things which we don't allow. Like I said, I don't want to go back home with my kids and they will ask me, 'What type of children did she bring up?' It would be a shame … to me and to my family, and I don't want that. [...] The only thing is I will not treat my kids like animals, but when it comes to discipline nobody will teach me what to do. … And you know yourself: you see my kids …
>
> Yeah, it is a big problem and from my experience here [...]. The diary itself in which the teacher records behaviour is a big thing for parents: if you write that the child has misbehaved and the child misses a stamp, then the next day you will see the parents here asking you to beat them! (Focus-group interview, 2010)

Many schools around Ireland operate a formal system of parent/teacher communication by using school journals or diaries. The issues that Bunmi spoke of above were reflected in the experiences of teachers using this system. Here is an extract from a focus-group discussion with teachers:

> TEACHER 1: I just know of circumstances where you might be aware if a student loses a stamp – we have a stamp system where children get two stamps a day – and if they lose a stamp they might say, 'Oh no, don't take a stamp off of me, I am going to get beaten,' you know that kind of way. It impinges then on the discipline system, because obviously you don't want the child to get hit, but obviously you want to get the message back that the child wasn't behaving, so it makes it kind of difficult to know what to do.

> TEACHER 2: I think it has caused behavioural issues in school from some African children, because they know that they can't, that we can't discipline them in the same way as their parents would at home, so they do play up in school – they become school devils and house angels. (Focus-group interview, 2010)

These complex and everyday issues required nuanced and everyday mediation. The school took issues such as discipline very seriously, and Bunmi played an important role in bringing parents on board, explaining school policy, and explaining parents' concerns to school staff. All in all, the efforts teachers made to understand and connect with parents in the surrounding neighbourhoods was evident continually and shared like a school ethos. As the principal explained during an interview:

> At the very early stage in this school, one of the Chairmen said, 'To work here you would have to be a missionary.' Well, I don't think he meant it …, well he did mean it in the religious sense, but he meant it in the caring sense. If a young teacher should come here even with tremendous teaching skills, unless they care about human beings they are not going to survive here, unless you care you are not going to bring about change. You can't go in, I remember … when I was first appointed here thinking, 'Well, right, we will turn this into a middle class school!' Well that was ignorance on my part: you need to meet the needs of the people where they are at.

[...] Also, schools serving areas of disadvantage have been quite fortunate in the development of home school liaison: ... schools were encouraged to engage parents in their children's education. We bought into that at a very early stage. It's possible to say that it was part of that whole caring or missionary zeal to provide opportunity, and that was part of it. And even before revised curriculum or new teaching methodologies or whatever there was an emphasis in that initiative to involve parents and the community, and I think that's it, a school can't operate in isolation! (Interview, 2010)

One of the most obvious expressions of the ways in which St Joseph's approaches 'interculturalism' is its International Day, which is held each year, usually during May. In 2010, International Day was a well-organised event for the community in which the school was opened for a variety of drop-in activities. The schoolchildren were encouraged to participate in a number of quizzes in the gym area. The children sat around tables aiming to win prizes by answering questions about capital cities, famous international singers, different kinds of food and various cultural facts and curiosities. Food and drinks were served in the staffroom, and parents sat chatting to one another in Polish, Russian, Yorùbá and English sampling each other's dishes. Some parents and teachers poked at suspicious-looking dishes before trying them, and the exotic quality of some of the food proved to be a powerful icebreaker. Bunmi arrived with a large pot of Nigerian food. She heated it up on the staffroom cooker and shared it out. The principal and vice-principal mingled with the parents, chatting about their own children.

Soon noises from a rehearsal could be heard throughout the corridors. A large number of children from Poland, Latvia and Lithuania dressed in traditional outfits ran through their routines in the gym, coached by a Lithuanian classroom assistant. The gym began to fill with parents and teachers, and the children were escorted in, one class after another, led by their teachers. The performances of traditional music and dance were often very professional looking. Everyone seemed to enjoy themselves. The highlight of the afternoon was a performance by Bunmi's daughters and their semi-professional dance group, Crystal Ice, which had achieved a remarkable level of local fame. The children jumped up and down, clapping and cheering when the dance group was introduced – a few children took the opportunity to act a little too crazily and had to be calmed by parents and teachers; some younger children clapped and jumped up and down enthusiastically but seemed unsure as to what exactly was happening. The dancers followed an energetic routine to contemporary R&B and pop music. A few children were picked to join them on stage. To great applause, Bunmi climbed on to the stage towards the end of the performance and danced with the children.

If one were to attend St Joseph's International Day one would be greeted by an extraordinarily new vision of schools in Ireland. Here is a denominational school making heroic efforts to include parents from a disadvantaged neighbourhood in an intercultural learning environment. It is a school aware of the potential for hidden biases in practice and the dangers of racism. St Joseph's empowers parents and teachers, promotes inclusion and celebrates diversity – they seem, to borrow from a former government minister, to have 'handled it quite well.' And the managers, parents and teachers recognise that it is *they* who have handled the situation. As one teacher put it, 'We didn't get any help from outside, you know? We are very adaptable as staff – that is one of our resources!' (Interview, 2010) But in order to fully evaluate the school experience for immigrant parents and children we move our narrative out through the school's gates to follow the stories of parents and children. We look to the ways in which they engage with education and the points of contestation they perceive.

Hallelujah Halloween

The parents of children attending St Joseph's often walk along a thin line which separates their closely held beliefs from the ethos of the school. Many parents frame their experiences as a series of negotiations, balancing acts or trade-offs during which their children's well-being, their desire for integration and their relationships with the school are at stake. These everyday, behind-the-scenes negotiations become especially delicate when they have to consider opting out of the ritual life of the school. But in a different set of ways, teachers also think about how to come to terms with the competing claims of the religious ethos, intercul-turalism and their own sense of how the school is handling things.

At the beginning of the schoolchildren's Holy Communion year, St Joseph's sends a letter to parents offering them the option of opting out of the ritual. During the year in which we completed this project, several parents elected to instruct the school to allow their children to opt out. This cohort was mainly composed of parents who migrated from African countries where they adhered to Islam. 'I remember,' said one teacher, 'I had a child who would take out the Koran, he would sit down and read the Koran on his own, and the father didn't want him to have anything to do with Christianity.' According to the teachers, others 'just quietly opt out.' However, many were welcomed by the local Church. According to one teacher:

> Even though they weren't of Catholic background the priest acknowledged that and said, 'You are very welcome to our ceremony,' and gave them a blessing, so they were allowed to get all dressed up and everything, which I thought was really nice and inclusive. So it meant that for the – God knows how many hours you spend on Communion – they weren't excluded for all of the time, you know going up to the Church and coming back down and that kind of thing. (Interview, 2010)

But Holy Communion is a Church/school event marked off as an obviously Christian ritual, even for very young children. One may even venture to suggest that Communion is ring-fenced as 'religion,' thus offering an obvious and expected flash-point for conflict. Therefore, parents and teachers work actively to avoid conflicts. But, interestingly, outside of the expected boundaries of culture and religion there are other flash-points. St Joseph's has witnessed conflicts over the panoply of seemingly innocuous figures that inhabit the everyday worlds of children – figures that children take extremely seriously. Battle-lines have been drawn up over Santa Claus, the Tooth Fairy and especially the witches and devils of Halloween.

Teachers described to us instances in which children, having first checked with their parents, arrived at school and informed their classmates that Santa Claus did not in fact exist. Therefore, they reasoned, they could not be judged harshly if Santa Claus did not visit their homes. Teachers also reported that the Tooth Fairy's delivery failures resulted in 'big problems!' However, it was Halloween that presented the greatest difficulties. Each year some classes in St Joseph's hold an in-school Halloween parade, and many children arrive at school without costumes on their parents' instructions. According to one teacher, 'When they get into the line and see all the other children dressed up. ...You can see it in them that they feel isolated, not by anyone or anything like that' (Interview, 2010). The empathy with which this teacher approached the situation was also evident among her colleagues, with some staff worrying about the dread Halloween was generating for African children raised to fear witches and believe in the power of Satanism. Another teacher recorded experiencing the sharp end of the tail:

> The Nigerian kids came in [*to class*], and they were quite a religious family, and they came in to the school and said, 'Witches are the work of the devil!' They started shouting out, 'Well we can't talk about this because it's Satan,' and they were really upsetting the other kids. We had really only been doing it as fun. And then the mothers said that we were pagans, that we're all pagans, and started saying that to the child. That was really quite hard to deal with. (Interview, 2010 [our interpolation])

It is not possible to dismiss these issues as the trivial concerns of kids at school, like the closing pages of *Lord of the Flies* in which the intense conflicts and dramatic world of the children is ruptured by the arrival of reasonable adults – 'What have you been doing? Having a war or something?' (Golding 2002: 223). Halloween is not child's play, because large-scale issues of societal integration manifest themselves to schoolchildren in immediate and everyday ways. And Halloween is not child's play for teachers either. During a focus-group session, one teacher expressed the issues thus:

> I think the Irish traditions and all that are very important. I feel that it is unfair to expect those to be put aside, but I do appreciate where they are coming from, but I think it's unfair to suggest it shouldn't be taught. [...]
>
>   I don't know where to start – maybe I am digging a bit of a hole here – but, you know, the way we were talking about Halloween, and they were coming in telling us that, well, no Santa, no Tooth Fairy. Well I feel that those communities should also be spoken to and told to respect our culture and also teach that to their children. We would never go in to criticise their culture, it works two ways. (Focus-group interview, 2010)

Other teachers agreed that broader issues were at stake and that Halloween really mattered:

> TEACHER 1: Irish culture [*is*] not subdued but is sometimes brushed over to accommodate the customs and beliefs of newcomer students, or maybe say, 'I better not teach that today as that might affect such and such, or he might not like that.' It could be something that's very relevant [...]

> TEACHER 2: Or not even that there is a danger in trying to be too welcome or too supportive in that you are emphasising difference instead of emphasising similarity, you know we feel that we have to explore the Nigerian culture for one, or the Polish for another, or whatever it happens to be, we feel the need to discuss it and talk about it or explore it but very often what we need to do is find what the similarities are and get on with our teaching. (Focus-group interview, 2010)

We found teachers implicitly recognised an important issue which is also raised in the international literature on multicultural education. A wealth of data has long demonstrated that school systems that disregard pupils' cultural backgrounds tend to exclude and marginalise immigrant children, potentially leading to underachievement. Data from the United States especially indicate that those students with a strong sense of their cultural background and 'heritage' perform well in the education system (Zhou 2003; Zhou and Kim 2006; White and Glick 2009). However, some commentators have claimed that the celebration of diversity for its own sake and attendant promotion of cultural awareness may lead to a sense of 'culturelessness' among 'native' students (Glazier and Seo 2005). The research evidence to support this claim is extremely weak, although this has not prevented the uncritical repetition of this claim in studies of integration and education in Ireland (Hinchion and Hennessy 2009: 7–22). However, there is an important point that should not be missed: 'interculturalism' as a pedagogical strategy to value diversity is perceived by many teachers as a weak approach. Our research suggests a lack of comfort among teaching staff with the aims, core principles and likely outcomes of interculturalism, together with a widely held view that there are little or no continuing professional development opportunities in this area. Government at a distance, in the case of intercultural education, seems to have resulted in classroom experiences in which the objectives are also at an uncomfortable distance. Little wonder then that Halloween should present intercultural dilemmas.

It is noteworthy that Halloween presented a lightning rod for the tensions of multicultural education more so than matters of organised religion. The importance that many children place on rituals such as Halloween over and above organised religion is certainly *part* of the story. But the voices of parents must be included to fully understand the nuances of what is at stake. One parent took a conciliatory approach, expressed in the language of culture:

> Every culture, every African has their own culture and they have what they believe in. Like, in my own understanding, this Halloween – questions came, and I told my children, we have Christians in Nigeria, we have Muslims, we have idol worshippers, and they have their seasons. [...] So my children they don't

worship idols, so they are not meant for the Halloween, even though they respect the holiday, are you getting me? When they wanted me to buy it in the house, I said no! If I can buy a Bible, I will buy you a cross, but I can't buy you a mask for Halloween, NO, no, no! ... We have to balance it, it is not everything given to you that you have to take, you only take what you need and leave the rest alone. (Focus-group interview, 2010)

Another parent focused on the impact of Halloween upon her children:

My children, when we first came here, they didn't want to walk even in the shopping centres at Halloween, coz there were so many witches hanging there. It was affecting them. They say, 'No, I don't want to see that!' Even my daughter, she was crying, screaming, and even when she was walking the street she just wanted to cry out. (Focus-group interview, 2010)

Bunmi's perspectives on the problems generated by Halloween were, as one might expect, conciliatory. 'Integration,' she said, 'is a two way thing: but the way the government have handled it ... is like assimilation, and they're two different things. We want to meet half way' (Interview, 2010). But whereas negotiations and trade-offs with the local Church and the school's ethos were practicable, Halloween, even for Bunmi, raised questions about the extent of the intercultural understandings that had developed. 'Assimilation is not a word in our dictionary,' she argued.

I don't want my children to lose their identity. I don't want them to lose their cultural values, which are very, very important. Like respect for adults – that's important in my house. Our food – they must know how to cook and eat it as well – our religion: it's very, very, very important. We are Christians, but we are not Catholics or Protestant, we are Pentecostals and we hold onto that. (Interview, 2010)

But Bunmi is an exceptional figure, with deep and horizontal connections across her locality. As we saw in a previous chapter, she also has strong connections to transnational politics in Nigeria. Few African parents would dispute the hugely important role that she has played in mediating with local institutions. However, there are other important forces in operation. In contrast to Bunmi's diplomatic and conciliatory approach to intercultural matters in her local school, others seek to rearticulate Irish traditions and incorporate them into their own meaningful schemes. Many African families perceive a landscape in which there are official structures and institutions as well as legitimate shadow structures and institutions provided by Pentecostal churches.

We spoke in detail to one Mountain of Fire and Miracles Ministry pastor who, like many other church leaders, operates a Sunday school in his church. The pastor initially outlined the important faith instruction sessions within the school but soon turned to juxtapose Irish society and the Irish education system with his Church's objectives. 'The Church is a school,' he said. In that school the aim, he said, is to produce 'full Christians' and 'soul workers.' 'They,' he said referring to Ireland, 'built schools, but schools that are man-made.' You cannot produce full Christian people, especially children, if you regard education as something that happens only within man-made buildings, he argued. For the pastor, and likewise for many other Pentecostal worshippers with whom we spoke, the Irish education system was sectional, partial and secular, even within ostensibly Catholic schools. The pastor perceived one of his missions to be to develop alternative education for Pentecostal children, funded by Pentecostal parents and faith-based in its teaching. He saw education as a moral matter which should aim to influence all aspects of a child's life: 'The physical, morals, manners, prosperity, personal relationships – true believers in all things' (Interview, 2011). Little wonder, then, that Halloween now has a rival ritual among many African schoolchildren – Hallelujah Night.

According to another Pentecostal pastor from the Redeemed Christian Church of God (RCCG) based in Mosney asylum seeker accommodation centre, word spread around the surrounding towns that children were suffering because of the iconography of Halloween. 'I don't disprove of any faith,' the pastor said. But, 'what I know is what I believe in, and what my Bible tells me.' For the pastor, Halloween offered images of precisely the figures that his Church preached against and, moreover, it represents both a 'demonic' tradition and one that celebrates consumerism for its own sake. 'That is why we decided on this Hallelujah Night, so we are not actually against any faith, Catholic or whatever' (Interview, 2010). The churches responded to the perceived suffering of schoolchildren and the deep concerns held by parents over the style and message of Halloween traditions.

Hallelujah Night is marked off as different from other evening services within the churches. Normally, adults, young people and small children engage in different but simultaneous activities, but on Hallelujah Night these 'separate groups' come together for 'very awesome Christian music.' 'We have a lot of music, Gospel, preaching as well, and that's what we do,' the RCCG pastor told us. The children are not, however, simply a passive audience for performances. In many churches the school-going children are encouraged to dress up in traditional clothes, they are facilitated in staging Christian-themed plays. Part antidote to the perceived ills of a permissive society, and part an extension of the power of Pentecostal churches to organise the resistance and accommodation strategies of African families in Ireland, Hallelujah Night offers an example of what integration is driven by and what it means in the everyday experiences of migrants.

Educating the new Irish

Education is at the frontline of Ireland's struggle to deal with multicultural populations and envision a more inclusive society. Perhaps more so than civic and political integration, labour market participation or matters of faith, education really matters precisely because it always references the future while speaking of the present. Ireland's education system emerged in the nineteenth century in response to many crucial national questions; it took on the contours of a largely denominational system that was largely blind to differences throughout the twentieth century. Now, under great pressure to change from secularising forces and increasing cultural diversity, the system is transforming slowly.

The specific ways in which education is responding to the challenges posed by integration has been our concern in this chapter. In the case of African parents and children, we have documented a number of challenges and points of contestation, together with showing the quotidian experiences in classrooms and the often heroic efforts by teachers, managers, parents and even children to get on with things in practical ways. Consistently, however, larger questions have been raised about the education system, the extant policies that inform practice and the philosophical goals of education in Ireland. The UK, the United States or France, with its infamous conflict over the wearing of Muslim hijabs in schools, are often cited as 'failed experiments,' case studies of systems that offer lessons about what not to do. Those advocating multicultural policies are assumed to be regressive types, overly fond of hollow liberal rhetoric and insufficiently concerned with protecting the cultural treasures of national identity and traditions. Discussions of education always tend, therefore, to depart from the practical and day-to-day and make reference to large-scale issues and concerns. To discuss a school or its pupils is to evoke a future society and its citizens.

Throughout the EU education is understood as a foundation pillar in efforts to build a more cohesive, secure and integrated Europe. Indeed, the term integration, as applied to immigration and social cohesion in Europe, was first used to describe the situations of and problems facing migrant workers and their school-going children during the 1970s (Maguire and Titley 2010: 1–19). An illustrative example of current EU policy is available in the 2008 *Green Paper on Migration and Mobility* (Commission of the European Communities 2008). This policy directs Member States to provide education to dependants of workers from another Member State in an official host language and teach the mother tongue and native culture of the country of origin. Beyond this, the Green Paper recognises that while migration policy is within the competence of the EU (especially Schengen Area countries) education policy is a matter for individual Member States. The overall project informing the Green Paper is that of Europe-building and, thus, school-going children from an immigrant background present particular concerns. The Green Paper highlights the spatial clustering of migrant families in European cities and the resulting de facto segregation from the mainstream resulting from high concentrations of immigrant pupils within small numbers of schools. Ireland, however, seems to offer a blurred picture of contradictory trends within the European frame. Data from the Organisation for Economic Cooperation and Development (OECD) PISA indicate serious problems with levels of education performance among immigrant children across Europe, though data on Ireland indicate that across several measures there is a small gap between immigrant students and their Irish-born peers in terms of performances. But, the EU Migrant Integration Policy Index (MIPEX) highlights the failures of the education system to provide targeted measures for immigrant children and, indeed, the closure or withdrawal of services and institutions since the onset of the current economic recession.[14] What is at stake in this blurred and contradictory image of integration and education that Ireland projects? How is it that Ireland has managed to reassure itself that we are on a different path towards integration and that, all in all, we have handled things well?

Throughout our ethnographic research, teachers in St Joseph's commented on the need for greater emphasis on language support, implicitly recognising one of the key issues in the integration of immigrant schoolchildren across Europe. During the years of the so-called Celtic Tiger resources were put in place and today many of those resources are being withdrawn in the face of a severe economic recession. It is noteworthy, however, that the principal of St Joseph's called attention to the effects of the economic recession on the ways in which integration is imagined, and remembered:

> I remember listening to David McWilliams [*the popular economic journalist*]. I am a great believer in David McWilliams: to date he has called it all! And I remember specifically in one of his programmes he said, 'I don't know why we must get it right – and this is the case with newcomer people and integration into our culture – no body else has.' I think he was making the point that because we were buoyant and everyone was floating high, the notion of difference wasn't really as obvious as it is about to become as the economy begins to wane. I think he spoke the reality there. I think we are only now seeing the downsides of people resenting others. (Interview, 2010 [our interpolation])

The principal's comments demand that we look not to integration measures in Ireland before and after the economic recession, but, rather, to the heart of intercultural education policy.

Throughout the twentieth century Ireland operated a largely denominational education system at primary and post-primary levels. Constitutionally, the rights of parents and the roles of churches superseded the 'guardian' state – the plumber who only turned up if called upon. Especially from 2000 onwards the traditional approaches and systemic practices of Irish education were forced to shift, albeit slowly, in the face of societal challenges such as ever-greater cultural diversity. But the denominational core of the system remained intact and was overlain by a discourse of interculturalism. The blurred and indistinct picture of integration and education in Ireland is in fact a simple one on close inspection. Interculturalism became the preferred rubric for discussing diversity in education because it dovetailed with an emergent EU-level policy-language code while simultaneously encoding an attack on 'failed' multiculturalism (discussions of multiculturalism would, of course, have resulted in demands for targeted interventions and challenges to the largely denominational system). Interculturalism denoted activities to foster the inclusion of new immigrant populations, members of the Travelling Community, those with disabilities and those from disadvantaged backgrounds in the mainstream schooling systems (McGorman and Sugrue 2007: 11). Interculturalism, then, became the slippery and elusive term for inclusiveness policies emanating outwards from the largely denominational mainstream. Interculturalism meant business as usual – an Irish solution for multicultural problems. In this arena, education policy today is characterised by a suspiciously neo-liberal form of government-at-a-distance, and integration is left to be worked out by those on the ground – 'Every school needs a Bunmi.'

In 1899 William James delivered a lecture to college students titled, *What Makes a Life Significant?* He opened with a recollection of a week he spent in the model-American society of the Chautauqua camp in New York State wherein he found:

> a serious and studious picnic on a gigantic scale. Here you have a town of many thousands of inhabitants, beautifully laid out in the forest and drained, and equipped with means for satisfying all the necessary lower and most of the superfluous higher wants of man. [...] You have kindergartens and model secondary schools. You have general religious services and special club-houses for the several sects. You have perpetually running soda-water fountains, and daily popular lectures by distinguished men. ... You have no zymotic diseases, no poverty, no drunkenness, no crime, no police. ... You have, in short, a foretaste of what human society might be, were it all in the light, with no suffering and no dark corners. (James 1899: 14–15)

James left the model schools and public soda-water fountains and caught himself, 'quite unexpectedly and involuntarily saying: "Ouf! What a relief!"' He found Chautauqua deadening and longed for everyday 'common life' (James 1899: 15). Today, Chautauqua is recalled only as a historical footnote, but James's visit to the quasi-utopian camp helped form his position on pluralism. The ideal American world he encountered was made up of a self-selecting population of God-fearing middle-class folk; diversity was non-existent; camp-goers volunteered for their own segregation. Understandably, many parents today may wish for an education for their children that is shielded from the dangers of common life, but as James realised the 'atrocious harmlessness of all things' (James 1899: 15) in Chautauqua was inimical to freedom of thought and creativity. In later years, William James wrote *A Pluralistic Universe* (1909) in which he dismissed the simplistic equations between diversity and unity, contestation and cohesion. Somewhat hesitantly, he committed himself to the view that:

> The pluralistic world is thus more like a federal republic than like an empire or a kingdom. However much may be collected, however much may report itself as present at any effective centre of consciousness or action, something else is self-governed and absent and unreduced to unity. ... For pluralism, all that we are required to admit as the constitution of reality is what we ourselves find empirically realised in every minimum of finite life. (James 1909: 324)

James's work influenced a number of his students who paid particular attention to education, diversity and racialisation. Among them was W.E.B. Du Bois, who eschewed simplistic visions of societal unity in favour of attention to lived experiences, sentiment, the soul, affect and empowerment. For Du Bois, pluralism held out the possibility that one day people might draw back the racial veil and become 'co-workers in the kingdom of culture' (Du Bois 1897: 195). The scholarship and activism of William James and W.E.B. Du Bois are worthwhile recalling today because both shunned utopian thinking and instead demanded attention to lived experiences and the everyday. It is in the everyday that one may perceive the agency of school managers, parents, teachers and children as they negotiate between their beliefs and practical requirements and show respect for traditions and while establishing new ones – it is in everyday life that people cultivate pluralism.

Everyday life is the consistent focus throughout this book. But especially with regard to the education system in Ireland, it is important to recognise that attention to the everyday is not simply a research frame. Rather, because of the government-at-a-distance practised in the Irish context, activities in local and ordinary life have the power to keep the system going and potentially subvert it. In short, there is no Chautauqua-like, model Irish form of education of society available for citizens to visit; no utopian future is imagined for education in the Republic of Ireland. Earlier in this chapter we noted the manner in which government spokespersons avoided discussions of racialisation, criticised the 'failed' multiculturalism in other jurisdictions, and congratulated Ireland for its apparent successes. One may find a particularly insightful glimpse into this government-level thinking in a 2006 speech delivered to the annual Patrick McGill Summer School by former Minister for Justice, Equality and Law Reform, Michael McDowell, TD. The former minister framed Ireland as different from the French approach to integration, 'which is that your daughters will not wear a veil to school, your sons will not wear skull caps to school, you must learn French, you must learn to be a citizen of the French republic, you must effectively go under the yoke of French republicanism to participate in French society, and diversity will be frowned upon to the extent that it conflicts with those aims' (McDowell 2006: 61). Instead of striving for utopias of shared common values and a state-driven education machine Ireland follows a 'middle course,' he argued, which, 'most Irish people understand instinctively.'[15] Thus, 'We have in this country in the past accorded to the Protestant and the Jewish faiths the right to organise their education as they see it. Whether that is wise or unwise is a matter for debate, but we cannot now withdraw that right from newer migrant groups into Irish society. I don't think we can say that the draw-bridge now comes up and that everyone must conform to a single form of state secular education in pursuit of social cohesion' (McDowell 2006: 62). The line of thinking here is clear: against the failed experiments in multicultural diversity in some countries and the far-too-rigid statism of France, Ireland's middle course is both reasonable and respectful of the unique traditions and sentiments of the land.

But the Irish solutions to the problems of multiculturalism and pluralism in education have not been composed of local resources alone. Few if any commentators on multiculturalism and education in Ireland have drawn on historical examples or on pluralist intellectual traditions. Rather, the Irish solutions tend to be neo-liberal ones, the 'middle course' is ad hoc and hands-off. Little wonder then that teachers, parents and children are the ones who are negotiating what pluralism means and shaping integration on the ground. As a Pentecostal pastor remarked to us, 'Education means everything to African families. We have our own ethos for schools: it's not by their colour that balloons fly, it's by their contents!'

Notes

1 The first volume was initially launched in 2007.
2 The RAPID Programme (Revitalising Areas through Planning Investment and Development) was launched in 2002 with the aim of delivering priority investment to designated disadvantaged areas. The term disadvantaged as used herein may refer to designated disadvantaged areas or to 'disadvantaged schools.' The Department of Education and Skills supports the Delivering Equality of Opportunity in Schools (DEIS) initiative. DEIS supports over 300 'disadvantaged' primary schools.
3 As of 2010, there were 3165 primary schools (excluding special schools) of which approximately 91 per cent were under Catholic patronage.
4 The national education owes its origins to 1831 when a multi-denominational system was introduced, which limited the remit of the state to secular learning while leaving matters of faith education within the competence of the churches. All of the churches in Ireland resisted this model and, thus, education in Ireland took on a denominational shape (Williams 1999). Article 44 (4) of the 1937 Constitution of Ireland, *Bunreacht na hÉireann*, clearly establishes that state aid for schools shall not discriminate between those under different denominations nor prejudice the rights of children. Bryan Fanning argues that this amounts to an early form of state-funded multiculturalism of a particular, national variety (Fanning 2009: 172). But, historically, one must also remember that until a referendum in 1972 Article 44 of the 1937 Constitution recognised the different churches but also 'the special position of the Holy Catholic Apostolic and Roman Church as the guardian of the Faith professed by the great majority of the citizens' (Government of Ireland 1937/1990). Indeed, a close reading of twentieth-century Irish history suggests that Ireland's 'multicultural' past shows only a weak role for the state. For example, the 1937 Constitution is enacted 'In the name of the Most Holy Trinity, from Whom is all authority [...] of men and States must be referred [...]' (*ibid.*). Of course, this is not an essential part of the Constitution but it does hint that state sovereignty is not especially straightforward. If we follow Wendy Brown in regarding one of the absolute, indispensable and irreducible conditions of sovereignty as being that the sovereign recognises no higher power and if we add this 'spirit' question to the on-the-ground ceding of responsibility and authority to the Catholic Church then the evidence mounts that 'the state' cannot be considered as a separable analytical category. Rather, the state is a set of institutions imbricated with other institutions such as the churches, in fact and in spirit, an idea, and apparatus, a fetish, but more than anything else a form of governmentality (Brown 2010).
5 The 1965 *Rules for National Schools under the Department of the Education* clearly states, 'Of all parts of a school curriculum, Religious Instruction is by far the most important. [... *And*] Religious Instruction is, therefore, a fundamental part of the school course, and a religious spirit should inform and vivify the whole work of the school' (Department of Education 1965: r68 [our interpolation]).
6 The lines of this debate are complex, constitutional, embedded in rights discourse and articulated in multiple ways on the ground. The debate over the provision of non-or multi-denominational education is likely to continue for the foreseeable future. Whereas, as Bryan Fanning has noted, there is a style of multiculturalism available in

the state's commitments to protect the rights of Catholic parents, the key issue is that their choices are rather different from parents who are not Catholics. A tiny percentage of schools are non- or multi-denominational and those are vastly oversubscribed. Moreover, many commentators argue that because the state funds education it cannot be discharging its duties if it does not allow equal access to schooling – simply stated, indirectly compelling parents to find alternatives to local denominational schools is not providing for education on an equal basis: one shouldn't be forced to sacrifice a fundamental right to exercise one's parental rights to denominational schools and a religious ethos.

7 During the summer of 2007, the crisis in school admissions continued to simmer. Parents applied to schools, and schools were required to reply to their application form or letter within twenty-one days. In cases where children were refused admission, parents were directed to the National Education Welfare Board (NEWB) and informed of their right to appeal to the Department of Education. That summer, up to forty families in Balbriggan, north Dublin, alone were without school places for their children.

8 Willis was interested in going beyond the obvious school structures and curriculum and examining the reproduction of class relations in schools. One of his important contributions was his demand for attention to the 'hidden curriculum' of pupil resistances (cultural production), which suggested a mode of engagement that both resisted and accommodated capitalist class culture (see Marsh 1977: 35; Marcus 1986: 165–194).

9 Although the circumstances were rather different, many people were struck by the resemblance between the 1970s' Boston bussing conflict and the violence that accompanied the so-called Holy Cross dispute in Belfast during 2001 and 2002. Mainly Catholic parents and children crossed loyalist communities in order to attend Holy Cross School. A loyalist picket prevented them from doing so in 2001, following accusations of vandalism and IRA spying. The dispute escalated and spread to other areas where children travelled through loyalist areas by bus in order to attend school. On 28 September 2001 several children were badly injured when the bus in which they were travelling to Hazelwood Integrated College was hit by a block. At one stage an improvised explosive device was found and defused, and at the height of the dispute in 2001 some 400 police officers were engaged in escorting children to school.

10 In 2002 integration policy for schools in Ireland began to be discussed openly. During that year, the Department of Education and Skills (DES) drafted recommendations for a National Action Plan on 'intercultural' education and signposted the development of curricula designed to reflect societal diversity (DES 2002: 11–12 passim).

11 According to the Department of Education and Skills (formerly Education and Science), 'The term interculturalism denotes acceptance not only of the principles of equality of rights, values and abilities, but also of the development of policies to promote interaction, collaboration and exchange with people of different cultures, ethnicity or religion. It refers to a recognition of gender issues, and addressing the challenges and barriers that many minority groups such as Travellers, people with disabilities, older adults, and people in disadvantaged areas may face' (DES 2002: 2).

12 The justification for intercultural education policy remaining aloof from specific issues and pushing activities down to schools, parents and children is clearly set forth in official documents. For example, the *Intercultural Education Strategy, 2010-2015* speaks of 'rights and responsibilities' throughout in an ostensibly philosophical manner. One does not have to read into this emphasis to realise that schools, parents and students

are in fact responsibilised as agents for intercultural education within a 'whole-school approach,' whereas government retains its comfortable role as the plumber who is rarely called in (see also Office of the Minister for State for Integration 2008: 36).

13 It is worth recording that many teachers regarded themselves as untrained to deal with issues of racism in the classroom. During a late-2010 focus group discussion five teachers were asked whether or not they felt that teacher training was keeping step with contemporary classrooms. The synchronicity with which everyone present shouted, 'No!' provoked laughter.

14 During recent years the National Consultative Committee on Racism and Interculturalism (NCCRI) has been discontinued and many language support and training initiatives have been curtailed severely or terminated altogether.

15 The same sentiment – characterised as 'a golden mean' – is to be found in an essay by Peter D Sutherland, former Attorney General, EU Commissioner and Director-General of the World Trade Organisation, and Special Representative for Migration and Development of the Secretary General of the United Nations (Sutherland 2008).

5

Miss Nigeria, and emergent forms of life

Invention and imitation, taken together, form, one may say, the entire warp and woof of human life, in so far as it is social. (William James)

Serena was running upstairs to the hotel dressing room when she saw Fiona Murphy. She tried to catch her breath while explaining that her best friend's makeup artist had yet to arrive. Part way through an account of her day's activities, she suddenly interrupted herself: 'Emmanuella is waiting; come on, we need to go!' She rushed towards the dressing room, chatting excitedly over her shoulder. It was 7.30pm, and only thirty minutes remained before the 2009 Miss Nigeria pageant was scheduled to begin. The scene in the hotel dressing room was a chaotic one. Open makeup cases were strewn across tables and on the floor, and a heavy bank of perfumes hung in the air. Several young women chatted breathlessly while applying their makeup or adjusting their dresses; a few others looked confused about what to do next. Bunmi seemed to be the only truly calm person in the room. She was wearing a traditional outfit made from a sparkling red material and stood at the side of the room chatting with two of her friends. 'Will you come over to me for a chat later?' she asked Fiona. 'I'll be at the VIP table,' she said in a mock-snooty voice. She nodded towards her daughter and smiled knowingly: the makeup artist was still stuck in traffic, and Emmanuella and Serena were threatening to take matters into their own hands.

A short while later Fiona returned to the lobby of the large and expensive Dublin hotel. The lobby was already full, but African families continued to arrive in a steady stream. If one follows the philosopher Slavoj Žižek in holding that subjectivity is a void filled in by appearances then the Miss Nigeria pageant offered a fascinating display of African-Irish subjectivities. A great many guests wore traditional outfits, while the others were immaculately turned out in expensive and often designer-label clothes. Guests strolled about the lobby in family groups, welcoming friends and colleagues with broad smiles. Most people took great care to greet notables, such as pastors and political activists. And for their part, the African-Irish elite glided about the lobby, shaking hands, smiling and exchanging a few words with as many people as possible. Occasionally, family groups or couples posed for photographs taken on digital cameras or expensive mobile phones.

Serena returned to the lobby shaking her head, 'Oh, come on Fiona,' she said in a tone of mock resignation, 'let's just sit down with my sisters.' She caught Fiona by the arm and guided her to the function room, which was already vibrating with loud dance music, laughter and shouted greetings. A number of African-Irish notables sat at tables at the front of the room – an elite group composed of members of non-governmental organisations, Nigerian-Irish networks, pastors from Pentecostal churches and various political activists. They, however, were up-staged by the musicians, dancers and other well-known members of the younger generation who arrived to claim the remaining VIP tables. They arrived fashion-ably late, dressed in urban-style clothes and accessorised with sunglasses or Trilby hats. Several young women in ballgowns wandered around wearing the sashes that marked them out as the winners of the Miss Kenya, Miss Africa and Miss Congo pageants. One of the pageant queens hung about next to a table which was assigned to the judges for the evening. Benedicta had agreed to be one of the judges for the second year running and was lost in conversation with Miss Congo. Finally, everything seemed to be ready: the room was full; the judges were at their table; the video and sound technicians moved in and out of the room double and triple checking the equipment; rumour had it that the contestants were dressed. Nothing happened, however. The pageant was scheduled to begin at 8pm, but by 9pm people were still chatting a lot and drinking a little – and nobody seemed to care too much. 'African time ...,' a person at Fiona's table explained.

Suddenly the room erupted with music: 'It's MILLAZ; it's MILLAZ! Naira, Naira, Naira, Naira – she hit the floor. Naira, Naira, Naira – she's a hustler, hustler, hustler on the floor.' The Nigerian-Irish band Millionaire Boyz, or 'Millaz,' were hugely popular with the crowd and their hit recording received loud applause. It was played again and again, and eventually people began to stand up and dance near their tables. While the evening was intended as a celebration of African-Irish culture, the large crowd included a great many young Irish teenagers who were there to support friends. The Millaz track was especially popular with teenagers who delighted in showing off the dance moves they had picked up on YouTube.

The hosts for the evening climbed up on to the stage and introduced the first act, Crystal Ice, Bunmi's daughter Emmanuella's semi-professional dance group from Dundalk. A popular song filled the room, and Crystal Ice began an energetic urban-style routine: individual dancers broke rank and reformed perfectly in time with the music. The audience were awestruck by the young dancers' abilities. But the performance ended after what seemed like a short time, and Crystal Ice left the stage to rapturous applause. The evening's hosts, a young Nigerian-Irish celebrity couple, took to the stage and introduced the judges, carefully noting their professional roles and various accolades. Then they introduced the eleven contestants one-by-one. The young women crossed the stage wearing shorts and tops in the Nigerian national colours, while the hosts stated their names, ages, courses of study or professional occupations. The young women formed a line and the guests in the room stood silently while Nofe Liberty, the vocalist from the

Dublin-based R&B band Amasis, sung the Nigerian anthem. More applause followed.

It was time for the contestants to perform. During the previous week they had trained hard at the Miss Nigeria 'Boot Camp.' 'We're in for a sexy evening,' the hosts said, 'and we're sure the contestants have friends in the audience.' And, with that, the contestants performed a dance routine to Beyonce's song, 'Single Ladies (Put a ring on it).' The contestants performed well, judging from the audience's reactions. In order to give the young women a break, the hosts introduced yet another act: Stone and Jezreel, a thoughtful R&B act whose American-style lyrics drifted around the room. 'Like 'roaches from the project, now they can't understand us, like we come from another planet. . . . Africans come to Dublin for a new lifestyle . . ., but they don't want to be in Ireland pushing a button.' The audience nodded and clapped to the soft R&B music.

The next act was Fabu-D, the popular Nigerian-Irish comedian. His act poked fun at African and Irish personalities, from the disciplining of children to racism. The audience was especially appreciative of his parody of the archetypical Nigerian-Irish pastor, which was delivered in a mixture of urban Nigerian and Dublin accents. The contestants were re-introduced and briefly walked about the stage to music wearing tasteful swimsuits and sarongs (rumour has it that this element of the pageant was done away with during subsequent years due to muttered complaints from pastors and parents). Next, a rap act took to the stage for a brief performance, followed by another set of routines by Crystal Ice. It was getting late by that point, and the contestants were welcomed back on stage in traditional attire – most of the young women wore clothes chosen to represent the specific regions of Nigeria where their families once lived. In turn, each contestant was asked open-ended questions by the hosts. For example, 'If a non-Nigerian was visiting Nigeria where would you tell them to visit?' one of the hosts asked, to which a contestant replied, 'Of course, I would bring them to the Igbo Harvest Festival, which takes place every August and is in Dublin now.' The same question was posed to Bunmi's daughter Emmanuella, who sparkled in a pink and peach-coloured outfit. She recommended the Eyo Festival in Lagos, assuring the audience, 'What Carnival is to Brazil, Eyo is to Lagos!' The audience was beguiled as she spoke in a soft Dundalk accent about the Eyo masquerade parade, describing the colourful hats, white robes and masks. She finished with a Yoruba saying, which translates as, 'If you do not come to Lagos state you will not see the Eyo masquerades.' The crowd responded with enthusiasm, and evidently proud, Bunmi jumped up from her seat and shook her hands in the air.

It was very late at this point, but the pageant showed no signs of ending. Rather, following a brief interlude, the audience was treated to a showcase of contemporary fashion and 'traditional' outfits. The fashion show lasted for about one hour, after which the contestants returned to the stage to present their special talents, which ranged from craft skills to a comedy act. Emmanuella stole this part of the show with contemporary lyrical and street-Hip Hop routines. The audience went wild: one or two people even jumped onto their chairs and attempted to ape her moves without moving their feet; the others danced and clapped while keeping – perhaps more sensibly – their feet on the ground.

It was time to mark the contributions of Nigerians in Ireland with a series of awards. A well-known figure who is active in a great number of non-governmental organisations and networks took the microphone: 'We are extremely proud to be Nigerians in Ireland,' he said.

> We are proud of where we are coming from and where we are going to go. For that reason I am going to address you as people of God, and you are going to respond with, 'Yes, yes, yes.' We are people who are passionate about God! [*The audience responded, 'Yes, yes, yes.'*] Today we are very pleased to honour three individuals who are recipients of this award.

The first award – the 'Beacon of Hope' award – went to a Brigidine Sisters missionary for her work in Africa and her role in founding a non-governmental organisation that helps African immigrants in Dublin. The 'Unsung Hero Award' went to a Nigerian-Irish woman who spent the past three decades organising overseas aid in support of water access projects in West Africa. The audience listened intently to her passionate acceptance speech. 'I try,' she said:

> To make sure all Nigerians, all black people, are accepted, that they can survive. We have to be proud of who we are. We are not different to anyone else: we are not criminals, we are not fraudulent; we are just people. But the difference is in the publicity we get; there is corruption all over the world. We should take back what we learn here. I always say, 'How can I do this in my own country?' And remember: we are here in the diaspora and you will never, never be regarded as Irish with your black colour. Remember your home!

As if to mark the tensions between the push of the transnational identification available in diaspora consciousness and the pull many people felt towards integration in Ireland, the final award went to Rotimi Adebari, the 'first black mayor' in Ireland and then County Councillor.

Finally, well into the following morning, it was time for the pageant contestants to return to the stage, one last time. The hosts asked each young woman: 'Why do you want to be Miss Nigeria?' Each of the contestants spoke about their desire to help with the integration of African immigrants in Ireland by teaching Irish people about the positive aspects of Nigerian culture. The judging began, and the lowest scoring contestants were eliminated. The hosts took every opportunity to build the tension in the room by pausing dramatically; speculation on the outcome among the audience heightened and seemed ready to tip over into outright gambling. Benedicta walked calmly up to the microphone to announce the judges' final decision – Emmanuella won. Bunmi nearly made it to Emmanuella first, but her daughters were slightly quicker. The family hugged and kissed Emmanuella. Photographic flashes lit up the stage like strobe-lighting; word began to spread about the 'after-party'.

The Miss Nigeria pageants are now annual events in Ireland, America, Holland, the UK, and Nigeria, of course. From the late 1950s onward the Nigerian events shared the basic features of Western-style beauty pageants,

5 Miss Nigeria Ireland, 2009

although efforts were made to emphasise African standards of beauty in judging. During the 1990s, however, Miss Nigeria became a target for criticism because of questions over public morality and issues of gender representation raised by the swimsuit parade. After a hiatus of several years, Miss Nigeria re-emerged as a family-friendly pageant that emphasised cultural values, individual talents and various forms of charm. As Rebecca Chiyoko King-O'Riain (2008) has observed, beauty pageants are often complex displays of ethnicity, 'race,' generations and divisions, and the 2009 Irish Miss Nigeria contest was no exception. The event allowed African families to gather together with friends, co-workers and community leaders. People strove to put their best foot forward in terms of appearances. Notable figures in the Nigerian-Irish 'community' performed their expected roles; and younger generation people marked themselves off as different by displaying their fluency in international fashion and modes of behaviour. The 2009 Irish Miss Nigeria contest also highlights the extraordinary cultural inventiveness of new immigrants in Ireland, from re-articulations of US-style and African R&B, Hip Hop and dance to distinctive forms of comedy. 'Tradition,' inventiveness and imitation, folded into one another in the 'warp and woof of human life' (James 1984: 212). But the frayed quality of people's everyday lives also showed itself: the challenges of integrating and the draw of diasporic structures of feeling; appearances, affective and emotional experiences, and racialisation. In short, the 2009 Miss Nigeria pageant offered us a privileged window onto many of the themes that we have endeavoured to explore throughout this book. Moreover, by situating a discussion of youth identity, generational differences and societal hope around this pageant, we may come closer to appreciating 'emergent forms' of African-Irish life (Fischer 1999). Against any reading of the pageant as a thin and surface-level event, one of the organisers explained his aims thus:

> I just believe, well, integration is a good word, but it is a very broad concept, so when it is said, 'integration,' you have to look at the elements of integration. What we need to do from the point of view of integration is first and foremost understanding and showing the beauty of our culture. When people see you first they don't know you, and they don't know who you are, so they don't know how to appreciate you. So what Miss Nigeria has been able to do is that people can see us, attend our event, and get to know us, get in touch with Miss Nigeria and ask her to attend their events. They are able to see that these people, well, they are not dummies . . .; it awakens something in them and then they engage. . . . When we say, 'black people,' people have this feeling that we climb the trees or something and they don't know anything. They have the opportunity to see the beauty of these people's culture, to see what they are made of. And, you know . . . it's a way of integrating, you know, because people will know that we have got something that we can appreciate from both worlds. [. . .] What it leads to . . . there is a genuine integration there, because it's not a forced one. It is these people are here, they believe in the same thing, so what is the difference? Colour?
>
> People watch it on TV, on Youtube, you might say – excuse my language – what is this fucking Miss Nigeria? Let's see what she is made of. Then you click on it and there she is. She has got sense, I would listen to her. (Interview, 2011)

For this organiser, then, the pageant offers hope for societal integration and cross-cultural communication. His words, however, also suggest the limits of those concepts and processes – one might well, he suspects, find racialisation at the end of the multicultural rainbow. And recall here the acceptance speeches during which one awardee warned their audience: 'we are here in the diaspora and you will never, never be regarded as Irish with your black colour. Remember your home!'

But for many young participants in these pageants the opportunities on offer for celebration and engagement presented the possibility of solidifying friendships and enhancing self-styling. One young research participant explained her participation in Miss Nigeria by describing the bonds of affection that she had established in Ireland and her feeling that the pageant somehow made sense as a way to celebrate Nigerian-Irish identity:

> So we moved then to Dundalk in 2000 and then . . . well, we have been in Dundalk ever since. Well I love Ireland. I absolutely love it. . . . I feel it is, well, the only awful thing was the hostel experience: I really didn't like it. . . But school was great, everyone was really lovely. . . especially throughout the asylum process, it was first of all denied and we had to appeal on humanitarian grounds, and every single one of the students in my class wrote letters. Like, it wasn't just my class: it was the whole of fifth year. They all wrote letters. It was amazing – they wrote letters to the Department of Justice [. . .]. (Interview, 2011)

For this young woman, Miss Nigeria represented the distance travelled from the asylum system, the years during which she studied and built up a great many friendships. The pageant also represented a different integration path to the one identified by her parents. She refuses the 'secluded' and self-reliant life available in Nigerian-Irish 'community life;' she perceives only a weak connection to an imagined homeland in Nigeria. It is to the perspectives, experiences and available horizons of members of the younger generation that we now turn – herein, we wish to explore emergent forms of life.

Thus far, our attention to everyday life has been inspired by the works of Jackson (1988; 2002; 2009) and, especially, Das (1998; 2007). In her ethnographic work on violence in South Asia, Das is interested in how large-scale events come to be folded into ongoing social relationships. She frames her approach by drawing on Ludwig Wittgenstein's *Philosophical Investigations*. There is a long history of anthropological engagements with Wittgenstein's later works (Geertz, 1973), especially with the concept of 'forms of life'. Veena Das, however, offers an important new reading.

'To imagine a language,' according to Wittgenstein, 'means to imagine a form of life' (1968: 19). This statement has been read as a provocation to abandon the pure, icy logic of abstract notions of language for the rough ground of what people actually say and do. 'Forms of life,' as Wittgenstein uses it, then, seems to denote an anthropology-friendly conception of communities composed of inter-woven language-games, conventional agreements and meaningful schemes. Thus, one commentator concludes, '[O]ur human form of life is fundamentally *cultural* (rather than biological) in nature' (McGinn 1997: 51 [original emphasis]; cf. Gellner 1998).[1] Das refuses this narrow-gauge reading and offers a broadened discussion of forms of *life*: 'the limit of what is considered human in a society; ... the conditions of the use of criteria as applied to others' (Das 1998: 180). Her investigations of everyday life are also explorations of limits – the limits of the human, the subject, knowledge and language, the knowable and the sayable. Her insights are of crucial importance, because everyday life, like 'forms of life,' is often taken as a synonym for culture. And during the recent past 'culture' has become a leitmotif in expressions of ethnic differences (Comaroff and Comaroff 2009), traditions and localities (Sahlins 1999; Appadurai 2011), and is a new mode of racialisation in the language of cultures rather than 'races' (Maguire and Cassidy 2009: 18). Especially when one considers the identities, family life, feelings and appearances of the younger generations of new immi-grants, one must move beyond a conception of culture that is fixed, essentialised, static and impenetrable. Instead, one is called to explore openness, fluidity, emotions and ethics, affect and appearances; one must take the culture of everyday life to be forever ringed by the limits of what can be known and expressed.

Emergent forms of youth

The majority of our research participants entered Ireland through the asylum system. Many migrated from countries such as Nigeria and the Congo because of well-founded fears of persecution; several experienced violence directly. Because the asylum determinations process in Ireland is an exceptionally long one with extraordinarily high levels of rejections, people remained warehoused for years while awaiting 'status.' For some of our research participants, violence in Africa was followed by structural violence in Ireland, from the conditions within the asylum system to the overtly hostile public reactions and often venomous media coverage (see, for example, NFP, EUMC 2003). In 2004, for example, an astonishing 79 per cent of Irish voters supported a constitutional amendment removing the automatic right to citizenship by birth, *jus soli*, in favour of granting citizenship through a combination of blood and residence rights, *jus sanguinis* and *jus domicile*. The media coverage and public statements during the referendum vilified asylum seekers as exploiters of Irish citizenship law, so-called 'maternity tourists' seeking residency rights as parents of Irish-born children (Maguire and Cassidy 2009). African immigrants felt criminalised and dehumanised. Bunmi, for example, spoke to us of the need 'to deal with the media, because the media was very negative, coming up with crazy headlines: 'Asylum Seekers are Spongers.' And it was what people read, they were feeding them with misconceptions. [...] Complaints that people were coming here to have babies' (Interview, 2010). The formative power of racialisation as a mode of legitimising life cannot be underestimated. After all, as Paul Gilroy reminds us, the racialised body represents a 'moment in the transmission of code and information' (Gilroy 2000: 36) and, therefore, politics at the level of life itself.

Throughout this account of the everyday lives of African immigrants in Ireland we have suggested the ways in which people have attempted to build their worlds, often in the face of enormous challenges. Racialisation showed itself time and again to have the power to disrupt normal life, block aspirations and cast doubt on hopes. As we have seen, taxi drivers attempting to earn a living under increasingly difficult circumstances in Drogheda and Dundalk frequently encountered racism. The illustrative comments of one driver indicated to us the affective ways in which racism is experienced and the shattering effects it may have on the level of life itself: 'I can't blame God for making me a black man, you know,' the driver said. 'It frustrates me, you feel bad, am I not a human being?' Racialisation was also evident as a powerful force during the local and European elections in 2009, on the doorsteps and on the graffiti that marked 'new immigrant candidates' posters. Moreover, the Jesus Walk that opened Chapter 3 above was held early in the morning to avoid (unsuccessfully, as it turned out) the public gaze. Racialisation, then, structures many aspects of the everyday lives of African immigrants; it limits those lives and calls reasons for hope into question. Racialisation elicits particular forms of African-Irish life, from various attachments to the local to modes of self-styling, and from the desire for integration to the sense that integration may not be possible no matter how hard one tries. And all of this translates into the ways in which children are raised.

Of all the parents we spoke with, Bunmi was most clear on the question of how to best raise children:

> I want to train my girls. ... They don't know who they will marry. They could marry Africans, who knows? ... So they go out and see other people, but not Irish, because the Irish are not like us. When they wake up in the morning they have a tendency to say, 'Hi Mummy,' or 'Good morning Mummy.' Well they have to kneel down, even at their age, as big as they are, to greet me. [...] It's ... a Nigerian practice. You kneel down when you greet someone older. I still kneel down for my parents, on my two knees. It's just a sign of respect. [...]
>
>   In the case of my [child], she has an accent, and I tell her to speak with an Irish accent. If you are listening to them talking to their friends, I don't understand them – it's pure Dundalk. (Interview, 2010)

Bunmi is a powerful figure in African-Irish life and she outlines the cultural values she wishes to inculcate in her children with confidence. Yet, even Bunmi hints at the limits of cultural identity: above, one may detect uncertainty and scepticism in her voice. This uncertainty was far more pronounced among other parents, especially when they turned to discussions of discipline in child-rearing. For example, one mother compared African cultural norms with the world available to children in Europe:

> A child doesn't want to be questioned. Why does he not want to work in the night, to do this, to do that? But if it is not done, which way, you understand? What I see in the European system: I am talking to my child, he is talking to me back, he doesn't even allow me to finish talking, telling me, I am talking, he is talking. (Interview, 2010)

Parents often expressed frustration at the permissiveness of Irish society and their inability to physically punish their children or find alternative ways to discipline them. Indeed, one parent who favoured 'grounding' their children as a means to penalise indiscipline wondered how it was that they had come to consider 'confiscating a Nintendo' to be a reasonable punishment. During conversations and interviews, members of the younger generation displayed a keen awareness of their parents' difficulties. As one young woman recalled, 'Most Irish kids, well they could turn around to their mother and say, "Mum, shut up." But in Nigeria, you could not say that – you would get a slap across the jaw or something' (Interview, 2011). Moreover, several parents found it difficult to resolve situations by drawing from or comparing with their own childhood experiences. 'How do you want the child to reason better in life?' one parent asked, before suggesting the difficulties involved in comparing their own experiences with 'soft' childhoods in Ireland:

> Let me give you a typical example: do you know what depression is, do you know what it means? I know those things which cause it: joblessness, not having enough to eat, not having enough money, nowhere to go to school, all these things happen in Africa! [Here] European rules and standards are coming up – everything must be perfect for them. (Interview, 2010)

Those parents who migrated from Africa with young children and subsequently raised Irish-born children felt keenly these tensions in childrearing. For example, the parent quoted below offered a vision of cultural mixing, especially around the challenge of building self-expression among their children:

> I have teenagers and younger ones born here, so I see both of them. They have got it in the mixture of both styles. Not everything in Africa that is good; not everything in Europe that is good. In my own understanding, [*you*] take the good things from both sides and try to build them into one. For example, the area of looking into people's eyes, I like it because it builds the children's confidence; it helps them to be expressive. When I was younger I couldn't speak with my parents because of this system we were just talking about, so I had to keep it in me, suffering in silence. Well part of this happened here as well with all your Catholic problems and so on, if you don't allow some expressive nature or something of expression in your children you may be blocking them from getting the facts which you need, they manage to correct on them before it's too late. It is one of those things that I appreciate. (Interview, 2010)

When one thinks about these descriptions of childrearing one is tempted to call to mind notions of assimilation, intergenerational conflict, or children growing up 'between two worlds' (Drachman et al 1996; cf. Maguire 2004). Because families are often the focus of migration studies, there has long been attention to the ethnic minority family as a microcosmic site of conflict between the forces demanding adherence to 'tradition' and the forces demanding change, as if the minority family is dysfunctional a priori (Kibria 1993). However, in many cases the tensions found in African-Irish new immigrant families are similar to tensions in a great variety of other households. For example, one Pentecostal pastor spoke to us about this concern with the cultural identities of young African-Irish, but situated against the backdrop of the challenges of childrearing in disadvantaged neighbourhoods:

> [W]ith that second generation there are a lot of problems. Some of our children they try to imitate in the target culture or new culture things which back home can be unacceptable. For them, this is the way that the young people live here.... But sometimes it's not acceptable, and you have this kind of conflict. So, you know, there are a lot of problems going on ... especially when they have grown up here, well they have culture one and now they are facing culture two [...].
>
> This is something related to your culture, not just your culture but the EU and so on. ... Like I was saying to one of the social workers, 'If you compare the old generation to the new generation, go to O'Connell Street in the old time you will not see what the young are doing in our time.' So, I think the discipline of the old generation is what we need today. ... And if the way that I discipline my children could be successful – to stop them from being on drugs, from being prostitutes – then that is the best way. 'But with your method, people are out there with drugs and prostitution.' (Interview, 2010)

Clearly there is a great deal to unpack in the above statement. Here we have the voice of a pastor setting himself off against the secular social worker. He compares African culture, especially *vis-à-vis* discipline, to secular and 'modern'

European culture. But, amid these comparisons one also finds the 'old ways' constructed as either Irish or African: a tradition of discipline becoming ever-more frayed by the powerful forces shaping the lives of young people today.

For African-Irish parents a variety of childrearing choices, tactics and strate-gies are available. Their room to manoeuvre is conditioned by their experiences, important institutions such as Pentecostal churches, and their ties to Africa. One might speak of African-Irish home life, then, as forms of life that are always-emergent and always in tension. But African-Irish home life is also set against limits, the limits of identification with new homes in Ireland or their former homes in Africa. Moreover, as Veena Das reminds us, one must also think in terms of forms of *life*, in this case the limits of true belonging: the ever-present threat that one might be crossed off from the community or *polis* on the grounds of 'race.' One parent discussed this issue by drawing attention to both the malleability of identity and the rigidity of 'race':

> The older ones say, 'Oh, these ones, they are Irish because they are born here.' So the older ones who were born in Africa says, 'How long will it take for me to be Irish?' and I say, 'Oh they are Irish because they are born here,' and she says, 'Yeah, but they are black, how long before they will be white?' (Interview, 2010)

It is certainly the case that many of our younger research participants described themselves as Nigerian or Congolese, but in many other ways they conceived of themselves as simply Irish. For some, countries like Nigeria were places to visit one's grandparents and were 'not clear' in their minds. 'I don't really have much to go to,' said Carri, a young African-Irish woman. Indeed, she described how her family were at that stage planning a vacation in Nigeria and the questions this was raising for her: her family's home-life included several phone conversations with overseas relatives each week, and she felt guilty when it occurred to her that she would prefer it if those relatives remained voices on the other end of a phone line. This admission then provoked her to explain that along with many in her generation, she sometimes felt ashamed that she was labelled 'Nigerian' and thus categorised along with 'Africans' and even those in her parents' generation. 'They are going to think we are all the same and so on, and I don't like the way some Nigerians here behave,' she said. 'Sometimes I'm ashamed of them.' What, one may ask, is this young woman's view on integration in Ireland and the forms of African-Irish life that have taken root? Her answers to these questions fold many themes together:

> I haven't experienced much racism here.... Well, the first few years were really bad, it would be from kids there, but it didn't bother me – I knew they didn't know any better. [...] There are a lot of problems here too. Well from what [*my sister*] has been telling me, there is a lot of young people that are doing things, well a lot of young people, well 12–13 year-olds having sex. It's just alarming basically. ... Obviously mum was raised a different way, and being in Ireland, and watching the way my friends interact with one another and their parents, yeah definitely influences us, like I go, 'And they do such and such in someone's

house,' and my mum is like, 'Oh my God!' [*Laughs*] Oh yeah, a lot and it causes a lot of disputes in the house. [...]

I dunno, well I think ... it is easier for me. I went to school here, and most of my friends are Irish. Even with the Nigerians who have kids here, encouraging their kids to have Irish friends, some kids tend to stick together. They go to the same church and so on. ... It really bugs me. ... There is no integration here in Ireland, and I think immigrants are mainly to be blamed for that. For example, the churches, they cause segregation more than anything. For example, the church here, there is only two or one Irish person that goes there. I was talking to my friend the other day and whenever she goes out at night to the pubs or whatever in Dundalk, she is like, 'Where are all the foreign people, where are all the black people?' because you see them during the day around the shops, but you don't see them at night. So it's absolutely non-existent in my opinion; it's basically seclusion I think. Like, basically, keeping to themselves. ... I think it is segregation not integration. (Interview, 2010 [our interpolation])

Tami, a young African-Irish girl and daughter of a taxi driver, spoke to us at length about her life in Ireland. In similar ways to the young woman quoted above, a variety of themes intersected in her description of life and integration in Ireland. She described migrating to Ireland at the age of twelve and spending several months within the asylum system:

I was just happy to be out of the life I was in when I was in Nigeria and to be here. I just didn't know anything: I was one of those kids who kind of moved along with everything; I didn't question anything; I was just happy. ... Things were alright then, there weren't many black people there: it was just a couple of us and a lot of Romanians. It was grand like. I was just having fun. So then I went to school. ... I went there and the experience was nice, people were great. I was one of the first black girls in the school, so everyone knew who I was. That didn't really bother me ... like, I made friends, I was happy. [...]

I remember in the hostel there were some Nigerians that we still know today and we all moved to Dundalk together. Like, I look back on Dundalk ten years ago, it has completely changed today: more buildings and more stuff like that. When we moved to Dundalk there weren't really any black people. [...] (Interview, 2011)

When discussing her sense of identity, Tami, like so many other young research participants described herself as Irish, but qualified her statements with a discussion of racialisation:

I consider myself Irish, like, I am from Ireland technically ... but, then, I am black, and they are like, 'I don't know that many black Irish people,' and I say, 'Well now you do!' Although I wasn't born in Ireland, I feel that all my experience (I can hardly remember what I did when I was eight or nine when I was in Nigeria, you know what I mean?), all that experience has been in Ireland. So when I look back, I think, well, I am Irish, most of the experience I remember has been from Ireland and not Nigeria or whatever. ... It's hard, well most of my memories are here in Dundalk. So yeah, I think it's a bit of a struggle: well, you want to fit in and you don't always. I am not ignoring the fact that I am Nigerian, but then again I am not Nigerian – I am Irish ... (Interview, 2011)

Tami's father also discusses his daughter's identity in terms of racialisation. He spends much of his free time with fellow worshippers in a local Pentecostal church. During the week, especially at night, he drives a taxi around Dundalk. Most of his customers are good people, he says, but often he runs a gauntlet of racial abuse. He says that he cannot help but bring his experiences home and warn his children:

> The government themselves are not even encouraged as far as I am concerned. That's what I tell my children. I said to them, 'Every time, whether you have ten Irish passports or not, you are not an Irish man, not an Irish woman. Having your passport does not make you be one of them, … because no matter what happens, you are not white, you are not that colour.' (Interview, 2010)

'My dad,' Tami explained to us, 'is always talking about the treatment of taxi drivers.' 'He really likes to express his views about it,' she told us with a grin. 'But seriously,' she said, 'he has had a lot of issues with the driving, especially over the past couple of months. He has had a lot of racism, attacks, and so on.' She also spoke abut difficult days when the family first moved to Dundalk: 'We had a lot of problems there, we had our tyres slashed. My dad would wake up and the tyres were slashed.' Tami has a good relationship with her parents but readily admits that a gulf is opening up between them in terms of shared experiences and values, yet she empathises with their struggles to parent effectively:

> It's just different, I mean in everything. My parents are very African minded. It's just the way they have been trained; it's what they know. Although they have lived here for so long, it's just what they know. It's like when you are young, you get influenced by everything, because you are learning, you take everything in from outside. Like I don't even know where to start with this … in things, like, well, it's everyway you live … the way you live your life, how you view stuff, marriage, anything, it's different. Although, I do have Nigerian culture, I still have the other side. [...]
>
> Like it's, 'You can't do this; you can't do that.' It is like I couldn't do anything until I was eighteen. Fair enough, but when you see your friends doing it, when you are sixteen or so, you watch TV and you see in the US they can get a car … Well stuff like that. You want to do what your friends do. I couldn't wear make-up 'til I was eighteen, I couldn't go out 'til I was eighteen. I remember when I was seventeen plus going to college and they still wouldn't let me do anything, I was like, 'I am going to *college* people – respect?' (Interview, 2011)

During conversations, Tami often wondered about what the future might hold for the next generation of African-Irish. 'I think,' she said, 'most Nigerians parents are too strict and they keep their children too closed. When they grow up, they tend to not be experienced or open to stuff, they are scared to do anything. … They don't understand that their kids learn from the culture here, they can't see that' (Interview, 2010). Like Carri, quoted above, she also spoke about the ever-more powerful roles of Pentecostal churches:

> I go to a mixed church, so to me I haven't had the experience of maybe exclusion, or not being part of something, or feeling left out, you know what I mean? … Or

maybe I just ignore it, I don't know, but I think everything is grand. I don't see that I am not included, so I don't look for the idea of integration. Maybe because I am blind to it, maybe I just don't see it. I just see everything is fine. In my church, our lives are together, I am not black to them or ... I don't go out with my African friends and then my Irish ones, everything is together. I don't see any kind of need for integration.

[*But, later she went into this issue in greater detail*]

When you go to a church that is all African, if you are black, well you feel safer there, so maybe you go to a black church, and before you know it, it is all African. If you are not black, maybe you don't feel very comfortable ... or you don't feel that you can fit in – a vast amount of black people might make you feel not included. People tend to go to what is familiar.

Here, Tami's voice demands that we consider the contradictions and tensions available in everyday African-Irish youth experiences and consider what if anything one might say about the broader patterns. What might one say to summarise those youth experiences?

One of the popular ways in which immigrant youth identity is explored in scholarly research is through the concept of 'acculturation.' Acculturation denotes, 'The process that occurs when people from one culture encounter and react to another culture' (MacLachlan and O'Connell 2000: 315). It is understood to occur at a group and/or individual level. In their recent and monumental study of international immigrant youth acculturation, Berry et al (2006) identify four distinct patterns followed by youths: a diffuse pattern characterised by uncertainty and confusion; a national pattern in which youth look to integrate into the national society; and an ethnic pattern characterised by orientation to one's own group; and, most importantly, an integration pattern in which youth identify with two cultures. Berry et al report that their data indicate that the overwhelming majority of immigrant youths surveyed were following the latter pattern. They were able to handle discrimination, experienced little stress and reported reasonably high levels of psychological wellbeing. Diversity, according to the authors, is the key: immigrant youth live in diverse worlds, and governments should heed their voices, because promoting and respecting diversity is good for societies. But acculturation is at best a problematic notion. Famously, Bronislaw Malinowski detested the concept and the word itself: acculturation, for Malinowski was a reified, hard-shelled notion of culture that poorly reflected culture as lived; moreover, it sounded like a cross between a hiccup and a belch. Even during the early twentieth century, Alfred Kroeber wondered, 'why these monotonous studies continue' (quoted in Beals 1982: 14). The early anthropologists' discomfort with the concept of acculturation reflected a distrust of 'culture' when used as an abstraction and a desire for the frictions and flows of everyday lives – the 'rough ground,' to borrow from Ludwig Wittgenstein (1968: 107). But Berry et al's studies of acculturation do suggest lines for further investigation. Is there, one may reasonably ask, a pattern available in emergent African-Irish youth identity?

The most important pattern that we identified in our research was the extent to which no clear pattern of youth identity was available. Rather, African-Irish youth identity seemed to be always-emergent, changing in response to a variety of circumstances, filled with tensions and contradictions – much like youth culture, or culture in general. As one young research participant put it:

> Well, I would say now I am Irish-Nigerian, *definitely*. And that makes me feel good, because before if you asked me this question, maybe three years ago, I would have said, 'I probably couldn't give you an answer, or I would have said one or the other.' ... Like, when I was in college I was, like, 'Irish, Irish-minded, Irish, Irish, Irish.' But, you know, it is just coincidence, most of my friends are Irish, and I grew up in secondary school with mostly just Irish people. A lot of Nigerian people would be, 'She is so ignorant, blah, blah, blah ... she doesn't talk to black people, she thinks she is white, she thinks she is Irish.' You know? ... I found it hard to be accepted in the Irish community and now I find it hard to be accepted in the Nigerian community, which is absolutely ridiculous. ... [*Later*] I guess I got more Nigerian. But right now I can sit here and say, 'I am an Irish-Nigerian,' because I feel so accepted by everyone here, and I just love Dundalk. ... I definitely feel accepted and appreciated in Dundalk. (Interview, 2011 [our interpolation])

As this one illustrative quotation from a recorded interview shows, identity forms itself amid the warp and woof of everyday experiences, it is always-emergent and tends to resist abstract categorisations. For example, for the young person quoted above, Nigeria is held together with Ireland in a transnational ecumene that includes her parents' Pentecostal church, overseas family members, long-distance phone calls, and occasional trips back home. But this is no 'ethnic pattern' of acculturation. Nigeria is important to her identity, her sense of family history and self, but it is crucially important in her everyday life as a source of cultural influences in the form of Nigerian R&B and Hip-Hop music. Like many African-Irish youth with whom we interacted, musical tastes were imbricated with transnational fashion styles, and various forms of self-styling. Cultural influences from 'home' could not be categorised as influences pushing for integration of ethnic segregation; rather, Nigeria represented a repository of materials from which to fashion one's identity in new and creative ways – and that is what really mattered to young people.

Contradictions, messiness, and an always-emergent set of sensibilities were also available in our discussions of racism and belonging. 'I was called Nigger and black and all these kinds of names,' one young research participant told us. 'But now, here in Dundalk it is a lot better.' As time moved on, this young person perceived a change in people's attitudes – familiarity, seemingly, bred acceptance. Like Tami, quoted above, many said that their parents' generation, especially because of their deep religious convictions, were following a different path. In contrast, the lives of our research participant were configured as 'open,' influenced by Nigerian and Irish 'culture,' and full of possibility. But, at the same time, racialisation was always present as a threat to hope. Interestingly, in all our discussions with African-Irish young people the fulcrum around which identity, self-styling and feelings of belonging turned was not some abstract notion of culture or identity, but, rather, home in very specific and everyday ways. According to one member of the younger generation:

> I feel safe in Dundalk; it is where I feel at home. Even when I was away, when I come to Ireland, I am home. I am almost home, when I get off the bus, and I see that Crowne Plaza there. I say, 'Yes, I am in Dundalk.' That's home for me: it is just something I am attached to. I am just attached to Dundalk – it is *my* home. (Interview, 2011)

We began this chapter with a description of the 2009 Miss Nigeria pageant, a description that showed the warp and woof of African-Irish social life. In this chapter we also explored generational differences, transnationalism and the role of racialisation. Here we are left with an open-ended set of questions about youth, the everyday and the local. Our abiding concern throughout this study of integration has been the power of the everyday and the force of the local. To conclude we turn to consider the everyday and the local in studies of integration more generally.

Note

1 Gellner argues that whereas Wittgenstein's early work was concerned with the relationship between the individual mind and the world, his later work refers to a world with culture – 'forms of life' wherein agreement is possible. Gellner rejects this later, *gemeinschaft*-like vision of culture because, he argues, it 'outlaws the very idea of social criticism by making every culture sovereign, self-validating, ultimate' (Gellner 1998: 105).

6

Conclusion

> Nothing could be more absurd than to hope for the definitive triumph of any philosophy which should refuse to legitimate, and to legitimate in an emphatic manner, the more powerful of our emotional and practical tendencies. (William James)

Beginning in the early 1990s, the period of the so-called Celtic Tiger was one of unprecedented economic growth. It was also a period of extraordinary migration patterns. Ireland, for so long imagined as a mono-cultural emigrant nursery, quite suddenly, it seemed, became a new host country for large-scale immigration. In a 2007 survey of 'Immigrants in a Booming Economy' economists Allan Barrett and Yvonne McCarthy explored the phenomenal growth in Ireland's 'non-national' population, from 7 per cent of the total population in 2002 to 10 per cent just four years later – the numbers of 'non-nationals' in the UK, they explained, increased by a smaller percentage over a thirty-year period (Barrett and McCarthy 2007: 790). Writing at the same time, the popular broadcaster and economist David McWilliams cast the situation thus:

> If the US were to match the per capita Irish figures, it would have taken in close to 15 million people in the past two years – twice the population of New York! The big question is whether this is desirable. How long can this go on? Is it always positive to have more and more migrants in the country? Does the narrow economic view – basically the more workers the merrier – always supersede ideas of ethnicity and ethnic coherence? ... We have essentially a laissez-faire approach [; ...] we have a 'sure it'll be grand' attitude – which has served us well thus far, but history shows that events can move quickly. (McWilliams 2006: no pagination)

Events did indeed move quickly. One year later Ireland was in the grip of an extraordinary economic recession. Beginning in 2007, Ireland experienced a massive 13 per cent decline in economic growth, which for an industrialised country is comparable only to the Great Depression of the 1930s. The extraordinary immigration levels declined; emigration returned. However, there has been no mass exodus of new immigrants since the onset of the economic recession (Koehler et al 2010: 13). In-flows of migrants have decreased sharply, but for a great many refugees, former asylum seekers and other immigrants Ireland is now home.

Our research was carried out during this extraordinary period in Irish history, from the twilight of the Celtic Tiger to the arrival of the International Monetary Fund in late 2010. During this period, the towns and neighbourhoods where we worked seemed drained of societal hope. Unemployment levels were increasing; a variety of public services were curtailed. The artist Seán Keating once described the period immediately after the British withdrawal from Ireland as a moment in which the nation held its breath, not knowing what to expect. Over the past three years we have seen towns and neighbourhoods enter into a dark period of insecurity in which the worst is always expected. Integration is certainly not seen as a priority.

In many ways, the central message of this book is that integration was never seen as a priority in Ireland, except by immigrants and those most closely associated with immigrants' lives. In our work on former asylum seekers and other immigrants in the taxi industry we showed how the deregulation of the industry under the banner of a neo-liberal agenda opened access to jobs but also opened a space for conflict, racism and rumours. 'Local' drivers faced an ever-more difficult working life characterised by increasing working hours, diminishing incomes and a rapidly transforming cultural landscape. Deregulation, in the words of one driver, resulted in 'a free-for-all' (Interview, 2011) characterised by regulation without certainty or hope for one's future. African drivers entered this industry in significant numbers; rumours spread about them; and, racism was directed at them. In the face of major conflicts and day-to-day antagonism on the streets and in their cars, African drivers showed a determination to stake out a place for themselves in the industry. The major problem in the industry, according to Yinka, was a systemic one, left to fester for years. And, our study of the taxi industry, especially in Dundalk and Drogheda, concurs with her analysis: deregulation, under the flag of neo-liberalism meant government-at-a-distance – the market was expected to be the ultimate regulator.

Integration was certainly not seen as a priority in the realm of politics either. Activists such as Benedicta and Yinka ran as candidates in the local and European elections in economically wounded localities and in the face of public scepticism and no small measure of hostility. They also ran within an unyielding political system. Extant research indicates that political parties have not gone far enough to encourage immigrant candidates and members of ethnic minorities (Chadamoyo et al 2007), but it is the dense local bonds of clientelism and brokerage, historical and national sentiment that 'new immigrant candidates' found it most difficult to overcome. The exhausting efforts of Benedicta and Yinka show the desire of immigrants such as former asylum seekers to have a voice in Irish politics, to act as role models for others, and to represent what really matters in their localities. Across Europe questions are being asked about political and civic integration; ways are being sought to measure civic integration, 'social capital,' political activism and 'opportunity structures.' Behind all of this, Christian Joppke (2007) detects an austere neo-liberalism whereby immigrants are regarded as responsible for their own integration.

Integration is also a deeply problematic issue in the Irish education system. Ireland's education system is a largely denominational one, and this has been the case since the foundation of the state. The rights of parents and the roles of churches are extremely powerful. As one Minister for Education put it, the role of government is like that of a plumber who is called in only when something goes wrong. The denominational core of the system remains intact but has recently been overlain by a discourse of 'interculturalism.' This is a slippery and elusive term for inclusiveness policies emanating outwards from the largely denominational mainstream. In many ways, interculturalism denotes business as usual, and integration is left to be worked out by those on the ground. The heroic efforts by schools such as St Joseph's and inspiring teachers and parents such as Bunmi occur in a space characterised by government-at-a-distance.

Throughout this book, then, we have described integration on the ground, within everyday lives. Though it was not in the original frame of our research project, we constantly ran up against the ramifications of neo-liberal government within people's lives. Taxi drivers railed against what they perceived as 'dehumanising' government policy. School teachers and parents worried about the weakness of official interculturalism as set against their day-to-day challenges. Political activists perceived a landscape composed of toothless networks, task-forces, and community groups: a soft and accessible imitation of the less-than-accessible political system. Because our work crossed different domains within people's lives, from religion and education to work and youth identity, we saw people struggle against discursive formations that shared a family resemblance.

In one of the most insightful essays on the topic of integration in Ireland, Breda Gray (2006) highlights the lack of attention in European discussions of integration to the ways in which immigrants 'adapt informally' (Gray 2006: 120). Instead, integration policies have been treated with great seriousness, as if there is an axiomatic relationship between policy rhetoric and practice. Moreover, integration policies have avoided sustained critical analysis. Her essay on the Irish situation draws from the insights of Michel Foucault (1991) to argue that migrants are today problematised, constructed as populations and subjected to a mode of neo-liberal governmentality. The aim, Gray argues, is to manage migration and render immigrants as responsiblised and self-empowering citizens:

> In other words, integration policies must foster self-sufficient and autonomous immigrants, who must work on themselves in order to be independent, and committed to contributing to the Irish economy and society, in order that they may be integrated. ... In line with neo-liberal modes of governance, individuals and groups are invited to be active and to take responsibility for their own integration. Refugees are imagined as choosing and advocating their way into neo-liberal citizenship in Ireland. (Gray 2006: 130)

For Gray, Irish integration policies, like similar policies across the European Union, are structured around an ideal of the migrant citizen, which is in turn benchmarked against a neo-liberal *homo-economicus*. To understand integration in Ireland, according to Gray, one must attend to the political mentalities involved in integration across different sectors of society, the actual interventions and the modes of subjectification. The key, she argues, is to understand the ramifications of neo-liberal governmentality today.

One may readily find the signatures of a neo-liberalism in Ireland's key integration policy statement, *Migration Nation* (2008), written in the hand of an Irish style of governmentality. Indeed, one is immediately struck by a lack of attention to integration in this Ministerial Statement of Policy on integration. The key actions envisaged in the statement include new immigration laws, more efficient asylum determinations' processes, the shoring up of residency and citizenship rights (predicated on the successful passing of language competency tests) and enhanced anti-discrimination policies and laws. As Michel Foucault pointed out in his discussion of the birth of neo-liberal governmentality in post-war Germany, neo-liberalism includes a new relationship between the economic order and the rule of law whereby law becomes the regulatory milieu or rules of the game for economic competition – instead of the reason of the state, *raison d'État*, we have governmentality via the rule of law, *l'État de droit* (Foucault 2008: 159–187).[1] Where integration is dealt with explicitly in *Migration Nation* it is framed not *vis-à-vis* 'the state' but rather as a set of ad hoc interventions in 'diversity management' (Office of the Minister for Integration 2008: 9). The techniques of government include a representative commission and taskforce, targeted support for diversity in certain schools, faith-based groups and non-governmental organisations. In essence, then, in order to avoid the mistakes of other countries – the so-called 'parallel communities' and the spectre of 'ghettoisation' – Irish integration policy involves migration management legislation, mainstreaming as a means to manage diversity, and leaving the rest to civil society and everyday life. Foucault's insights into *l'État de droit* resonate strongly. While much of the processes of integration may be left to civil society and everyday life, the trial and judgement of migrants' integration will likely be framed by neo-liberalism and benchmarked against a *homo-economicus*. 'Successful integration,' according to the Ministerial Statement, 'hinges on a vibrant civil society,' because, 'Integration lives and breathes, and indeed dies, at the level of community' (Office of the Minister for Integration 2008: 17, 22).

But more needs to be said here. Breda Gray's venturesome critique of integration and neo-liberal governmentality stops short upon identifying what is at stake theoretically. What, one might ask, are the specific ways in which neo-liberal governmentality operates in Ireland? While some commentators hold that it represents the fashionable outward ideological appearance of new imperialism – 'Empire,' to borrow from Hardt and Negri (2000; cf. Foucault 2008: 130) – others eschew descriptions of neo-liberalism as a singular and coherent ideology. David Harvey (2005), for example, argues that the history of neo-liberalism is characterised by 'uneven geographical development,' 'partial and lop-sided application from one state and social formation to another' (Harvey 2005: 13). So too with governmentality: Foucault's 'proposed analytical grid' (2008: 186) offers a starting point for analysis but does not offer a theoretical end point. In the light of discussions of neo-liberal governmentality, what, one might ask, are the impacts of EU-wide policies on the lives of migrants in Ireland? Our attention must surely shift to the local and the everyday.

For Michel Foucault the analysis of neo-liberal forms of governmentality is 'not confined by definition to a precise domain determined by a sector of the scale. ... In other words, the analysis of micro-powers is not a question of scale, and it is not a question of a sector, it is a question of a point of view' (Foucault 2008: 186). And here our point of view has been people's everyday lifeworlds, their experiences of the world and their always-limited perspectives on worlds forever ringed by something more. One of the unintended consequences of our research was that we elicited perspectives on neo-liberal governmentality in Ireland. For example, in a context of deregulation and racism in the taxi industry we found African drivers staking out a space and attempting to position themselves to build new lives. In trying to raise and educate their children, African families poured themselves energetically into attempts to reshape the schooling system. In these and other contexts that we studied, new immigrants were giving new life to sectors in which the politics of life itself was damaging to life itself.

Anthropologists have long been suspicious of attempts to bracket off 'the economy' as a research object and, instead, have shown the ways in which 'the economy' is imbricated by grounded local and global relational ties, bonds of familiarity and trust (Polanyi 1944; Isik 2010). This approach has never been more relevant than today. In a moment in which neo-liberalism denotes an important shift in government in which economic mentalities, rationalities and modes of intervention serve as a permanent economic tribunal for all forms of human behaviour, good government is no longer about social justice. Notions of the collective good or societal hope and wellbeing remain, to borrow from Friedrich Nietzsche, as the last smoke from an evaporating reality. In this context, anthropologists have written about the anxieties and uncertainties experienced affectively by people in their everyday lifeworlds (Verdery 2000; Tsing 2004). Herein, by descending into ordinary lives we have shown the ways in which former asylum seekers and other immigrants are giving new life in Ireland, reshaping the sectors and scales in which they live, from local politics to transnational politics and from education to working lives. Situated against the background of an extraordinary and deep economic recession, one may see emergent forms of life, not just survival in the face of adversity.

Throughout this book we have called attention to the power of Pentecostal beliefs in the different sectors and at the different scales of African-Irish life. We have shown how Pentecostal churches reach into asylum centres and give hope to asylum seekers. African taxi drivers reached for their beliefs as a means to survive in a harsh industry. Pentecostal churches were important staging grounds for local political campaigns. Furthermore, Pentecostal beliefs structured the interactions between parents, children and teachers in Irish schools. Faith is important, then, in any discussion of African-Irish life after asylum. But, what is more, Pentecostalism is growing as a frame through which African immigrants inhabit Irish localities, re-enchant towns and symbolic spaces and produce new homes while simply living their everyday lives. In a moment of deep economic recession, in which the dominant discourse is a neo-liberal one wherein the market is an all-powerful site of verediction and regulation, little wonder that former asylum seekers and other immigrants are finding meaning and hope in the everyday power of Pentecostalism. From beyond the limits and from within the lacunae of a neo-liberal world of market values and regulation, *l'État de droit*, new immigrants are generating alternate structures of meaning, new forms of self-styling and affective and emotional engagements with the world, a powerful, everyday *l'État de religion*.

Ethnographic research and writing elicits images, voices, spaces and moments. Here we have elicited numerous voices, together with the voices and stories of key research participants, to show the importance of the everyday to understanding moments in the taxi industry, in political and civic integration, in religious life and in the lives of young African-Irish people. But our work is not a still-life image: in a period of extraordinary societal change, we have tried to show the dynamics and complexities of the everyday. Today, Yinka has returned to take up an activist role in Nigeria, fulfilling her desire to act as a model of emulation in Nigerian politics; Benedicta is fulfilling her promise to take what she learned from Irish politics and apply it in Nigeria where she is acting as a special govern-ment aide. Bunmi is continuing in her role as an educator and is one of the key people pushing for new spaces to be designated in schools, which will be 'home-like' and friendly places for staff, students and parents to break down barriers together. Several of the pastors with whom we carried out our research continue to perceive a Christian world composed of souls in Ireland and Nigeria in need of saving and are committed to evangelising both countries. More than for the other research participants, *l'état de religion* expresses their sense of the world. But for many young African-Irish people the worlds of their parents and the existing taken-for-granted ways of the world in Ireland are not enough. Our work is not a still-life image, and their worlds are continually being remade.

Note

1 According to Foucault, 'Reason of state is not an art of government according to divine, natural, or human laws. It doesn't have to respect the general order of the world. It's government in accordance with the state's strength' (Foucault 1979: 229).

CAVAN COUNTY LIBRARY

Bibliography

Allport, Gordon Willard & Leo Postman. 1947. *The Psychology of Rumour*. New York: Holt, Rinehart & Winston.

Amnesty International: Irish Section. 2008. 'Note on Asylum Seekers and Mental Health.' www.amnesty.ie/amnesty/live/irish/action/article.asp?id=4570&page=3801 (accessed October 2010).

Anderson, Allen, Michael Bergunder, Andre Droogers & Cornelis van der Laan. 2010. *Studying Global Pentecostalism*. Berkeley: University of California Press.

Appadurai, Arjun. 2011. *Modernity at Large: Cultural Dimensions of Globalization*. Minneapolis: University of Minnesota Press.

Arendt, Hannah. 1973. *Illuminations*. London: Fontana/Collins.

Barrett, Alan & Yvonne McCarthy. 2007. 'Immigrants in a Booming Economy: Analysing Their Earnings and Welfare Dependence.' *Labour* 21(4–5): 789–808.

Barrett, Seán D. 2003. 'Regulatory Capture, Property Rights and Taxi Deregulation: A Case Study.' *Economic Affairs* 23(4): 34–40.

——. 2010. 'The Sustained Impacts of Taxi Regulation.' *Economic Affairs* 30 (1): 61–65.

Bateson, Gregory. 1975. 'Some Components of Socialisation of Trance.' *Ethos* 3: 143–156.

Bax, Mart. 1976. *Harpstrings and Confessions: Machine-style Politics in the Irish Republic*. Amsterdam: Van Gorcum & Co.

Beals, Ralph. 1982. 'Fifty Years in Anthropology.' *Annual Review of Anthropology* 11: 12–32.

Beesley, Arthur. 2011. 'Nearly all Asylum Requests Rejected.' *The Irish Times* (M30 March): 4.

Berry, J.W., Jean S. Phinney, David L. Sam & Paul Vedder (eds). 2006. *Immigrant Youth in Cultural Transition: Acculturation, Identity, and Adaptation across National Contexts*. New York: Lawrence Erlbaum Associates.

Bhabha, Homi. 2004. *The Location of Culture*. London and New York: Routledge.

Bialecki, Jon, Naomi Haynes & Joel Robbins. 2008. 'The Anthropology of Christianity.' *Religion Compass* 2(6): 1139–1158.

Boas, Franz. 1944. *The Function of Dance in Human Societies*. New York: Dance Horizons.

Boland, Rosita. 2007. 'Faith before Fairness.' *The Irish Times* (8 September): 1.

Bourdieu, Pierre. 1996. *The Rules of Art: Genesis and Structure of the Literary Field*. London: Polity Press.

Bourke, Eva & Borbála Faragó (eds). 2010. *Landing Places: Immigrant Poets in Ireland*. Dublin: The Dedalus Press.

Bowden, Matt & Louise Higgins. 2000. The Impact and Effectiveness of the Garda Special Projects, Final Report to the Department of Justice, Equality & Law Reform. Dublin: The Children's Research Centre, Trinity College Dublin.

Bowen, Elizabeth. 1975. *Pictures and Conversations*. London: Knopf.

———. 1995. *Bowen's Court & Seven Winters*. London: Vintage Classics, Random House.

Brandon, Andrew. 1987. *Health and Wealth*. Eastbourne: Kingsway.

Breen, Claire. 2008. 'The Policy of Direct Provision in Ireland: A Violation of Asylum Seekers' Right to an Adequate Standard of Housing.' *International Journal of Refugee Law* 20(4): 611–636.

Brown, Ryan & Rebecca A. Seligman. 2009. 'Anthropology and Cultural Neuroscience: Creating Productive Intersections in Parallel Fields.' *Progress in Brain Research* 178: 31–42.

Brown, Wendy. 2010. *Walled States, Waning Sovereignty*. New York: Zone Books.

Browne, Noel. 1998. 'Church and State in Modern Ireland.' In *Ireland's Evolving Constitution 1937–1997: Collected Essays*, Tim Murphy & Patrick Twomey (eds). Oxford: Hart Publishing, pp. 41–51.

Buckley, Vincent. 1985. *Memory Ireland: Insights into the Contemporary Irish Condition*. Melbourne: Penguin Books Australia.

Butler, Judith. 1997. *Excitable Speech: A Politics of the Performative*. London: Routledge.

Carroll, Robert & Stephen Prickett. 1998. *The Bible: Authorised King James Version*. Oxford: Oxford University Press.

Carter, Paul. 1987. *The Road to Botany Bay: An Essay in Spatial History*. London: Faber & Faber.

Carty, Kenneth. 1983. *Party and Parish Pump*. Waterloo, Canada: Wilfrid Laurier University Press.

Cavell, Stanley. 1989. *This New Yet Unapproachable America: Lectures After Emerson, After Wittgenstein*. Chicago: University of Chicago Press.

Chadamoyo, Neltah, Bryan Fanning & Fidèle Mutwarasibo. 2007. 'Getting into Politics.' In *Immigration and social change in the Republic of Ireland*, Bryan Fanning (ed.), Manchester: Manchester University Press, pp. 185–197.

Chubb, Basil. 1963. 'Going About Persecuting Civil Servants: The Role of the Irish Parliamentary Representative.' *Political Studies* 10(3): 272–286.

Coakley, John & Liam O'Dowd. 2005. *The Irish border and North-South Cooperation: An Overview*. IBIS Working Paper no. 47. Dublin: IBIS.

Coard, Bernard. 1974 [1971]. How the West Indian Child is Made Educationally Subnormal in the British School System: Scandal of the Black Child in Schools in Britain. London: New Beacon Books.

Coleman, Simon. 2000. *The Globalisation of Charismatic Christianity*. Cambridge: Cambridge University Press.

———. 2006. 'Studying "Global" Pentecostalism: Tensions, Representations and Opportunities.' *Pentecostudies* 5(1): 1–17.

Collins, Niamh & Eoghan Williams. 2004. 'Immigrants Look to set up FF Cumann in Mosney.' *Irish Independent* (February 8): 4.

Comaroff, Jean & John L. Comaroff. 2000. 'Millennial Capitalism: First Thoughts on a Second Coming.' *Public Culture* 12(2): 291–343.

———. (2009). *Ethnicity, Inc.* Chicago: University of Chicago Press.

Commission of the European Communities. 2008. Green Paper on Migration and Mobility: Challenges and Opportunities for EU Education Systems, COM(2008) 423 final. Brussels: European Commission.

Crowley, Niall. 2006. 'A Strategic Framework for Action on Equality and Cultural Diversity.' *Irish Journal of Anthropology* 9(3): 27–35.

Cullen, Pauline P. 2009. 'Irish Pro-Migrant Nongovernmental Organisations and the

Politics of Immigration.' *Voluntas* 20: 99–128.

Dáil Éireann. 2003. 'Taxi Regulation Bill 2003: Second Stage (Resumed).' *Dáil Debates* 569(1): 113–144.

D'Alton, John. 1844. *The History of Drogheda: With its Environs, and an Introductory Essay, Volume 1.* Dublin: Self-published.

Daniel, E. Valentine. 1996. 'Crushed Glass, or is there a Counterpoint to Culture,' In *Culture/Contexture: Essays in Anthropology and Literary Study*, E. Valentine Daniel & Geoffrey Peck (eds). Berkeley: University of California Press, pp. 357–377.

Das, Veena. 2007. *Life and Words: Violence and the Descent into the Ordinary.* Berkeley and LA: University of California Press.

Das Gupta, Monisha. 2006. *Unruly Immigrants: Rights, Activism, and Transnational South Asian Politics in the United States.* Durham: Duke University Press.

De Certeau, Michel. 2002. *The Practice of Everyday Life.* Berkeley: University of California Press.

Deleuze, Gilles. 1990. *The Logic of Sense.* New York: Columbia University Press.

DeParle, Jason. 2008. 'Border Crossings: Born Irish but with Illegal Parents.' *New York Times* (25 February): 1.

Department of Education. 1965. *Rules for National Schools under the Department of Education.* Dublin: The Stationery Office.

Department of Education and Skills. 2002. *Promoting Anti-Racism and Interculturalism in Education – Draft Recommendations towards a National Action Plan.* Dublin: The Stationery Office.

Department of Education and Skills and the Office of the Minister for Integration. 2010. *Intercultural Education Strategy, 2010–2015.* www.education.ie/servlet/blobservlet /mig_intercultural_education_strategy.pdf (accessed 6 August 2011).

Derrida, Jacques & Gianni Vattimo. 1998. *Religion.* London: Polity Press.

De Tona, Carla & Ronit Lentin. 2011. 'Networking Sisterhood, from the Informal to the Global: AkiDwA, The African and Migrant Women's Network, Ireland.' *Global Networks* 11(2): 1–20.

——. 2007. 'Overlapping Multi-centred Networking: Migrant Women's Diasporic Networks as Alternative Narratives of Globalisation.' In *Performing Global Networks*, Karen Fricker & Ronit Lentin (eds). Newcastle: Cambridge Scholars Press, pp. 67–88.

Directorate-General, Justice, Freedom and Security. 2009. *Handbook on Integration: For Policy-makers and Practitioners.* Brussels: EU Commission.

Doyle, Kathleen. 2010. 'The Liberalization of the Small Public Service Vehicle (SPSV) Market and its Impact on the Industry in Ireland'. Presentation by the Commissioner for Taxi Regulation, Kathleen Doyle, to the Taxi Network Meeting, Lisbon, Portugal, 13 July.

Doyle, Roddy. 2008. *The Deportees and Other Stories.* London: Viking.

Drachman, Diane, Young Hee Kwon-Ahn & Ana Paulino. 1996. 'Migration and Resettlement Experiences of Dominican and Korean Families.' *Families in Society* 77(10): 626–638.

DuBois, W.E.B. 1897. 'Strivings of the Negro People.' *Atlantic Monthly* 80: 194–198.

——. 2008 [1903]. *The Souls of Black Folk.* Oxford: Oxford University Press.

Eade, John & David Garbin. 2007. 'Reinterpreting the Relationship between Centre and Periphery: Pilgrimage and Sacred Spatialisation among Polish and Congolese Communities in Britain.' *Mobilities* 2(3): 413–424.

Economist. 2006. 'Christianity Reborn.' *The Economist* (December 23): 48–50.

English, Eoin. 2009. 'Taxi Driver Denies Accusations of Racism,' *The Irish Examiner* (1 April): 5.

EU-MIDIS. 2009. *European Union Minorities and Discrimination Survey*. Brussels: Fundamental Rights Agency (FRA).

European Union. 2006. 'Consolidated Versions of the Treaty on European Union and of the Treaty Establishing the European Community.' *Official Journal of the European Union* (C 321): 37.

Faber, Goodbody Economic Consultants and Irish Marketing Surveys. 1998. *Review of the Taxi and Hackney Carriage Service in the Dublin Area*. Dublin: Stationery Office.

Fanning, Bryan. 2009. *New Guests of the Irish Nation*. Dublin: Irish Academic Press.

Fanning, Bryan, Fidèle Mutwarasibo & Neltah Chadamoyo. 2003. *Positive Politics: Participation of Immigrants and Ethnic Minorities in the Electoral Process*. Dublin: Africa Solidarity Centre.

——. 2004. *Negative Politics, Positive Vision: Immigration and the 2004 Elections*. Dublin: Africa Solidarity Centre.

Fanning, Bryan, Kevin Howard & Neil O'Boyle. 2010. 'Immigrant Candidates and Politics in the Republic of Ireland: Racialisation, Ethnic Nepotism or Localism?' *Nationalism and Ethnic Politics* 16(3 & 4): 420–442.

Fanon, Frantz. 1967. *Black Skin, White Masks*. New York: Grove Press.

Favell, Adrian. 1998. *Philosophies of Integration*. London: Macmillan/New York: St. Martin's Press.

Feldman, Alice, Deo Ladislas Ndakengerwa, Ann Nolan & Carmen Frese. 2005. *Diversity, Civil Society and Social Change in Ireland: A North-South Comparison of the Role of Immigrant/New Minority Ethnic-Led Community and Voluntary Sector Organisations*. University College Dublin: Geary Institute.

Finegael.ie. 2007. www.finegael.ie/news/index.cfm/type/details/nkey/30416/pkey/653 (accessed 13 February 2011).

Fischer, Michael M.J. 1999. 'Emergent Forms of Life: Anthropologies of Late or Postmodernities.' *Annual Review of Anthropology* 28: 455–478.

——. 2003. *Emergent Forms of Life and the Anthropological Voice*. Durham: Duke University Press.

FLAC. 2003. *Direct Discrimination? An Analysis of the Scheme of Direct Provision in Ireland*. Dublin: FLAC Report.

Foucault, Michel. 1981. 'Omnes et Singulatim: Towards a Criticism of Political Reason.' In *The Tanner Lectures on Human Values II*, Sterling McMurrin (ed.). Cambridge and New York: Cambridge University Press, pp. 223–255.

——. 1991. 'Governmentality.' In *The Foucault Effect. Studies in Governmentality*, Graham Burchell, Colin Gordon & Peter Miller (eds). Chicago: University of Chicago Press, pp. 87–104.

——. 2008. *The Birth of Biopolitics*: Lectures at the Collège de France, 1978–1979. London: Palgrave Macmillan.

Gallagher, Michael. 2008. 'Does Ireland need a New Electoral System?' In *Irish Political Studies Reader*, Conor McGrath & Eoin O'Malley (eds). London and New York: Routledge, pp. 197–223.

Garda Commissioner. 1975. Garda Commissioner's Memo (signed Chief Superintendent) to Department of Justice, 1 August (3c/2042/75). Department of Justice, Equality and Law Reform 2005/155/6, Original reference number: S18/75.

Garner, Steve. 2007. 'Babies, Bodies and Entitlement: Gendered Aspects of Access to Citizenship in the Republic of Ireland.' *Parliamentary Affairs* 60(3): 437–451.

Gartland, Fiona. 2010. 'Racial Tension at the Taxi Rank.' *The Irish Times* (23 February): 6.

Garvin, Tom. 1974. 'Political Cleavages, Party Politics and Urbanisation in Ireland: The Case of the Periphery-Dominated Centre.' *European Journal of Political Research* 2: 307–327.

——. 1991. 'The Long Division of the Irish Mind.' *Irish Times* (28 December): 10.

Geertz, Clifford. 1973. *The Interpretation of Cultures*. New York: Basic Books.

Gellner, Ernest. 1998. *Language and Solitude: Wittgenstein, Malinowski, and the Habsburg Dilemma*. Cambridge: Cambridge University Press.

Giddens, Anthony. 1991. *Modernity and Self-Identity*. London: Polity.

Gilligan, Chris. 2010. 'Segregating Northern Ireland from the discussion on integration', a special issue of *Translocations: The Irish Migration, Race and Social Transformation Review on Integration*, Gavan Titley & Mark Maguire (eds), vol. 6(2). www.imrstr.dcu.ie (accessed 10 March 2011).

Gilroy, Paul. 2000. *Against Race: Imagining Political Culture Beyond the Colour Line*. Cambridge, MA: Harvard University Press.

Glazier, Jocelyn & Jung-A Seo. 2005. 'Multicultural Literature and Discussion as Mirror and Window?' *Journal of Adolescence and Adult Literacy* 48: 686–700.

Glendinning, Victoria. 1985. *Elizabeth Bowen: Portrait of a Writer*. Harmondsworth: Penguin.

Golding, William. 2002. *Lord of the Flies*. London: Faber & Faber.

Goodbody Economic Consultants. 2005. *National Review of Taxi, Hackney and Limousine Services*. Dublin: Commission for Taxi Regulation.

Goodbody Economic Consultants in association with Faber Maunsell and Irish Marketing Surveys. 2009. *Economic Review of the Small Public Service Vehicle Industry*. Dublin: Commission for Taxi Regulation.

Government of Ireland. 1990 [1937]. *Bunreacht na hEireann/Constitution of Ireland*. Dublin: Stationery Office.

——. 1992. *Education for a Changing World: Green Paper on Education*. Dublin: Stationery Office.

——. 1995. *Charting Our Education Future: White Paper on Education*. Dublin: Stationery Office.

——. 1998. *Education Act 1998*. Dublin: Stationery Office.

——. 2007. Response of Ireland to the Green Paper from the European Commission on the Future of the Common European Asylum System. http://ec.europa.eu/home-affairs/news/consulting_public/0010/contributions/member_states/ireland_en.pdf (accessed 6 January 2012).

Gray, Breda. 2006. 'Migrant Integration Policy: A Nationalist Fantasy of Management and Control?' *Translocations: The Irish Migration, Race and Social Transformation Review* 1(1): 118–138.

Gregg, Melissa & Gregory J. Seigworth. 2010. *The Affect Theory Reader*. Durham: Duke University Press Books.

Guha, Ranajit. 1983. *Elementary Aspects of Peasant Insurgency in Colonial India*. Oxford, UK and Delhi: Oxford University Press.

Hage, Ghassan. 2003. *Against Paranoid Nationalism: Searching for Hope in a Shrinking Society*. Sydney: Pluto Press.

Hannerz, Ulf. 1996. *Transnational Connections: Culture, People, Places*. London: Routledge.

Hardt, M. & A. Negri. 2000. *Empire*. Cambridge, MA: Harvard University Press.

Harvey, David. 2005. *A Brief History of Neoliberalism*. Oxford and New York: Oxford University Press.

Hinchion, Carmel & Jennifer Hennessy. 2009. 'Reading other Worlds, Reading my World.' *Development Education in Action* 9(Autumn): 7–22.

Hoffmann, Elizabeth A. 2006. 'Driving Street Justice: The Taxicab Driver as the Last

American Cowboy.' *Labour Studies Journal* 31(2): 1–18.

Holland, Kitty. 2005. 'Stuck in Ireland's Hidden Villages.' *The Irish Times* (9 April): 4.

Hollenweger, Walter. 1972. *The Pentecostals.* London: SCM Press.

Inglis, Tom. 1998. *Moral Monopoly: The Rise and Fall of the Catholic Church in Modern Ireland.* Dublin: University College Dublin Press.

Irish Council of Churches (ICC). 2003. *Research Project into Aspects of the Religious Life of Refugees, Asylum Seekers and Immigrants in the Republic of Ireland.* Belfast: Irish Council of Churches.

Irish National Teachers Organisation (INTO). 2005. *Immigration and Education.* Dublin: Irish National Teachers Organisation.

Irishtaxi.org, blog posted 14 July 2010, irishtaxi.org/forum

Isik, Damla. 2010. 'Personal and Global Economies: Male Carpet Manufacturers as Entrepreneurs in the Weaving Neighbourhoods of Konya, Turkey.' *American Ethnologist* 37(1): 53–68.

Jackson, Michael. 1988. *Paths towards a Clearing: Radical Empiricism and Ethnographic Inquiry.* Bloomington: Indiana University Press.

———. 2002. *The Politics of Storytelling: Violence, Transgression, and Inter-subjectivity.* Copenhagen: Museum Tusculanum Press.

———. 2009. *The Palm at the End of the Mind: Relatedness, Religiosity, and the Real.* Durham: Duke University Press.

James, William. 1984. *Talks to Teachers on Psychology and to Students on Some of Life's Ideals.* Cambridge, MA: Harvard University Press.

———. 1996 [1909]. *A Pluralistic Universe.* Nebraska: University of Nebraska Press.

———. 2006 [1899]. 'What Makes a Life Significant?' In *Leading Lives that Matter,* Mark Schwehn & Dorothy Bass (eds). New York: Eerdmans, pp. 14–28.

Joppke, Christian. 2006. *Immigrants and Civic Integration in Western Europe.* Montreal: Institute for Research on Public Policy.

———. 2007. 'Transformation of Immigrant Integration: Civic Integration and Antidiscrimination in the Netherlands, France, and Germany.' *World Politics* 59(2): 243–273.

Juchno, Piotr. 2009. *Eurostat Statistics in Focus: Population and Social Conditions.* Brussels: European Commission.

Kapferer, Bruce. 1988. *Legends of People, Myth of State.* Washington: Smithsonian Institution Press.

Kiberd, Declan. 1996. *Inventing Ireland: The Literature of a Modern Nation.* London: Vintage.

Kibria, Nazli. 1993. *Family Tightrope: The Changing Lives of Vietnamese-Americans.* Princeton, New Jersey: Princeton University Press.

King, Jason. 1999. 'Porous Nation: From Ireland's 'Haemorrhage' to Immigrant Inundation.' In *The Expanding Nation: Towards a Multi-ethnic Ireland, Vol. 1,* Ronit Lentin (ed.). Dublin: Trinity College Publication, pp. 49–55.

King-O'Riain, Rebecca Chiyoko. 2008. 'Making the Perfect Queen: The Cultural Production of Identity in Beauty Pageants.' *Sociology Compass* 2: 74–83.

Kissane, Bill. 2003. 'The Illusion of State Neutrality in a Secularising Ireland.' *Western European Politics* 26(1): 73–94.

———. 2008. 'The Not-so-Amazing Case of Irish Democracy.' In *Irish Political Studies Reader,* Conor McGrath & Eoin O'Malley (eds). London and New York: Routledge, pp. 15–41.

Kleinman. Arthur, 1988. *The Illness Narratives: Suffering, Healing and the Human Condition.* New York: Basic Books.

Koehler, Jobst, Frank Laczko, Christine Aghazarm & Julia Schad. 2010. *Migration and the Economic Crisis in the European Union: Implications for Policy*. Brussels: IOM.

Komito, Lee. 1985. 'Politics and Clientelism in Urban Ireland: Information, Reputation, and Brokerage.' Unpublished PhD thesis: University of Pennsylvania.

——. 1989. 'Voters, Politicians, and Clientelism: A Dublin Survey.' *Administration* 37(2): 171–196.

——. 1992. 'Brokerage or Friendship? Politics and Networks in Ireland.' *Economic and Social Review* 23(2): 129–145.

——. 1993. 'Personalism and Brokerage in Dublin Politics.' In *Irish Urban Cultures*, Chris Curtin, Hastings Donnan & Thomas Wilson (eds). Belfast: Institute of Irish Studies, Queen's University of Belfast, pp. 79–98.

Koopmans, Ruud. 2004. 'Migrant Mobilisation and Political Opportunities: Variation among German Cities and a Comparison with the United Kingdom and the Netherlands.' *Journal of Ethnic and Migration Studies* 30(3): 449–70.

Kopkind, David. 1974. 'Banned in Boston: Busing into Southie.' *Ramparts* XIII: 34.

Kopytoff, Igor. 1987. 'The Internal African Frontier: The Making of African Political Culture.' In *The African Frontier*, Igor Kopytoff (ed.). Bloomington & Indianapolis: Indiana University Press, pp. 3–84.

Kozol, J. 2005. 'Overcoming Apartheid.' *The Nation* (December 19): 26.

Labov, William. 1972. *Language in the Inner City: Studies in the Black English Vernacular*. Philadelphia: University of Pennsylvania Press.

Lawrence, D.H. 2000. *The Rainbow*. London: Penguin Books.

Lee, Joseph J. 1989. *Ireland, 1912–1985: Politics and Society*. Cambridge: Cambridge University Press.

Lefebvre, Henri. 1991. *The Production of Space*. London: Blackwell.

——. 1992. *Critique of Everyday Life, Vol. 1*. London: Verso Books.

Lenihan, Brian. 2004. 'Citizenship Change Common Sense.' *The Irish Times* (28 May): 18.

Lentin, Ronit. 2009. 'Migrant Women's Networking: New Articulations of Transnational Ethnicity.' In *Ethnicities and Values in a Changing World*, Gargi Bhattacharyya (ed.) Farnham and Burlington VT: Ashgate Publishing, pp. 65–82.

Lentin, Ronit & Robbie McVeigh. 2006. *After Optimism? Ireland, Racism and Globalisation*. Dublin: Metro Eireann Publications.

Lewis, Anthony. 1971. 'Weary, Fearful Refugees from Ulster Crowd into Ireland.' *The New York Times* (13 August): 3.

LMFM Podcasts. 2009. 'Michael Reade Show, 23–9–09 and 22–9–09,' www.lmfm.ie/on-air/show/the-michael-reade-show/32aa5f5f-7d34–40ec-8e47–e5fcc860f5a7 (accessed 12 October 2010).

Lock, Margaret. 1993. 'Cultivating the Body: Anthropology and Epistemologies of Bodily Practice and Knowledge.' *Annual Review of Anthropology* 22: 133–155.

Los Angeles Times. 1906. 'Weird Babel of Tongues.' *LA Times* (18 April): 1.

Luibhéid, Eithne, 2004. 'Childbearing against the State? Asylum Seeker Women in the Irish Republic.' *Women's Studies International Forum* 27: 335–349.

Lynch, James. 1986. *Multicultural Education: Principles and Practice*. London: Routledge & Kegan Paul.

Lynch, Kathleen & Ann Lodge. 2002. *Equality and Power in Schools*. London and New York: Routledge/ Falmer.

MacCormaic, Ruadhán. 2009. 'A Fast Track to Deportations.' *The Irish Times* (12 September): 6.

Mac Éinrí, Piaras. 2007. 'Integration Models and Choices.' In *Immigration and Social Change in the Republic of Ireland,* Bryan Fanning (ed.). Manchester: Manchester University Press, pp. 214–237.

Mac Éinrí, Piaras, & Allen White. 2008. 'Immigration into the Republic of Ireland: A Bibliography of Recent Research.' *Irish Geography* 41(2): 151–179.

MacLachlan, Malcolm & Michael O'Connell (eds). 2000. *Cultivating Pluralism: Psychological, Social and Cultural Perspectives on a Changing Ireland.* Dublin: Oak Tree Press.

Maguire, Mark. 2004. *Differently Irish: A Cultural History of Vietnamese-Irish Life.* Dublin: The Woodfield Press.

Maguire, Mark & Tanya Cassidy. 2009. 'The New Irish Question: Citizenship, Motherhood and the Politics of Life Itself.' *Irish Journal of Anthropology* 13(2): 12–32.

Maguire, Mark & Gavan Titley. 2010. 'The Body and Soul of Integration.' *Translocations: Migration and Social Change* 6(1): 1–19.

Mansergh, Martin, 2004. 'Back Door to EU Citizenship is the Key Issue.' *The Irish Times* (24 April): 16.

Marcus, George E. 1986. 'Contemporary Problems of Ethnography in the Modern World System.' In *Writing Culture: The Poetics and Politics of Ethnography,* James Clifford & George Marcus (eds). Berkeley: University of California Press, pp. 165–194.

Marcus, George E. 2002. *The Sentimental Citizen: Emotion in Democratic Politics.* Pennsylvania: Pennsylvania State University Press.

Marsh, Colin. 1997. *Key Concepts for Understanding Curriculum: Perspectives, Vol. 1.* London: Falmer Press.

Marx, Karl. 2004. *Capital: Critique of Political Economy, Vol. 1.* London: Penguin.

Mauss, Marcel. 1935. 'Techniques of the Body.' *Economy and Society* 2: 70–88.

Mawhinney, Alison. 2007. 'Freedom of Religion in the Irish Primary School System: A Failure to Protect Human Rights?' *Legal Studies* 27(3): 379–403.

Mbembé, J. Achille & Steven Rendall. 2002. 'African Modes of Self-Writing.' *Public Culture* 14(1): 239–273.

McBride, Caitlin. 2009. 'Taxi Drivers Clash in Car Park over Radio Race Row.' *The Evening Herald* (September 24): 25.

McConnell, Daniel. 2009. 'Dáil Family Trees show Clans who Rule Ireland.' *Sunday Independent* (December 27): 9.

McDonald, Henry. 2007. 'Ireland Forced to Open Immigrant School.' *The Guardian* (25 September). www.guardian.co.uk/world/2007/sep/25/schools.internationaleducationnews (accessed 6 January 2012).

McDowell, Michael, TD, 2004. 'We must be Able to Manage Migration in a Sensible Fashion.' *The Irish Times* (24 April): 15.

——. 2006. 'Immigration, Integration and Cultural Identity.' In *The Soul of Ireland: Issues of Society, Culture and Identity,* Joe Mulholland, (ed.). Dublin: Liffey Press, pp. 56–63.

McGarry, Patsy. 2004. 'Immigrants Praised for "Huge Impact" on Church.' *The Irish* Times (February 25): 4.

McGinn, Marie. 1997. *Wittgenstein and the Philosophical Investiga*tions. London: Routledge.

McGorman, Enda & Ciaran Sugrue. 2007. *Intercultural Education: Primary Challenges in Dublin 15.* Dublin: Social Inclusion Unit of the Department of Education and Science.

McMorrow, Conor. 2010. *Dáil Stars: From Croke Park to Leinster House.* Dublin: Mentor Books.

McWilliams, David. 2006. 'Let's Come to Our Census on Immigration.' *David McWilliams*

Personal Web Page, July 19. www.davidmcwilliams.ie/2006/07/19/lets-come-to-our
-census-on-immigration (accessed 6 January 2012).

Meyer, Birgit. 1999. *Translating the Devil.* Edinburgh: Edinburgh University Press.

Migrant Rights Centre Ireland (MRCI). 2010. *Racism and Migrant Workers in Ireland.*
Dublin: MRCI.

Mitra, Diditi. 2008. 'Punjabi American Taxi Drivers: The New White Working Class?'
Journal of Asian American Studies 11(3): 303–336.

Moss, Warner. 1933. *Political Parties in the Irish Free State.* New York: Columbia University
Press.

Murphy, Liam D. 2002. 'Demonstrating Passion: Constructing Sacred Movement in
Northern Ireland.' *Journal of the Society for the Anthropology of Europe* 2(1): 22–30.

National Consultative Committee on Racism and Interculturalism (NCCRI). 2001. *Anti-
Racism Election Protocol for Political Parties in Ireland and Declaration of Intent.*
Dublin: NCCRI.

National Consultative Committee on Racism and Interculturalism (NCCRI). 2007.
Reported Incidents Relating to Racism, January – June 2007. Dublin: NCCRI.

National Council for Curriculum Assessment (NCCA). 2005. *Intercultural Education in
the Primary School. Enabling Children to Respect and Celebrate Diversity, to Promote
Equality and to Challenge Unfair Discrimination.* Dublin: NCCA.

National Focal Point (NFP), EU Monitoring Centre on Racism and Xenophobia (EUMC).
2003. *Case Study: Media Coverage of Refugee and Asylum Seekers in Ireland.* Dublin:
NCCRI and the Equality Authority.

Nee, Martina. 2009. 'Headford Man Fined for Racist Attack on Taxi.' *Galway Advertiser*
(December 23): www.advertiser.ie/galway/article/20467 (accessed 6 January 2012).

Neuman, Russell, George E. Marcus, Michael MacKuen & Ann N. Crigler. 2007. *The Affect
Effect: Dynamics of Emotion in Political Thinking and Behaviour.* Chicago: University
of Chicago Press.

Northside People. 2010. 'Taxi Drivers hold Vigil for Colleagues.' (July 22): www.dublin-
people.com/content/view/3517/55/ (accessed 23 July 2010).

O'Connell, Rory. 2000. 'Theories of Religious Education in Ireland.' *Journal of Law and
Religion* 14(2): 433–523.

O'Connor, Alison. 2004. 'Asylum Seekers told they can't form FF Cumann.' *The Irish
Independent* (May 27): 3.

O'Connor, Frank. 1994 [1957]. 'A Minority.' In *A Frank O'Connor Reader,* Michael
Steinman (ed.). New York: Syracuse University Press, pp. 182–190.

Office of the Minister for Integration. 2008. *Migration Nation: Statement on Integration
Strategy and Diversity Management.* Dublin: Stationery Office.

O'Halloran, Marie, 2004. 'Citizenship System Being Abused.' *The Irish Times* (31
March): 6.

Organisation for Economic Co-operation and Development (OECD). 2009. *OECD
Reviews of Migrant Education: Ireland.* Paris: Organisation for Economic Co-
operation and Development.

O'Shea, Owen. 2011. *Heirs to the Kingdom: Kerry's Political Dynasties.* Dublin: The O'Brien
Press.

O'Toole, Fintan. 1997. *The Ex-Isle of Ireland: Images of a Global Ireland.* Dublin: New
Island Books.

Phelan, Helen & Nyiel Kuol. 2005. *Survey of Persons with Refugee and Leave to Remain
Status in Limerick City.* Limerick: Reception and Integration Agency (RIA) and
Limerick City Development Board.

Phenninx, Rinus, Dimitrina Spencer & Nicholas Van Hear. 2008. *Migration and Integration in Europe: The State of Research.* Oxford: ESRC Centre on Migration, Policy and Society (COMPAS), University of Oxford.

Polanyi, Karl. 1944. *The Great Transformation.* New York: Farrar and Rinehart.

Poloma, Margaret M. 2000. 'The Spirit Bade Me Go: Pentecostalism and Global Religion.' Paper Prepared for Presentation at the Association for the Sociology of Religion Annual Meetings, August 11–13. Washington, DC.

Proust, Marcel. 2004. *Swann's Way.* London: Modern Library.

Punch. 1862. *Punch* 43 (18 March): 153.

Putnam, Robert. 2001. *Bowling Alone: The Collapse and Revival of American Community.* New York: Simon & Schuster.

Robateau, Albert J. 2001. *Canaan Land: A Religious History of African Americans.* Oxford: Oxford University Press.

Robbins, Joel. 2004a. 'The Globalization of Pentecostal and Charismatic Christianity.' *Annual Review of Anthropology* 33: 117–143.

———. 2004b. *Becoming Sinners: Christianity and Moral Torment in a Papua New Guinea Society.* Berkeley: University of California Press.

———. 2009. 'Pentecostal Networks and the Spirit of Globalization: On the Social Productivity of Ritual Forms.' *Social Analysis* 53(1): 55–66.

———. 2010a. 'Anthropology, Pentecostalism, and the New Paul: Conversion, Event, and Social Transformation.' *South Atlantic Quarterly* 109(4): 633–652.

———. 2010b. 'Anthropology of Religion.' In *Studying Global Pentecostalism: Theories and Methods*, Allen Anderson (ed.). Berkeley: University of California Press, pp. 156–178.

Robinson, James. 2005. *Pentecostal Origins: Early Pentecostalism in Ireland in the Context of the British Isles.* Milton Keynes: Paternoster.

Rose, Nikolas. 1999. *Powers of Freedom: Reframing Political Thought.* Cambridge: Cambridge University Press.

Rowley, Paul & Nicky Gogan. 2008. *Seaview.* Dublin: Still Films.

Ruane, Medb. 2000. 'Floating Reminder of Shamed Policies.' *The Irish Times* (27 March): 16.

Rudé, George. 1959. *The Crowd in the French Revolution.* Oxford: Clarendon Press.

Sahlins, Marshall. 1999. 'Two or Three Things that I Know about Culture.' *Journal of the Royal Anthropological Institute* 5(3): 399–421.

Salako, Olubunmi. 2008. *Tales by Moonlight: African Stories for Children, Vol. 2.* Dublin: Cornerstones.

Scarry, Elaine. 1985. *The Body in Pain.* Oxford: Oxford University Press.

Schlesinger, Arthur M. 1991. *The Disuniting of America: Reflections on a Multicultural Society.* New York and London: WW Norton and Company.

Schuster, Liza. 2005. 'A Sledgehammer to Crack a Nut: Deportation, Detention and Dispersal in Europe.' *Social Policy and Administration* 39(6): 606–621.

Shandy, Dianna J. 2008. 'Irish Babies, African Mothers: Rites of Passage and Rights in Citizenship in Post-Millennial Ireland.' *Anthropological Quarterly* 81(4): 803–831.

Sharrock, David. 2007. 'Ireland Opens its First All Black School.' *The Times* (September 24) www.timesonline.co.uk/tol/news/world/europe/article2522914.ece (accessed 3 August 2011).

Shibutani, Tamotsu. 1966. *Improvised News: A Sociological Study of Rumour.* Indianapolis: Bobbs-Merrill.

Soja, Edward W. 1999. 'History: Geography: Modernity.' In *The Cultural Studies Reader,* Simon During (ed.) London and New York, Routledge, pp. 113–126.

Sökefeld, Martin. 2002. 'Rumours and Politics on the Northern Frontier.' *Modern Asian Studies* 36(2): 299–340.

Smyth, Emer, Merike Darmody, Frances McGinnity & Delma Byrne. 2009. *Adapting to Diversity: Irish Schools and Newcomer Students.* Dublin: Economic and Social Research Institute

Smyth, Emer, Selina McCoy & Merike Darmody (eds). 2004. *Moving Up: The Experience of First-Year Students in Post-Primary Education.* Dublin: The Liffey Press in association with The Economic and Social Research Institute.

Smyth, Jamie. 2011. 'Refugee Recognition Rate Draws Concern.' *The Irish Times* (25 May): 6.

Spiller, Keith. 2001. '"Little Africa:" Parnell Street, Food and Afro-Irish Identity.' *Chimera* 17: 37–43.

Statham, Paul & Emily Gray. 2005. 'Becoming European? The Transformation of the British pro-migrant NGO Sector in Response to Europeanization.' *Journal of Common Market Studies* 43(4): 877–898.

Sutherland, Peter. 2008. 'A Golden Mean between Multiculturalism and Assimilation.' *Studies* 97(Spring): 80–118.

Taussig, Michael. 1987. *Shamanism, Colonialism and the Wildman: A Study in Terror and Healing.* Chicago and London: University of Chicago Press.

Titley, Gavan. 2008. 'Backlash! Just in Case: 'Political Correctness', Immigration and the Rise of Preactionary Discourse in Irish Public Debate.' *The Irish Review* 308: 94–110.

Tsing, Anna L. 2004. *Friction.* Princeton: Princeton University Press.

TV3 News Podcasts at 5.30, 30 March 2009, www.tv3.ie/news.php (accessed 3 August 2011).

Ugba, Abel. 2004. *A Quantitative Profile Analysis of African Immigrants in 21st Century Dublin.* Dublin: Department of Sociology, Trinity College Dublin.

——. 2006. 'Between God and Ethnicity: Pentecostal African Immigrants in 21st Century Ireland.' *Irish Journal of Anthropology* 9(3): 56–63.

——. 2009. *Shades of Belonging: African Pentecostals in Twenty-first Century Ireland.* Trenton, NJ, Asamara, Eritrea: Africa World Press.

Van Gennep, Arnold. 1960. *The Rites of Passage.* London: Routledge & Kegan Paul.

Verdery, Katherine. 2000. 'Privatization as Transforming Persons,' In *Between Past and Future: The Revolutions of 1989 and their Aftermath*, Sorin Antohi & Vladimir Tismaneanu (eds). Budapest: Central European University, pp. 175–197.

Vogel, Dita & Anna Triandafyllidou. 2005. 'Introduction: Civic Activation of Immigrants,' In *Building Europe with New Citizens? An Inquiry into the Civic Participation of Naturalised Citizens and Foreign Residents in 25 Countries*, Dita Vogel & Carl von Ossietzky (eds). Oldenburg: Universität Oldenburg Press, pp. 5–21.

White, Michael J. & Jennifer E. Glick. 2009. *Achieving Anew. How New Immigrants do in American Schools, Jobs, and Neighbourhoods.* New York: Russell Sage Foundation.

Williams, Kevin. 1999. 'Faith and the Nation: Education and Religious Identity in the Republic of Ireland.' *British Journal of Educational Studies* 47(4): 317–331.

Willis, Paul. 1977. *Learning to Labour: How Working Class Kids Get Working Class Jobs.* Westmead, UK: Saxon House.

Wittgenstein, Ludwig. 1968. *Philosophical Investigations.* New York: Macmillan.

——. 1999. 'Philosophical Investigations, sections 65–78.' In *Concepts*, Eric Margolis & Stephen Laurence (eds). Massachusetts: Massachusetts Institute of Technology Press, pp. 171–175.

Zhou, Min & Susan S. Kim. 2006. 'Community Forces, Social Capital, and Educational Achievement: The Case of Supplementary Education in the Chinese and Korean

Immigrant Communities.' *Harvard Educational Review* 76(1): 1–29.

Zhou, Min. 2003. 'Urban Education: Challenges in Educating Culturally Diverse Children.' *Teachers College Record* 105(2): 208–225.

Žižek, Slavoj. 2003. *The Puppet and the Dwarf: The Perverse Core of Christianity.* Massachusetts: Massachusetts Institute of Technology Press.

Index

Note: 'n.' after a page number indicates the number of a note on that page.